Longman

21st Century Science

GCSE Additional Science Foundation

Series Editor:
Penny Johnson

Iain Brand
Mark Levesley
Penny Marshall
Michael O'Neill
Gary Philpott
Steve Woolley

PEARSON
Longman
Edinburgh Gate
Harlow, Essex

Contents

P5 Electric circuits

B6 Brain and mind

How to use this book

Each module starts with a double page that introduces some of the ideas that you will learn more about in the module.

It also has questions that will help you to start thinking about the ideas in the module.

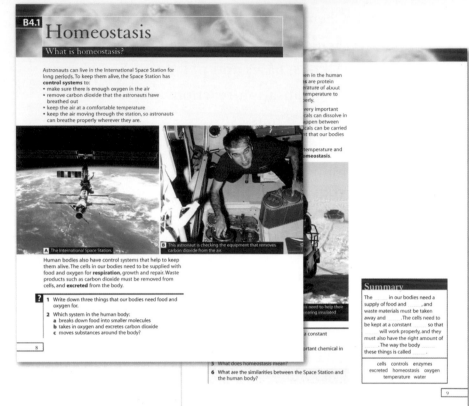

Each module is divided into 12 topics. Each topic is a double page.

You should be able to answer this question when you have finished this topic.

The questions will help you to understand what is on the page.

These boxes give you ideas for practical work or other activities.

The words in **bold** are important scientific words. You can check their meanings by looking at the glossary at the end of the book.

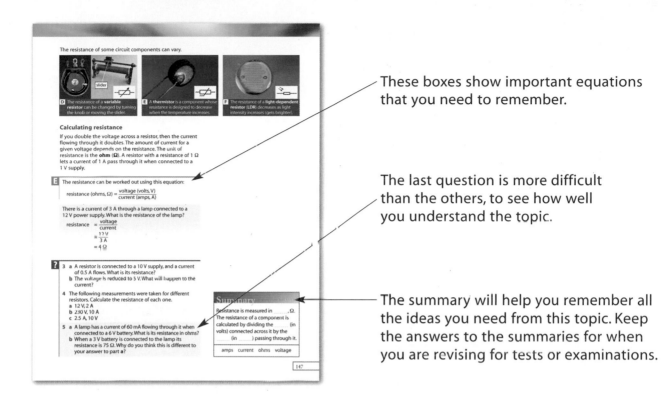

The resistance of some circuit components can vary.

D The resistance of a **variable resistor** can be changed by turning the knob or moving the slider.

E A **thermistor** is a component whose resistance is designed to decrease when the temperature increases.

F The resistance of a **light-dependent resistor** (LDR) decreases as light intensity increases (gets brighter).

Calculating resistance

If you double the voltage across a resistor, then the current flowing through it doubles. The amount of current for a given voltage depends on the resistance. The unit of resistance is the **ohm** (Ω). A resistor with a resistance of 1 Ω lets a current of 1 A pass through it when connected to a 1 V supply.

E The resistance can be worked out using this equation:

$$\text{resistance (ohms, Ω)} = \frac{\text{voltage (volts, V)}}{\text{current (amps, A)}}$$

There is a current of 3 A through a lamp connected to a 12 V power supply. What is the resistance of the lamp?

$$\text{resistance} = \frac{\text{voltage}}{\text{current}}$$
$$= \frac{12\,\text{V}}{3\,\text{A}}$$
$$= 4\,Ω$$

? 3 a A resistor is connected to a 10 V supply, and a current of 0.5 A flows. What is its resistance?
  b The voltage is reduced to 5 V. What will happen to the current?

4 The following measurements were taken for different resistors. Calculate the resistance of each one.
  a 12 V, 2 A
  b 230 V, 10 A
  c 2.5 A, 10 V

5 a A lamp has a current of 60 mA flowing through it when connected to a 6 V battery. What is its resistance in ohms?
  b When a 3 V battery is connected to the lamp its resistance is 75 Ω. Why do you think this is different to your answer to part **a**?

Summary

Resistance is measured in _____, Ω. The resistance of a component is calculated by dividing the _____ (in volts) connected across it by the _____ (in _____) passing through it.

amps current ohms voltage

147

These boxes show important equations that you need to remember.

The last question is more difficult than the others, to see how well you understand the topic.

The summary will help you remember all the ideas you need from this topic. Keep the answers to the summaries for when you are revising for tests or examinations.

The last two pages have revision questions that will help you check how much you have remembered from this module.

C4.13 The alkaline earth metals
What patterns are there in other groups of elements?

The elements in Group 2 of the Periodic Table are called the alkaline earth metals. These elements, which have several important uses, show patterns in their chemical and physical properties.

Alkaline earth metal	Symbol	Proton number	Relative atomic mass	Density (g/cm³)
beryllium	Be	4	9	1.85
magnesium	Mg	12	24	1.74
calcium	Ca	20	40	1.54
strontium	Sr	38	88	2.60
barium	Ba	56	137	3.51

A

The elements of this group have many similarities. They are all fairly soft, silvery-coloured metals. They are all shiny when polished. They are fairly reactive elements and tarnish quickly in moist air.

1 The elements in Group 2 are all metals. List four common properties of metals.

2 a Draw a graph of density against proton number for the alkaline earth metals using axes like these.

C

  b How does the density change as you go down the group?

3 a Copy and complete this table.

Metal	Protons	Electrons	Electron arrangement
beryllium			
magnesium			
calcium			

  b How are the electron arrangements these metals:
    i different ii similar?

B A barium meal allows the intestines to show up on X-ray images.

4 Draw a labelled diagram showing the structure of a beryllium atom. Include the following labels.

electrons protons neutron
nucleus first electron shell
second electron shell

5 Why do elements in the same group have similar chemical properties?

... 2. Like sodium ... and calcium ... rogen gas and an

_____ + _____ H₂ (g)
_____ + hydrogen

... eacts violently ... of magnesium

... ride

... h metal, with ... rs. However, all ... with halogens to ... lids contain ions ... ium chloride ... mide contains

... up 2 metals.

... etal halides is MX₂, ... for the symbol of the metal and X stands for the symbol of the non-metal. Write the formula for:
  a barium fluoride
  b beryllium chloride
  c magnesium iodide

8 Copy and complete the word and symbol equations for the reaction of barium with water.
  _____ + _____ → _____ + hydrogen
  _____ + 2H₂O (l) → Ba(OH)₂ (aq) + _____

9 Copy and complete the word and symbol equations for the reaction of calcium with bromine.
  _____ + bromine → _____
  _____ + _____ → CaBr₂ (s)

10 Barium has some similar properties to sodium metal.
  a Why is it stored under oil?
  b What safety precautions should be observed when handling the metal?

11 a What are ions and how are they formed?
  b Write down the electron arrangements of a chlorine atom (Cl) and a chloride ion (Cl⁻).
  c Explain why chlorine forms a Cl⁻ ion.

12 Care has to be take when handling certain compounds of alkaline earth metals as they can be dangerous. Explain the safety precautions required when handling chemicals which show the following hazard symbols.
  a
  b
  c

13 The flame test for barium produces green flashes of colour.
  a What other element produces a green colour in a flame?
  b What is the name of the technique that can be used to produce a spectrum for an element?
  c What does a spectrum show?
  d How can this be used to confirm the identity of an element?

58

59

Homeostasis

What is homeostasis?

Astronauts can live in the International Space Station for long periods. To keep them alive, the Space Station has **control systems** to:
- make sure there is enough oxygen in the air
- remove carbon dioxide that the astronauts have breathed out
- keep the air at a comfortable temperature
- keep the air moving through the station, so astronauts can breathe properly wherever they are.

A The International Space Station.

B This astronaut is checking the equipment that removes carbon dioxide from the air.

Human bodies also have control systems that help to keep them alive. The cells in our bodies need to be supplied with food and oxygen for **respiration**, growth and repair. Waste products such as carbon dioxide must be removed from cells, and **excreted** from the body.

?

1 Write down three things that our bodies need food and oxygen for.

2 Which system in the human body:
   a breaks down food into smaller molecules
   b takes in oxygen and excretes carbon dioxide
   c moves substances around the body?

Most of the chemical reactions that happen in the human body are controlled by enzymes. **Enzymes** are protein molecules, and they work best at a temperature of about 37 °C. Our bodies have to be kept at this temperature to make sure all the enzymes can work properly.

Your body is about 65% water. Water is a very important substance because many different chemicals can dissolve in it. Chemical reactions in our cells often happen between dissolved chemicals, and dissolved chemicals can be carried around our bodies in blood. It is important that our bodies always have the right amount of water.

The way our bodies keep factors such as temperature and the amount of water constant is called **homeostasis**.

C People living in extreme environments like this need to help their bodies maintain a constant temperature by wearing insulated clothing.

?

3 Why do our bodies have to be kept at a constant temperature?

4 Give two reasons why water is an important chemical in our bodies.

5 What does homeostasis mean?

6 What are the similarities between the Space Station and the human body?

Summary

The _____ in our bodies need a supply of food and _____, and waste materials must be taken away and _____. The cells need to be kept at a constant _____ so that _____ will work properly, and they must also have the right amount of _____. The way the body _____ these things is called _____.

cells   controls   enzymes   excreted   homeostasis   oxygen   temperature   water

Smells spread through the air by **diffusion**. In drawing A, smelly molecules from the meat get into the air. There are a lot of smelly molecules in the air near the meat, so we say they have a high concentration. There are not as many smelly molecules further away, so they are at a lower concentration. The molecules are moving in all directions all the time. This movement will make them spread out (diffuse) from a place where they are at a high concentration to a place where they are at a low concentration.

A

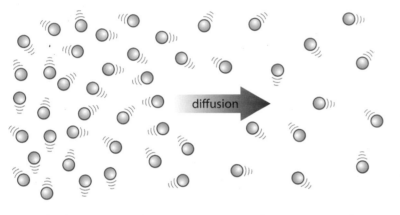

diffusion

higher concentration   lower concentration

B

Substances can move in and out of cells in your body by diffusion. To do this, they usually have to move through a cell membrane. Many membranes have small holes in them that allow small molecules through, but not large ones. Membranes like this are called **partially permeable membranes**.

?

1 How do smells spread out through the air?

2 Look at drawing A. Which dog should smell the meat next? Explain your answer.

3 Why is the smell of perfume strongest when you are standing close to someone wearing it?

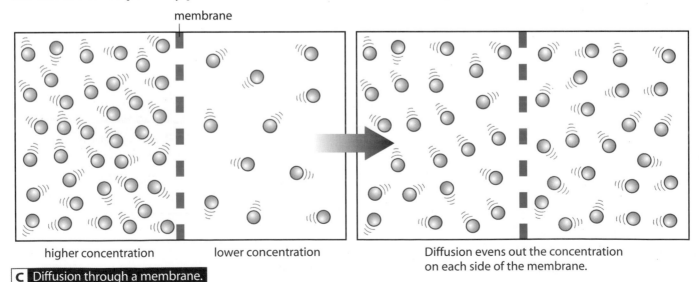

membrane

higher concentration   lower concentration

Diffusion evens out the concentration on each side of the membrane.

C Diffusion through a membrane.

Diffusion allows food substances to pass from the gut into the blood, and from the blood into the cells in the rest of your body.

?

4   What is a partially permeable membrane?

5   Why do only small food molecules diffuse into the blood?

A   Iodine molecules are small, and starch molecules are quite large. Starch makes iodine solution turn black.
- How can you use starch and iodine to show that Visking tubing is a partially permeable membrane?

When you breathe in, there is a higher concentration of oxygen in the air in your lungs than there is in your blood. So there is an overall movement of oxygen from your lungs to your blood (diffusion). The blood carries oxygen to the cells in your body. The concentration of oxygen in your blood is higher than the concentration of oxygen in your cells, so oxygen diffuses into the cells. Carbon dioxide is removed from cells in a similar way.

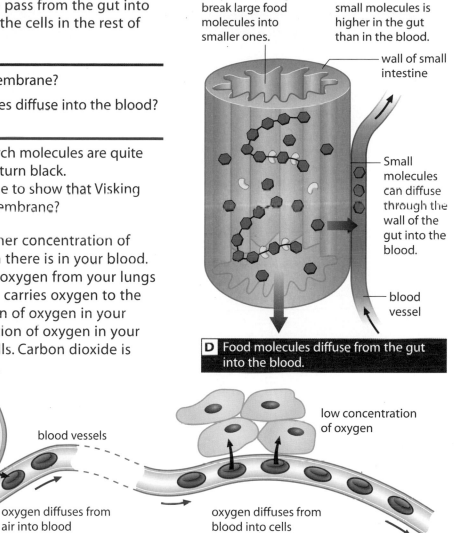

Enzymes in the gut break large food molecules into smaller ones.

The concentration of small molecules is higher in the gut than in the blood.

wall of small intestine

Small molecules can diffuse through the wall of the gut into the blood.

blood vessel

D   Food molecules diffuse from the gut into the blood.

air in lungs

high concentration of oxygen

blood vessels

low concentration of oxygen

lower concentration of oxygen

oxygen diffuses from air into blood

oxygen diffuses from blood into cells

E   How oxygen is taken to cells.

?

6   Name three things that go into or out of cells by diffusion.

7   Which is the odd one out: food molecules, oxygen, carbon dioxide? Explain your answers.

8   Explain how carbon dioxide is removed from cells and breathed out, using ideas about concentration and diffusion.

Summary

Molecules move around all the time, and overall they move from areas of _____ concentration to areas of low _____. This is called _____. Diffusion can occur through _____ permeable _____, which have holes big enough to let small _____ through. Food substances, _____ and carbon _____ move in and out of cells by _____.

concentration   diffusion   dioxide   high   membranes   molecules   oxygen   partially

Osmosis

How does water move in and out of cells?

Diffusion can have some unexpected results. Diagram A shows an experiment with a partially permeable membrane. There is pure water on one side of the membrane, and a sugar solution on the other. After a little while, the fluid level has *risen* on the side with the sugar solution, because some of the pure water has moved into the sugar solution. The diffusion of water into a concentrated solution is called **osmosis**.

? 1 What does a partially permeable membrane do?

2 What is diffusion?

3 What is osmosis?

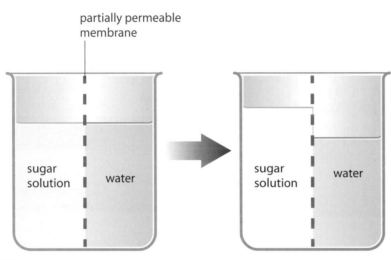

A

To understand why this happens we need to think about what individual molecules are doing. Diagram B shows the same apparatus with pure water on each side of a partially permeable membrane. The molecules of water are moving all the time, and some of them pass through the tiny holes in the membrane. However, equal numbers pass through in each direction, so the water levels on the two sides stay the same.

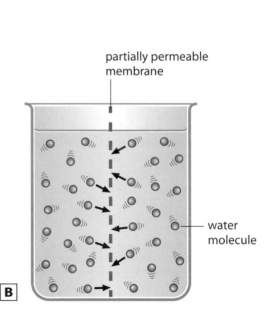

B

? 4 Look at diagram B. Why does the water level stay the same on both sides?

Diagram C shows what happens when you have sugar solution on one side of the membrane. The sugar molecules are too big to go through the holes in the membrane. If we have the same volume of liquid on each side, there are more water molecules in the pure water than in the solution. That means that there are more water molecules that can move from Y to X than in the other direction. The number of water molecules in X will increase, until the numbers of water molecules on each side are the same.

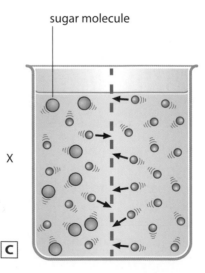

C

A similar thing happens if you have two solutions. Water molecules will move from the more dilute solution (the one with more water molecules) into the more concentrated one, until the concentrations are equal. The solutions do not have to contain the same chemicals. For example, water will move from a dilute salt solution into a concentrated sugar solution.

? 5 a Which contains more water molecules: a concentrated solution or a dilute solution?
 b Why is there an overall movement of water from a dilute solution into a concentrated one?

It is important that the liquids in your body are at the right concentrations, otherwise water might move by osmosis and stop cells working properly.

A Potato cells contain water with lots of chemicals dissolved in it.
 • How can you find the concentration of the solution inside potato cells?

E

? 6 Look at the photos in D. Explain what has happened using ideas about osmosis.

7 The concentration of glucose in a cell is decreasing. Write down as many different explanations for this statement as you can.

8 Shipwreck survivors in lifeboats must never drink seawater. Explain why.

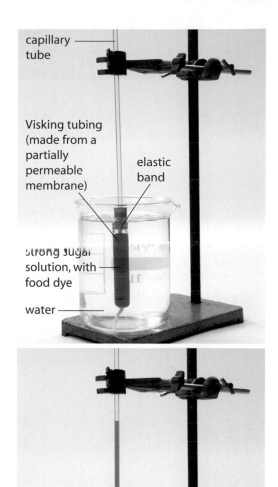

capillary tube

Visking tubing (made from a partially permeable membrane)

elastic band

strong sugar solution, with food dye

water

D Osmosis makes the level of the liquid in the tube rise.

Summary

If you have two _____ separated by a partially _____ membrane, water will move from the _____ solution into the _____ one. This is called _____.

concentrated   dilute   permeable
osmosis   solutions

Enzymes and temperature

Why do enzymes work best at a particular temperature?

Enzymes are **proteins** that speed up reactions in the body. There are thousands of different enzymes in your body, and each one speeds up a different chemical reaction.

A reaction happens when the **reactants** join up. The enzyme makes it easier for the reaction to happen by bringing the reactants close together. After the reaction happens the **products** leave the enzyme. The enzyme can then speed up another reaction between more reactants.

Each kind of enzyme can only speed up one kind of reaction, because only molecules with the right shape can fit into the enzyme. This is called the **'lock and key' model**.

A Amylase enzymes in saliva will break up the starch in the toast into smaller sugar molecules. Amylase does not work on other substances such as proteins or fats.

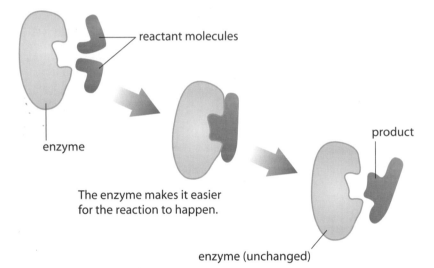

reactant molecules

enzyme

The enzyme makes it easier for the reaction to happen.

product

enzyme (unchanged)

B An enzyme helping to make large molecules from small ones.

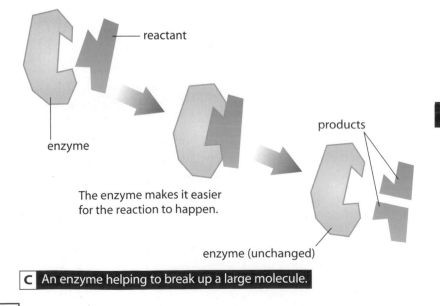

reactant

enzyme

The enzyme makes it easier for the reaction to happen.

products

enzyme (unchanged)

C An enzyme helping to break up a large molecule.

?
1 What kind of chemical are enzymes made from?

2 **a** What does amylase do?
   b What will happen if you add amylase to cheese, which is mainly protein?
   c Explain your answer to part **b**.

3 How does an enzyme speed up a reaction?

Molecules in a liquid are moving around all the time. A reaction happens when the reactant molecules bump into an enzyme molecule and stick to it. If you warm up the liquid the particles move around faster, so the reactants are more likely to bump into the enzyme. Because they have more energy, they are also more likely to stick to the enzyme and react. This means that the **rate of reaction** increases if you increase the temperature.

However, if you make an enzyme too hot, the protein molecule changes shape and the enzyme does not work as well. This is called **denaturing**. This means that enzymes must be at just the right temperature to work properly – warm enough for the reaction to happen quickly, but not so warm that the enzyme is damaged. The best temperature for the enzyme is called its **optimum temperature**. Enzymes in the human body have an optimum temperature of about 37 °C.

A How can you find out the optimum temperature for an enzyme?

• What apparatus will you need?

powdered milk mixture

trypsin solution

D

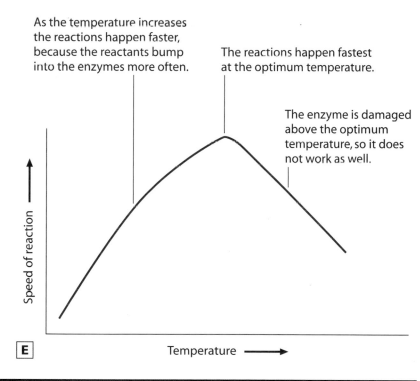

As the temperature increases the reactions happen faster, because the reactants bump into the enzymes more often.

The reactions happen fastest at the optimum temperature.

The enzyme is damaged above the optimum temperature, so it does not work as well.

Speed of reaction

E

Temperature

?
4 a What happens to molecules in a liquid if you warm it up?
 b How does warming up a liquid increase the rate of a reaction?

5 a What is the normal temperature of the human body?
 b Explain how you worked out your answer to part **a**.

6 Think of a plus, a minus, and an interesting point about this statement: Enzymes should work best at 20 °C.

7 Why will amylase break down starch faster if you chew your food well?

Summary

Enzymes are _____ that speed up chemical _____. Each _____ only works on _____ set of reactants. Enzymes work _____ at higher temperatures because the _____ move around faster, and they are more likely to _____ into the _____ and stick to it.

| bump | enzyme | faster | one |
| proteins | reactants | reactions | |

Control systems

How do control systems work?

A

These sharks are being kept in an aquarium so that people can see them. The water in the aquarium has to be kept at the right temperature so the sharks stay warm enough. This can be done automatically using a **temperature control system**.

A thermometer detects the temperature of the water.

If the water is too cold, a thermostat switches on the heater.

The heater warms the water up.

B How an aquarium is kept warm.

In the control system of the aquarium:
- the thermometer is a **receptor** which detects **stimuli** (changes in its surroundings)
- the thermostat is a **processing centre**
- the heater is an **effector**, which makes a change.

The processing centre receives information from a receptor and decides what to do. It triggers the **response** (the action needed) by sending instructions to an effector.

?
1 Why does an aquarium need a temperature control system?

2 What is:
   a a receptor
   b an effector
   c a stimulus?

3 What does a processing centre do?

Babies who are born prematurely have to be looked after very carefully. They cannot control their body temperatures properly, so they are kept in incubators. The incubator has a thermometer to detect the temperature inside it, and a small computer. It also has a heater to warm it up, and a fan to blow warm or cool air into the incubator. The incubator is kept at the right temperature automatically, without a nurse having to check it.

Sometimes your brain is the processing centre in a control system. For instance, if you are reading and it is getting dark, you may decide to switch on the light. You would move your hand to press the light switch.

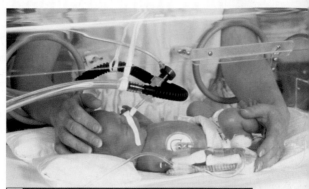

C An incubator used for a premature baby.

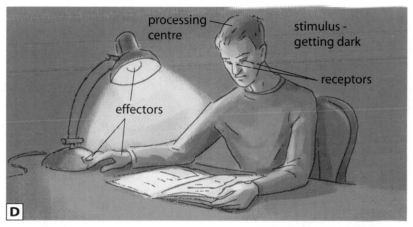

D

Your body also has lots of automatic control systems, which keep the conditions inside your body constant without you having to think about them. All these systems have receptors and effectors and processing centres. You will find out how some of these control systems work later on in this module.

? 4 In a premature baby incubator:
  a what is the receptor
  b what is the processing centre
  c what are the effectors?

? 5 The sunshine is too bright for your eyes, so you put some sunglasses on. In this situation:
  a what is the stimulus
  b what are the receptors
  c what is the processing centre
  d what are the effectors?

6 You can help your automatic control systems to keep you at the right temperature by adjusting your clothing or your surroundings. What effectors could you use if you feel:
  a too hot
  b too cold?

7 Which is the odd one out: stimulus, receptor, effector? Explain your answers.

8 Choose two control systems in the International Space Station and explain which kinds of receptors and effectors would be needed for each system. You may need to look back at Topic B4.1.

Summary

Control _____ keep conditions constant. They have _____ to detect _____. The processing _____ decides what _____ is needed, and sends instructions to an _____.

centre   effector   receptors
response   stimuli   systems

17

Homeostasis and energy

How does your body gain and lose heat?

A Strenuous exercise can lead to overheating and **dehydration** (loss of water).

B Mountaineers can become cold and dehydrated.

C People who live in hot climates must be careful not to get too hot and to make sure they have enough water.

D Scuba divers need to make sure they get enough oxygen and keep warm.

The conditions in your body need to be kept steady or you may become ill. Some of the conditions that need to be kept constant are:
• body temperature
• the amount of water in the body.

?

1 List two things that need to be kept constant in your body.

2 Write down one situation where you could get too:
a hot
b cold.

Your body **core** contains all the important organs, such as the heart, liver and brain. Your body is warmest inside, because this is where most of the heat is produced by respiration. The heat is taken to other parts of the body in the blood, and is transferred to tissues in the arms and legs to keep them warm. If the air around your body is cooler than body temperature, your body will lose heat to the air. Your hands and feet can often feel colder than the rest of your body because they have a large surface area and lose heat easily.

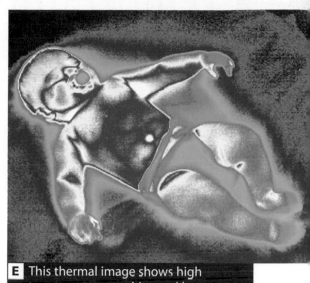

E This thermal image shows high temperatures as white, and low temperatures as purple.

A How does the temperature of your skin change along your arm?

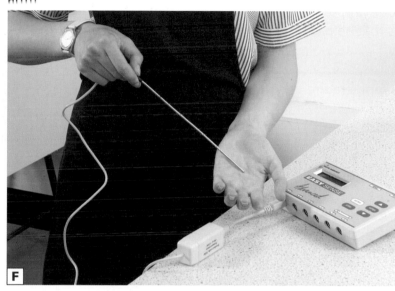

F

You are producing and losing heat all the time, and most of the time the heat gains and losses are balanced. If something makes you hotter, you need to lose more heat to help you to cool down again. If something makes you colder, you need to gain more energy to warm you up, or lose less heat. You can help to keep your energy gains and losses balanced by wearing suitable clothes or controlling the temperature of your surroundings.

?
3 **a** How is most of the heat in your body produced?
   b How does heat energy get to your hands and feet?
   c Why are your hands and feet often colder than the rest of your body?

4 If your body is producing more heat than it is losing, what will happen to your temperature?

5 Look at photos B and C.
   a How are these people trying to control their body temperatures?
   b Explain why this will work, in as much detail as you can.

Summary

Your body needs to be kept at a _____ temperature. It needs constant amounts of _____. _____ produces heat energy, which is taken around the _____ in the _____. Energy is _____ from the skin. _____ gains and losses need to be _____ to maintain a constant _____.

balanced	blood	body	constant
	energy	lost	respiration
		temperature	water

19

Temperature control
How does your temperature control system work?

Your skin has temperature receptors, which detect the temperature of the air around you. You can help to control your body temperature by wearing suitable clothes, and by keeping your surroundings at the right temperature. However, you also have an automatic control system that helps you to maintain a steady core body temperature.

Receptors in the brain detect the temperature of the blood flowing through it. The brain also acts as the processing centre, which decides what action is needed and sends instructions to the effectors. The effectors that help to control temperature are mainly in the skin.

A Elephants spray themselves with water to cool down.

? 1 **a** Where are the two receptors in your temperature control system?
   b What acts as the processing centre?
   c Where are the effectors?

Cooling down

Diagram B shows what the skin does when your body is too hot.

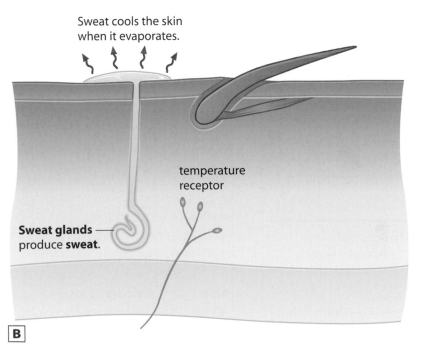

Sweat cools the skin when it evaporates.

temperature receptor

Sweat glands produce **sweat**.

B

When you are too hot your skin feels hot. The hot skin can lose energy to the air near it, which warms up. If you are standing in a breeze, the warm air and evaporated sweat is moved away, making it easier for your skin to lose more energy.

? 2 Name one effector in your temperature control system.

3 Why does a breeze help you to keep cool?

How can you show that sweat helps to cool us down?

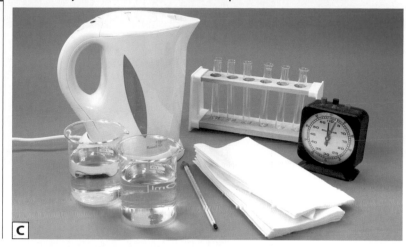

C

Keeping warm

Diagram D shows what the skin does when your body is too cold.

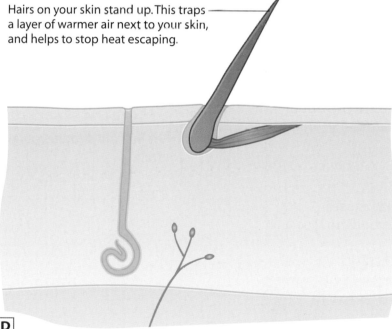

Hairs on your skin stand up. This traps a layer of warmer air next to your skin, and helps to stop heat escaping.

D

If you get very cold, you may start to **shiver**. Your muscles produce lots of energy from respiration when you are shivering, and some of this energy becomes heat which helps to warm up the body.

?
4 How do hairs on our skin help to keep us warm?

5 How can our muscles help to keep us warm?

6 Explain why someone who is dangerously hot might be wrapped in a wet sheet to cool them down.

Summary

The skin and the brain have temperature _____. The _____ is the processing centre. _____ helps you to cool down. Shivering and the hairs on your _____ help you to keep _____ .

brain   receptors   skin
sweating   warm

Heat stroke

What happens if your body temperature gets too high?

When your surroundings are very hot, or you have been exercising hard, you produce a lot of sweat to help you to cool down. If you do not replace the water by drinking, you may become dehydrated. Sweat contains salt, so someone who is sweating a lot may also be short of salt.

? 1 Which two substances do our bodies lose when we are very hot?

A person who is becoming dehydrated may suffer from **heat exhaustion**. They may have a headache and feel dizzy, and they may also feel confused and sick. They will look sweaty and pale, and may have muscle cramps. Someone with heat exhaustion must be taken to a cool place and given drinks to replace the lost water.

If a person with heat exhaustion does not cool down and drink, they may develop **heat stroke**. Because they are dehydrated they do not sweat as much, and so their bodies cannot cool down. If their core body temperature becomes too hot, their temperature control system does not work properly. Their body temperature continues to rise out of control and if they are not treated, they may die. Heat stroke can also happen very suddenly.

Heat stroke usually happens to:
* people who are not used to the heat
* people who have a fever or an illness that causes vomiting or diarrhoea (which causes the body to lose a lot of water)
* people who have taken drugs such as ecstasy.

A Footballers need to stay cool during a match, and make sure their bodies have enough water and salt.

? 2 a What are the symptoms of someone suffering from heat exhaustion?
  b What first aid should you give them?

B These people are at a high risk of heat stroke.

A person with heat stroke will have a headache and feel dizzy and confused. Their skin will be red, hot and dry, and their pulse rate will be fast. It is important to cool them down as quickly as possible by putting them in a bath of cold water, or covering them in cold wet sheets. A person with heat stroke must be seen by a doctor.

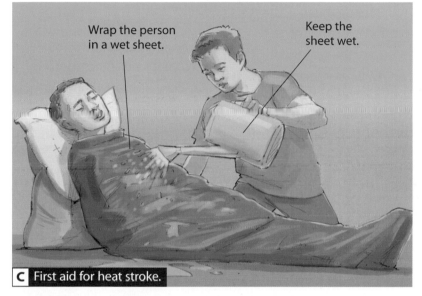

Wrap the person in a wet sheet.

Keep the sheet wet.

C First aid for heat stroke.

It is obviously better to avoid getting too hot in the first place!

D Some of these people may get heat stroke.

?

3 a Why does someone with heat stroke stop sweating?
b What are the other symptoms of heat stroke?

4 What first aid should you give to someone with heat stroke?

?

5 Look at diagram D.
a Which group of teenagers is most likely to get heat stroke?
b Explain your answer.

6 What other harm may come to some of the people in drawing D?

Summary

If you get too hot, you lose a lot of _____ through sweat and may _____. This stops you _____, and your temperature may _____ out of control. A person with heat _____ will have red, _____, dry skin, a rapid _____ rate, and may be _____ and confused. They must be _____ down quickly or they may _____.

cooled	dehydrate	die	dizzy	hot
pulse	rise	stroke	sweating	water

Hypothermia

What happens if our body temperature gets too low?

The normal core body temperature in humans is 37 °C. If a person's core body temperature drops to 35 °C they have **hypothermia**. If the core cools to 30 °C they will lose consciousness, and they will probably die once it drops to about 25 °C.

Many people think of hypothermia happening when people are caught outside in very cold weather, but it can happen at any time when the heat lost by the body is greater than the heat being produced.

?
1 What is the normal core body temperature?

2 a How cold is someone with hypothermia?
   b What causes hypothermia?

A Rain and wind can cool the body, even when the air temperature is quite warm. The cooling effect of the wind is called **wind chill**.

B Elderly people sometimes cannot afford to keep their houses warm, and they often cannot move around enough to keep warm.

D Babies' temperature control systems do not work very well, so they have to be kept warm.

C Cold water cools the body much faster than cold air. Many people who fall into water die from hypothermia, not from drowning.

?
3 Describe two situations when a person might get hypothermia.

A What affects the rate at which a body cools down?

You could investigate clothing, wind, or being wet.
- What apparatus will you need?
- How many different conditions will you test?
- How will you make sure your results are reliable?

E

A person with hypothermia may:
- be shivering
- have cold, pale and dry skin
- be confused
- lose coordination
- have slurred speech
- become drowsy.

Someone with hypothermia must be warmed up. This can be done by taking them to a warm place. If they are wet, give them warm, dry clothes. Wrap them in blankets or more warm clothes, and give them warm drinks. They should not be given alcohol as this widens the blood vessels near the skin and would make them cool down even faster.

?
4 Write down four symptoms of hypothermia.

5 How should you treat someone with hypothermia?

6 Why shouldn't you give alcohol to someone with hypothermia?

7 A person's hands could be 15 °C, but they are not suffering from hypothermia. Explain this observation.

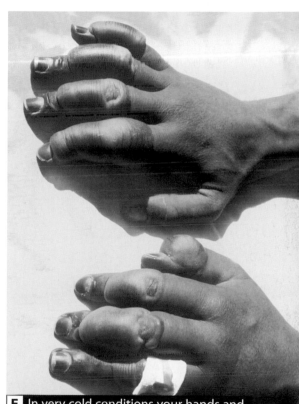
F In very cold conditions your hands and feet cool down even faster than the rest of your body, because blood flow is less. If the cells freeze they die – this is called frostbite. Noses and ears may also get frostbitten.

Summary

Hypothermia occurs when the _____ body temperature falls below _____. A person with _____ may be pale, _____, confused and drowsy. They should be _____ up and given warm _____.

35 °C	core	drinks	hypothermia
	shivering	warmed	

Water balance

How is the amount of water in your body controlled?

About 65% of your body weight is water. You have an automatic control system to balance the amount of water you gain with the amount of water you lose.

Your body gains water:
• in drinks
• in food
• by respiration (which converts glucose and oxygen into carbon dioxide and water).

A How can you find out how much water is in different foods?

B

A Meerkats can go for months without drinking because they get the water they need from their food.

Your body loses water:
• through sweating
• through breathing
• in faeces
• in **urine**.

The liquid part of blood is called **plasma**. It carries blood cells and lots of dissolved chemicals around the body. You need the right amount of water in your body to keep the concentration of blood plasma correct.

If blood plasma is too concentrated, water will be drawn out of cells by osmosis (see Topic B4.3). If blood plasma is too dilute, water may diffuse into other organs, which will swell up and may not be able to work properly.

?
1 Write down three ways that your body gets water.

2 Write down four ways in which your body loses water.

The **kidneys** produce different amounts of urine depending on the conditions in the body. Table C shows how your kidneys help to keep your water levels balanced.

You…	Your blood plasma…	Your kidneys produce…
…are in a warm place, or you have been exercising.	…becomes more concentrated because you have lost a lot of water through sweat.	…concentrated urine, so you do not lose any more water.
…have drunk a lot of water.	… becomes more dilute.	…dilute urine, to get rid of the extra water.
… have eaten a lot of salty food.	…becomes more concentrated, because of the extra salt.	…concentrated urine, to get rid of the extra salt.

C

D At high altitudes there is not much oxygen in the air, so mountaineers have to breathe faster. This means they lose more water in their breath, and they may become dehydrated.

3 a What is plasma?
  b What does it carry around the body?

4 What could happen if your blood plasma is:
  a too concentrated
  b too dilute?

5 a What do your kidneys do if your blood plasma is too dilute?
  b What do they do if you have been eating lots of salty food?

6 Concentrated urine is dark yellow, and dilute urine is almost colourless. Look at photo D. How can a mountaineer tell if he or she is drinking enough liquid? (*Hint*: there are two ways.)

Summary

Your body needs to _____ the amount of _____ it gains and loses. You get water from _____, drink and _____, and you lose it in _____, breathing, faeces and _____. Your _____ produce _____ or concentrated urine, depending on the _____ of your blood _____.

balance   concentration   dilute   food   kidneys   plasma   respiration   sweat   urine   water

Kidneys

How do your kidneys work?

Your kidneys are important for keeping water levels in your body balanced, but they also excrete (get rid of) other substances. For instance, proteins in your food are broken down by the digestive system into amino acids. Your body uses the **amino acids** to make new proteins for growth and repair, but it cannot store any leftover ones. If you have more amino acids than you need, your **liver** breaks them down and make a substance called **urea**, and this is excreted by the kidneys.

?
1 Write down two things that your kidneys do.

2 a Why does the body need to get rid of amino acids?
  b Where are amino acids turned into urea?
  c What happens to the urea?

The liver breaks down extra amino acids to form urea.

The kidneys remove urea and some water and salts from the blood.

Urea and other substances are carried around the body in the blood.

Urine is stored in the bladder until you go to the toilet.

A Part of the human excretory system.

The kidneys filter small molecules such as water, sugar, salt and urea out of the blood, and then they reabsorb any of these substances that the body needs. This all happens in tubes called **kidney tubules**. Diagram C shows what happens in the tubules.

?
3 What happens to urine when it has been made?

Each kidney is made of hundreds of thousands of tubules. Only one is shown here, so you can see its position.

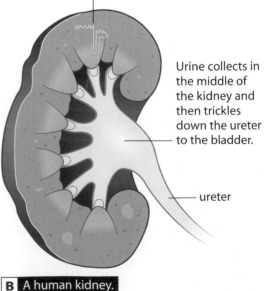

Urine collects in the middle of the kidney and then trickles down the ureter to the bladder.

ureter

B A human kidney.

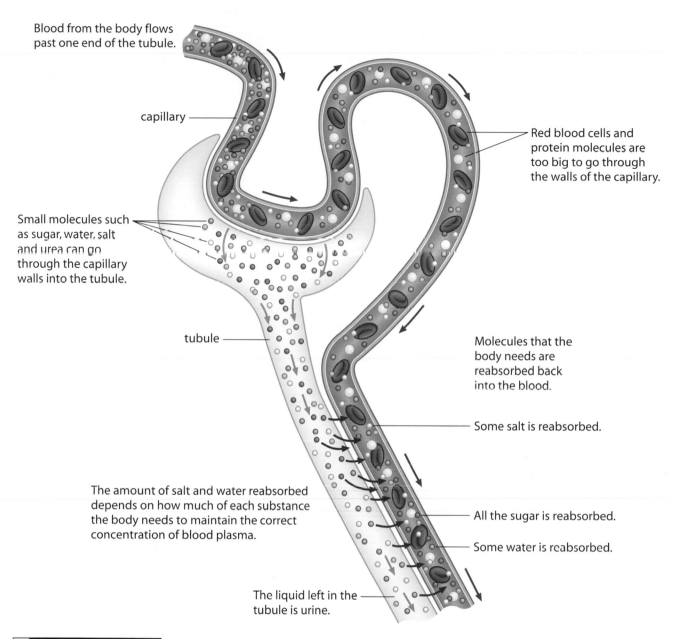

Blood from the body flows past one end of the tubule.

capillary

Red blood cells and protein molecules are too big to go through the walls of the capillary.

Small molecules such as sugar, water, salt and urea can go through the capillary walls into the tubule.

tubule

Molecules that the body needs are reabsorbed back into the blood.

Some salt is reabsorbed.

The amount of salt and water reabsorbed depends on how much of each substance the body needs to maintain the correct concentration of blood plasma.

All the sugar is reabsorbed.

Some water is reabsorbed.

The liquid left in the tubule is urine.

C How the kidneys work.

?

4 Which molecules are too big to go into the kidney tubule?

5 Which molecules are all reabsorbed into the blood?

6 Which molecules are not reabsorbed into the blood at all?

7 Why does the kidney sometimes reabsorb different amounts of salt and water?

8 a Describe a situation where the kidney will reabsorb a lot of salt and only a little water.
b What would your urine be like if your kidney did this?

Summary

Amino _____ are broken down to make urea in the _____, and _____ is excreted by the _____. The kidneys also filter _____, salt and water out of the blood. All the sugar is _____, and also as much salt and _____ as the body needs.

| acids | kidneys | liver | reabsorbed |
| sugar | urea | water | |

Drugs and water
How can drugs affect your water balance?

Your kidneys control the amount of water in your body, by changing the concentration of the urine they excrete. The kidneys are the effectors in the water control system. Some drugs can affect the way the kidneys work.

Drinking alcohol affects the kidneys, and makes them produce lots of dilute urine. This means that the body is getting rid of more water than usual. Drinking a lot of alcohol can therefore lead to dehydration. A 'hangover' after drinking a lot of alcohol is partly caused by dehydration.

A Drinking these can dehydrate you.

?

1 Write down three ways by which our bodies gain water.

2 Write down four ways by which our bodies normally lose water.

3 Why can drinking alcohol lead to dehydration?

Other drugs can also affect water balance. One of these is ecstasy, which makes the kidneys produce only small amounts of concentrated urine. Many people know that dehydration is bad for the body, but it is also possible for too much water to be harmful. In 1995, a teenager called Leah Betts died after taking ecstasy at a party. She died because she drank too much water.

Ecstasy kills

Leah Betts, who fell into a coma after taking Ecstasy at a party, died today without regaining consciousness.

B Leah Betts is not the only person to die after taking ecstasy, but her death hit the headlines at the time.

C A lot of water is lost as sweat while dancing.

Ecstasy can stop people feeling the effects of heat and thirst, and they can carry on dancing until they become dehydrated and may suffer from heat stroke. Most people who use ecstasy know this, so they drink lots of water. However, ecstasy also stops the kidneys working properly, and reduces the amount of urine they produce. This means that if you drink too much water, your body may not be able to get rid of it.

This is what happened to Leah. She drank a lot of water, but her body was not getting rid of it. Her blood became too diluted, and water moved into cells in her brain by osmosis. The cells swelled up, and the pressure on her brain caused her to become unconscious and die.

A doctor recommends that people who are going to use ecstasy should take a 2-litre bottle of soft drink with them, and add 4 teaspoons of salt to it. Drinking this mixture should stop them suffering from the effects of too much water. However, this does not mean that ecstasy is safe to use – there are fears that using the drug could permanently affect brain cells.

?

4 A person who has taken ecstasy at a party normally loses a lot of water.
  a Which is the main way that they lose water?
  b Explain your answer to part **a**.

5 a If you drink more water than your body needs, how does your body get rid of the extra water?
  b Why doesn't this happen for someone who has taken ecstasy?

6 What caused Leah Betts' death?

7 Explain why a soft drink with added salt is better than pure water for party-goers using ecstasy. Use the word 'concentration' in your answer.

Summary

Alcohol makes the _____ make a lot of _____ urine. This can lead to _____. _____ makes the kidneys produce a _____ amount of _____ urine. This can lead to the body having too much _____.

concentrated	dehydration	dilute
ecstasy	kidneys	small	water

Survival school

How does the human body survive in different conditions?

SURVIVAL SCHOOL

A

The human body is amazing – you can survive in extreme environments if you know how!

But EVERYONE needs survival skills – you can die of heat or cold even in Britain!

If you understand how your body works, you have a better chance of surviving.

The temperature of your body must be kept constant to allow enzymes to work properly.

1 **a** What do enzymes do?
   b What are they made from?
   c In a reaction involving enzymes, what happens if you change the temperature? Explain in as much detail as you can.

2 **a** What process in your body produces heat?
   b Where is most of this heat produced?
   c How is the heat transferred to other parts of the body?
   d Explain why your hands and feet are often cooler than other parts of your body.

3 Control systems have different parts. Explain what each of the following words means, and give an example of each.
   a a stimulus
   b a receptor
   c a processing centre
   d a response
   e an effector

4 In the control system that maintains your body temperature:
   a name two receptors
   b describe two effectors
   c name the part that acts as the processing centre.

Your control systems may not work in all conditions!

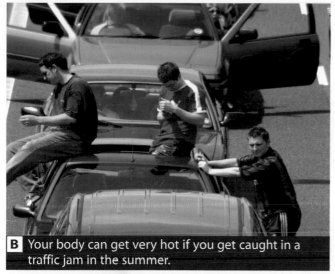

B Your body can get very hot if you get caught in a traffic jam in the summer.

5 Explain how sweat helps to keep you cool.

6 a Describe the symptoms of heat stroke.
  b What first aid should you give to someone who is suffering from heat stroke?
  c Explain how this first aid will help them.

C You can also get extremely cold in some situations!

7 a Explain how shivering can help to keep you warm.
  b How do the hairs on your skin help to keep you warm?

8 a What is hypothermia?
  b Describe three situations in which someone might get hypothermia.
  c What are the symptoms of hypothermia?
  d What first aid treatment should you give to someone with hypothermia?

The amounts of water and salts in your body also have to be controlled, to keep your blood plasma at a steady concentration.

9 Substances move in and out of cells by diffusion and osmosis.
  a What is diffusion?
  b Give one example of diffusion happening.
  c What is osmosis?
  d What will happen to a cell if the fluid outside it is too dilute?

10 Your kidneys control the water level in your body, and also excrete other substances.
  a Where is urea made?
  b What happens to urea in the kidneys?
  c What happens to salt in the kidneys?
  d Why don't protein molecules get into the kidney tubules?
  e What happens to urine after it is made in the kidneys?

D Your kidneys have to control water and salt levels in lots of different conditions.

11 Look at the teenagers in the drawing. Give two reasons why their blood plasma may become more concentrated.

12 Describe one situation when your kidneys would make:
  a a lot of dilute urine
  b a small amount of concentrated urine.

13 How do these drugs affect the urine that the kidneys produce?
  a alcohol
  b ecstasy

Chemical patterns

How do we use elements and compounds?

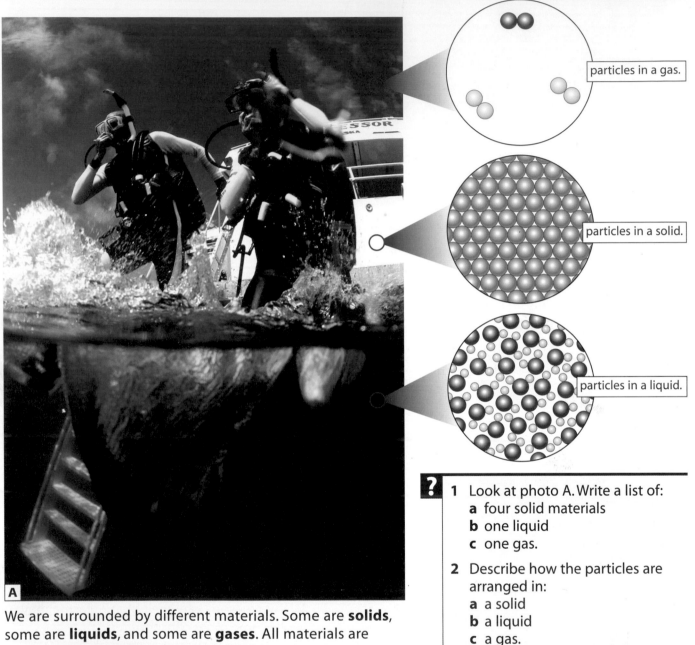

particles in a gas.

particles in a solid.

particles in a liquid.

A

We are surrounded by different materials. Some are **solids**, some are **liquids**, and some are **gases**. All materials are made of tiny particles.

Divers need to carry oxygen with them so they can breathe underwater. Oxygen is an **element**, made of only one kind of **atom**. You cannot break oxygen atoms into anything simpler. Water is a **compound**. It is made of oxygen and hydrogen atoms bonded together. Water can be split up into hydrogen and oxygen. The properties of water are very different from the properties of the two elements that make it up.

?

1 Look at photo A. Write a list of:
   a four solid materials
   b one liquid
   c one gas.

2 Describe how the particles are arranged in:
   a a solid
   b a liquid
   c a gas.

3 What is the difference between an element and a compound?

4 **a** How can you test a gas in the laboratory to see if it is oxygen?
   b What is the test for hydrogen?
   c What would happen if you tried these tests with water?

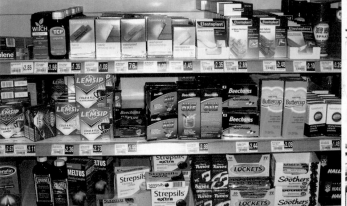

B We need to understand the properties of elements so that we can develop and use new compounds, like medicines, dyes and cosmetics.

C Helium is an unreactive gas used to fill balloons. It makes balloons float because it has a very low **density**. Alloys of iron are used in lamp-posts and buildings, as iron is strong and fairly cheap.

D Alloys of aluminium are used to build helicopters because aluminium has a low density. Aluminium is an expensive metal.

E Analytical chemists can investigate the elements and compounds present in a sample.

There are about 100 different elements, and they all have different properties and uses. Everything around us is made of elements, or of compounds made with elements. Scientists and engineers need to know about the **properties** of elements and compounds to help them to choose the right material for the job, or to make new materials.

?

5 Hydrogen has a lower density than helium, so it is lighter. Why do you think balloons are filled with helium rather than hydrogen?

6 a Why is iron used to build lamp-posts and not aluminium?
  b Why is aluminium used to build helicopters and aeroplanes?

7 Think of a plus, a minus and an interesting point about this statement: The atmosphere should be made of helium.

8 The elements on this page can be put into different groups. Think of different ways of grouping them, and explain your reasons for each grouping.

Summary

Materials are all made of _____. In an _____ all the atoms are the same. Two or more _____ kinds of atom joined together form a _____. We choose materials for particular jobs because of their _____.

atoms	compound	different
	element	properties

Classifying elements

How can we sort elements into groups?

Chemists often sort elements into groups according to their properties. This makes them easier to understand and study. Elements can be classified in several ways. For example, they can be put into groups according to their state. At room temperature 11 elements are gases, two are liquids, and the rest are solids.

? 1 Draw up a table of elements showing seven solids, two liquids and four gases. Start your table like this:

Solids	Liquids	Gases

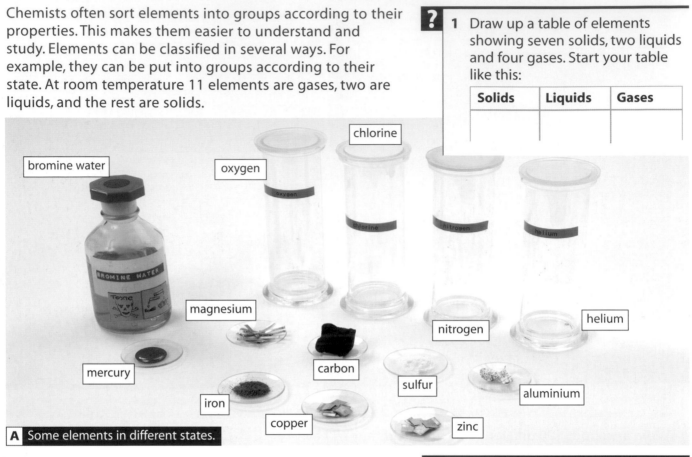

A Some elements in different states.

Elements can also be classified as **metals** or **non-metals**, depending on their properties. About three-quarters of the known elements are metals and the rest are non-metals.

? 2 Write down the names of:
a three metals
b five non-metals.

B Metals.

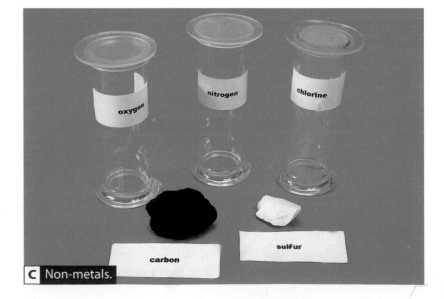

C Non-metals.

Metals are generally:
- hard shiny solids, with high melting points (only mercury is a liquid at room temperature)
- good conductors of heat
- good conductors of electricity
- strong and hard to break
- malleable and ductile, so they can be hammered into shape and drawn into wires.

Non-metals are generally:
- dull solids, liquids or gases, with low melting points (only carbon, silicon and boron have very high melting points)
- poor conductors of heat (they are good insulators of heat)
- good insulators of electricity (except carbon in the form of graphite, which does conduct electricity)
- brittle solids, weak and easily broken.

?

3 a Write down three properties of metals.
  b Write down three properties of non-metals.

4 Mercury is a liquid at room temperature.
  a Will mercury conduct electricity?
  b Explain your answer.

5 Look at the elements in photo E.
  Which is the odd one out? Explain your answers.

E

gold

iron

sulfur

6 A new element is discovered. It is a solid and it bends easily without breaking.
  a Is this new element a metal or a non-metal? Explain your answer.
  b What other tests might you do to find out?

A How can you compare the properties of metals and non-metals?

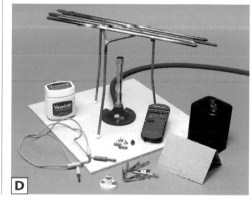

D

Summary

About _____ % of the elements are _____ and the rest are _____.

Metals are generally strong, _____ solids that are _____ conductors of heat and electricity.

Non-metals are generally weak solids, liquids and gases. Most of them have _____ melting points. They are poor _____ of heat and electricity.

| conductors | good | low | metals |
| non-metals | shiny | 75 | |

Atomic structure

What are atoms made from?

All atoms are made up of three types of smaller particle called protons, neutrons and electrons.

? 1 What are atoms made of?

The three types of particle have different properties.

Particle	Charge	Relative mass
proton	positive	1
electron	negative	negligible
neutrons	no charge	1

A

The mass of these particles is so small that we do not measure it in grams. We say that protons and neutrons have a relative mass of 1. The mass of the electrons is so small that we can ignore it. We say that electrons have a **negligible** mass. Atoms always have the same number of protons as electrons. This makes the atoms **neutral** as the charges cancel out.

? 2 a If an atom has four protons, how many electrons does it have?
b Explain your answer.

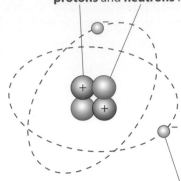

protons and **neutrons** in the **nucleus**

electrons move around the nucleus

B The structure of a helium atom.

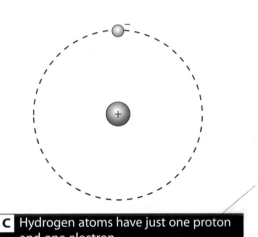

C Hydrogen atoms have just one proton and one electron.

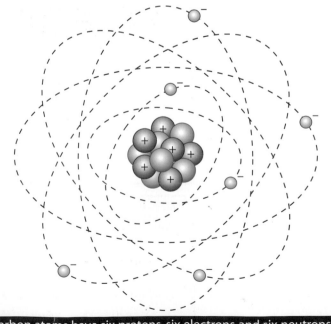

D Carbon atoms have six protons, six electrons and six neutrons.

The **proton number** (or **atomic number**) of an atom is the number of protons in its nucleus. Atoms of the same element always have the same number of protons, so they always have the same proton number. The **mass number** of an atom is the total number of protons and neutrons in the nucleus. Atoms of the same element can have different numbers of neutrons, so they can have different mass numbers.

The masses of atoms are measured by using **relative atomic masses** (RAM). In this scale the lightest atom, hydrogen, is given a relative atomic mass of 1. Other elements are measured relative to hydrogen. So helium, which is four times heavier, is given the RAM of 4.

This is the mass number of the element. It is the total number of protons and neutrons in the atom.

This is the proton number of the element. It is the number of protons in the atom.

12
C
6
carbon

E This is the way that information about elements is shown in the Periodic Table.

Symbol	Name	Proton number	Mass number	Numbers of		
				protons	neutrons	electrons
Ar	argon	18	40	18	22	18
Br	bromine	35	81	35	46	35
Ag	silver	47	108	47	61	47

F The atomic structures of some atoms of common elements.

The **Periodic Table** on page 40 contains information about the elements, including their symbols and proton numbers.

3 The element sodium can be shown like this:

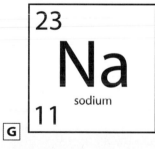

23
Na
sodium
11

G

a What is the proton number of sodium?
b What is the mass number of sodium?
c How many proton and electrons does an atom of sodium have?

4 a Write down two ways that protons and neutrons are similar.
b How are protons and neutrons different?

5 If an atom has 15 protons, what else does this tell you about the atom?

6 Which is the odd one out: proton, neutron, electron? Explain your answers.

7 Find out why many Periodic Tables show chlorine with a mass number of 35.5 (*Hint*: you cannot have half a proton or neutron in the nucleus.)

Summary

An atom is described by its proton number (or _____ number) that equals the number of protons. The atom is _____ as the number of electrons equals the number of _____.

Particle	Charge	Where found
proton		in nucleus
neutron	no charge	in _____
electron		

around nucleus   atomic
negative   neutral   nucleus
positive   protons

The Periodic Table

Why is the Periodic Table useful?

The Periodic Table is a useful way of classifying the elements. In this table the elements are arranged in order of their proton number into rows, called **periods**. The vertical columns in the Periodic Table are called **groups**.

A In the modern Periodic Table the elements are arranged in order of their proton number.

The position of the elements in the Periodic Table tells us something about how the elements react. Elements in the same group have similar chemical properties, so they react in similar ways.

As we travel from left to right across a period the properties of the elements gradually change. Metals are always found on the left of the period and non-metals on the right. There are 90 naturally occurring elements. Three-quarters of these elements are metals. They are mostly found in Groups 1 and 2, and in the central block called the **transition metals**. The metals in the transition block all have fairly similar chemical properties, but they are not exactly the same.

?

1 In the Periodic Table what is meant by:
   a a period
   b a group?

2 Name a non-metal that is:
   a in the same group as oxygen
   b in the same period as oxygen.

Summary

In the Periodic Table the elements are arranged in order of increasing _____ number. The elements with similar _____ properties are arranged in columns called _____. The rows of elements are called _____. In each period metals are on the _____ and non-metals are on the _____. Most metals are found in groups _____ and _____ and in the middle block, called the _____ metals.

chemical	groups	left	periods
proton	right	transition	1 2

?

3 What is special about elements in the same group of the Periodic Table?

4 Where are the metals found in the Periodic Table?

5 Write down the names of:
   a three metals with similar properties
   b three non-metals with similar properties.

6 Think of a plus, a minus and an interesting point about this statement: There should only be 50 different elements.

7 Write down the name and symbol for an element which:
   a is a metallic element in Group 4
   b is in the second period of Group 7
   c is a transition metal in the fourth period.

Formulae and equations

Why are chemical formulae and equations useful?

A chemical formula gives information about an element or compound using symbols. The formula of an element is usually just its symbol.

carbon – C   iron – Fe   sodium – Na   silicon – Si
magnesium – Mg   aluminium – Al   phosphorus – P

In some elements two atoms join together to form a molecule, called a **diatomic molecule**. We show this by writing a formula for the molecule with a little 2 after the symbol. Elements that form diatomic molecules are oxygen, nitrogen, hydrogen, and all the elements in Group 7 of the Periodic Table.

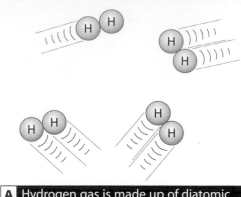

A Hydrogen gas is made up of diatomic molecules, H_2.

?

1 What is the difference between an element and a compound?

2 What is a diatomic molecule?

3 Write the formulae of all the diatomic elements. You may need to look at the Periodic Table on page 40.

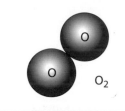

B Oxygen forms diatomic molecules.

Atoms of different elements can join together to make compounds. Diagram C shows some molecules of compounds and their formulae.

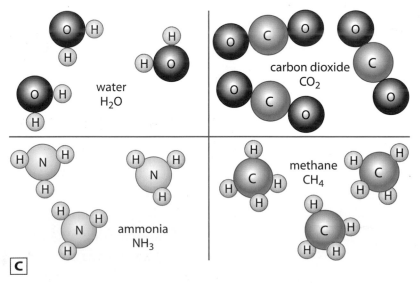

water
H_2O

carbon dioxide
CO_2

methane
CH_4

ammonia
NH_3

C

Some compounds do not form individual molecules. Diagram D shows how the different atoms are arranged in iron sulfide. Here the **formula** tells us the ratio of atoms of each element in the compound. The formula for iron sulfide is FeS, which tells us that there is one iron atom for every sulfur atom atom.

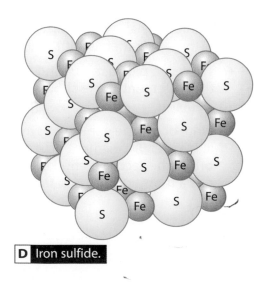

D Iron sulfide.

4 Write down the formula for each of the molecules shown in diagram E.

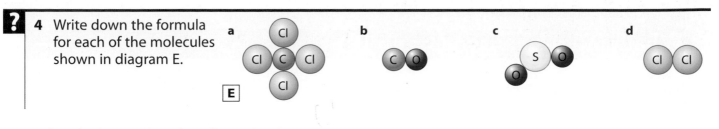

A **chemical equation** describes what happens in a chemical reaction. The arrow shows that the **reactants** have changed into the **products**.

This is the **word equation** for the reaction between hydrogen and oxygen:

hydrogen + oxygen → water
(reactants)   (product)

This can also be written as a **symbol equation** using the formulae of the elements or compounds in a reaction.

State symbols are used in some equations. These are: (s) solid; (l) liquid; (g) gas; and (aq) dissolved in water.

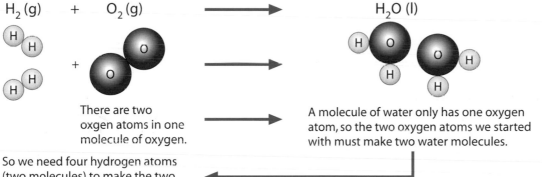

H_2 (g) + O_2 (g) → H_2O (l)

There are two oxgen atoms in one molecule of oxygen.

A molecule of water only has one oxygen atom, so the two oxygen atoms we started with must make two water molecules.

So we need four hydrogen atoms (two molecules) to make the two water molecules.

F

However this symbol equation is not quite right. Chemical reactions involve rearranging atoms and molecules to form new substances. During a reaction atoms are not lost or created. There is always the same number of atoms at the end as there was at the beginning. Diagram F shows that we need two molecules of hydrogen to react with one molecule of oxygen. We show this by writing a large number in front of the formula. This is now a **balanced symbol equation**.

$2H_2$ (g) + O_2 (g) → $2H_2O$ (l)

5 Write symbol equations for the following word equations. (*Hint*: you can find all the formulae on these pages.)
   a sulfur + oxygen → sulfur dioxide
   b carbon + oxygen → carbon dioxide

6 The carbon dioxide gas formed in a coal fire sometimes combines with more solid carbon to form the poisonous gas carbon monoxide. Write a word equation to represent this change.

Summary

The formula of an element is usually just its _____. A few elements are diatomic, such as oxygen (_____) and _____ (H_2).

The formula of a compound tells us the number of _____ of each element in a _____, e.g. water is _____ and _____ is CO_2.

atoms   carbon dioxide   hydrogen
molecule   symbol H_2O O_2

The alkali metals

What patterns exist in Group 1?

Group 1 in the Periodic Table contains the very reactive **alkali metals**.

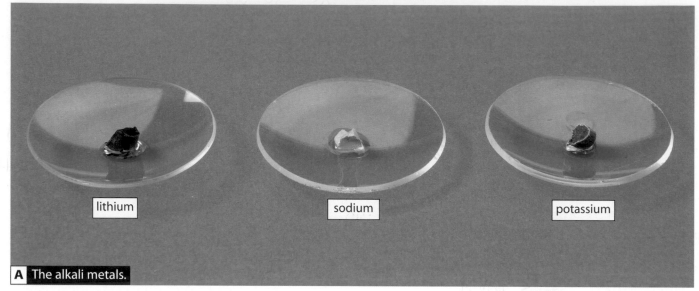

A The alkali metals.

The alkali metals are all in the same group of the Periodic Table because they react in a similar way. Their properties change gradually down the group.

Element	Symbol	Proton number	Melting point (°C)	Boiling point (°C)	Density (g/cm³)	Reactivity
lithium	Li	3	181	1342	0.53	least reactive
sodium	Na	11	98	883	0.97	
potassium	K	19	63	760	0.86	
rubidium	Rb	37	39	686	1.53	
caesium	Cs	55	29	669	1.90	most reactive

B

Alkali metals have a shiny metallic surface when you cut them. They react very quickly in moist air, so they soon **tarnish** and become dull. They also react quickly with cold water to produce hydrogen gas and a metal hydroxide. The metal hydroxides all dissolve in water to form **alkaline** solutions (pH above 7). The general formula for all alkali metal hydroxides is MOH (M is the general symbol for an alkali metal).

metal + water → metal hydroxide + hydrogen

For example, the balanced symbol equation for the reaction of sodium with water is:

sodium + water → sodium hydroxide + hydrogen
$2Na (s) + 2H_2O (l) → 2NaOH (aq) + H_2 (g)$

?

1 Which of the alkali metals has:
   a the highest boiling point
   b the highest density?

2 How do the melting points change as you go down Group 1?

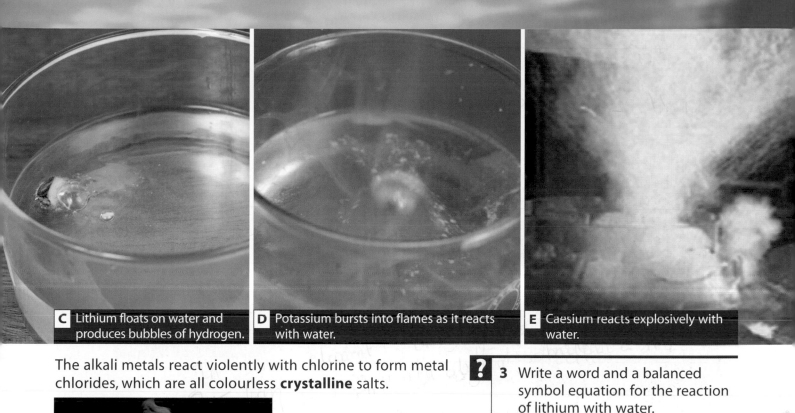

C Lithium floats on water and produces bubbles of hydrogen.

D Potassium bursts into flames as it reacts with water.

E Caesium reacts explosively with water.

The alkali metals react violently with chlorine to form metal chlorides, which are all colourless **crystalline** salts.

F Sodium chloride being formed.

The equation for the reaction of sodium with chlorine is:

sodium + chlorine → sodium chloride

$$2Na \ (s) + Cl_2 \ (g) \rightarrow 2NaCl \ (s)$$

The sodium chloride formed in this reaction is common salt. The general formula for all alkali metal chlorides is MCl.

? 5 Look at the photos on this page. How can you tell that the alkali metals get more reactive as you go down the group?

6 Think of a plus, a minus and an interesting point about this statement: All alkali metals should have the same reactivity.

7 Which of the metals will float on water? Explain your answer. (*Hint*: the density of water is 1 g/cm³.)

? 3 Write a word and a balanced symbol equation for the reaction of lithium with water.

4 Why are the Group 1 metals called the alkali metals?

Summary

The alkali metals are found in _____ in the Periodic Table. They are all very _____.

metal + water → metal hydroxide + _____

metal + _____ → metal chloride

The reactivity _____ down the group.

chlorine	Group 1	hydrogen
	increases	reactive

45

The halogens

What patterns exist in Group 7?

Group 7 in the Periodic Table contains the reactive non-metals called the **halogens**. They all have diatomic molecules and their chemical reactions are similar. However, their appearances and physical properties are different.

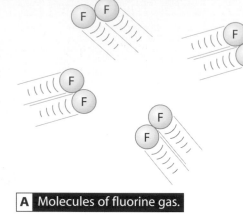

A Molecules of fluorine gas.

Fluorine is a pale yellow gas.

Chlorine is a green gas.

Bromine is a brown liquid that forms a brown gas.

Iodine is a black shiny solid that forms a purple gas when it sublimes (goes straight from a solid into a gas with no liquid state).

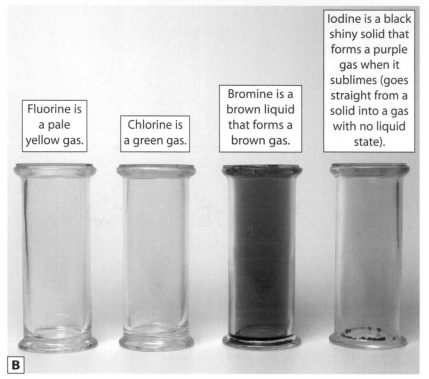

B

The halogens show regular patterns in their physical and chemical properties.

Element	Symbol	Proton number	Formula	Melting point (°C)	Boiling point (°C)	Appearance at room temperature and pressure	Reactivity
fluorine	F	9	F_2	−220	−188	yellow gas	most reactive
chlorine	Cl	17	Cl_2	−101	−35	green gas	
bromine	Br	35	Br_2	−7	59	brown liquid	
iodine	I	53	I_2	114	184	black solid	least reactive

C

As you go down Group 7, melting points and boiling points increase, and the colour becomes darker.

When halogens react with metals they form solid salts called metal **halides**. Sodium chloride and iron bromide are examples of halide salts.

metal + halogen → metal halide

?

1 Which halogen has the highest boiling point?

2 Which halogens would be gases at −100 °C?

3 Write down the formula for fluorine gas.

The reactivity of the halogens decreases down the group. For example, when iron wool is heated and comes into contact with halogen vapour it:
• immediately bursts into flames in fluorine
• starts to glow brightly in chlorine
• glows a dull red in bromine
• slowly changes colour in iodine.

The word equation and the balanced symbol equation for the reaction of chlorine with iron are shown below.

iron + chlorine → iron chloride
$Fe (s) + Cl_2 (g) → FeCl_2 (s)$

D Chlorine reacting with iron wool.

E Chlorine **bleaches** (removes the colour from) damp litmus paper.

? 4 **a** Write a word equation for the reaction of fluorine with iron.
   b Write a symbol equation for the formation of iron bromide ($FeBr_2$).

5 Look at photo E. Describe two different chemical tests to show the difference between samples of oxygen and chlorine gas.

6 How can you use the reactions of the halogens with iron to put them into an order of reactivity?

7 Chlorine reacts with sodium bromide (NaBr) to form sodium chloride (NaCl) and release bromine vapour. Represent this reaction using:
   a a word equation
   b a symbol equation
   c a balanced symbol equation with state symbols.

Summary

The _____ are reactive _____ found in Group 7 in the Periodic Table. They exist as _____ molecules. Halogens react with _____ to form metal _____. The reactivity _____ down the group.

| decreases | diatomic | halogens |
| halides | metals | non-metals |

Using chemicals safely

How can we make sure we use chemicals safely?

The halogens, and certain compounds of them, can be used to kill bacteria in water. They can also bleach dyes and other materials. Household bleach often contains chlorine and is used to kill bacteria in toilets and to remove stains. Iodine used to be used as an antiseptic, but today we often use other chemicals that are less harmful to human skin.

A Chlorine kills bacteria in swimming pools.

B Iodine tablets can be added to water to make it safe to drink.

? **1** Describe two ways in which the halogens can help to stop us becoming ill.

2 Why should you be careful not to spill bleach on your clothes?

The halogens are all toxic and corrosive; this is what makes them useful for killing bacteria, but it also means that we have to be very careful when using them. Gloves and safety glasses must be worn when handling any halogen, and care must be taken to avoid breathing any halogen gases.

The alkali metals are also hazardous as they are corrosive and react violently with water. This means that they could react with the water present in your skin. They are all stored in oil, tongs must be used to pick them up and safety glasses must be worn.

? **3** Suggest why the alkali metals are stored in oil.

Many chemicals can be dangerous if not handled properly. We use **hazard symbols** to show the hazards of different chemicals (table C).

Symbol	Meaning	Precautions
X i	**Irritant** – will make the skin blister or turn red.	Wear eye protection. Wash any splashes off the skin straight away.
X h	**Harmful** – a risk to health (although not likely to kill you)	Wear eye protection. Wash any splashes off the skin straight away.
☠	**Toxic** – can cause death if swallowed or breathed in.	Wear gloves and eye protection. Wear a mask over the mouth and nose, or use a fume cupboard.
	Corrosive – attacks living tissue such as skin or eyes.	Wear gloves and eye protection.
🔥	**Highly flammable** – catches fire easily.	Keep the chemical away from flames or sparks, and also keep it away from oxidising substances.
🔥	**Oxidising** – helps other substances to burn.	Wear eye protection. Keep away from flammable substances, including clothing.

C

Dilute acids and alkalis that are used in school laboratories are irritants. More concentrated acids and alkalis can be harmful or even corrosive. Sometimes a substance can have more than one hazard label.

D Ethanol is harmful and highly flammable.

?
4 What hazard symbol would you put on a bottle containing potassium?

5 Why should you wear a mask that covers your nose and mouth if you are using a toxic chemical?

6 What precautions should you take when you are using alkalis in the school lab?

7 Why wouldn't you expect to see a 'harmful' hazard symbol on a container as well as a 'corrosive' symbol?

Summary

Chlorine and the other _____ can be used to kill _____ in water and to bleach _____. Many chemicals are hazardous and _____ precautions must be taken when using them. Hazard _____ tell us about the hazards of a chemical.

bacteria	dyes	halogens
	safety	symbols

49

Electron arrangements

How are the electrons arranged in atoms?

Different elements have different properties. For example, some elements are metals and some are non-metals. Some elements are very reactive and others hardly react at all. The chemical properties of an element depend on its **electron arrangement**.

In all atoms:
- the protons and neutrons are found in the nucleus with electrons circling round it
- protons have a positive charge and electrons have a negative charge
- the proton number equals the number of protons (and electrons if the atom is neutral).

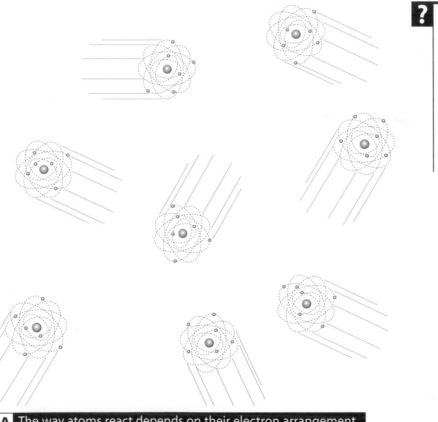

? 1 Which particles are found:
  a in the nucleus
  b circling around the nucleus?

2 Why is the electron arrangement the most important part of the atomic structure to chemists?

3 a What is the charge on a proton?
  b Why are atoms usually neutral?

A The way atoms react depends on their electron arrangement.

In all atoms the electrons are arranged in **electron shells** or **energy levels**. Each shell can only hold a certain number of electrons. The first shell holds two electrons and when it is full the second shell starts to fill. The second shell can hold eight electrons and then the third shell starts to fill. When the third shell has eight electrons the fourth shell starts to fill. The inner shells always fill first. Bigger atoms have more electrons and more electron shells.

? 4 What is the maximum number of electrons in the:
  a first shell
  b second shell?

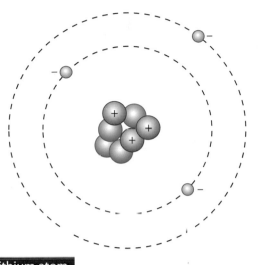

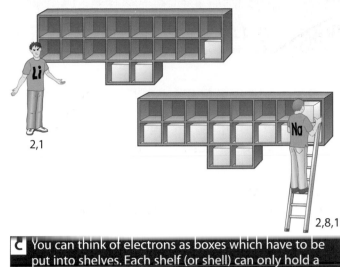
2,1

2,8,1

C You can think of electrons as boxes which have to be put into shelves. Each shelf (or shell) can only hold a certain number of boxes (or electrons).

B A lithium atom.

We sometimes show electron arrangements by drawing diagrams like diagram D. However, as some elements have nearly 100 electrons, these diagrams could be very large! An easier way is to just write the number of electrons in each shell. For example, the electron arrangement of potassium would be written as 2, 8, 8, 1.

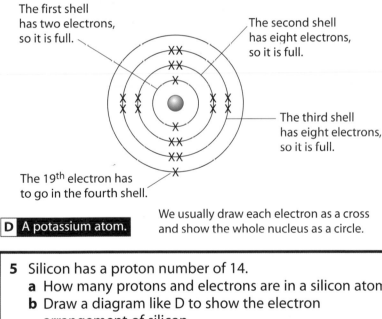

The first shell has two electrons, so it is full.

The second shell has eight electrons, so it is full.

The third shell has eight electrons, so it is full.

The 19th electron has to go in the fourth shell.

D A potassium atom.

We usually draw each electron as a cross and show the whole nucleus as a circle.

?

5 Silicon has a proton number of 14.
 a How many protons and electrons are in a silicon atom?
 b Draw a diagram like D to show the electron arrangement of silicon.
 c Write the electron arrangement for silicon in numbers.

6 The electron arrangements for some different elements are given below.
 A 2, 8, 6   **B** 2, 8, 2   **C** 2, 8, 1   **D** 2, 7   **E** 2, 8, 7   **F** 2, 1
 a Which of these elements are metals and which are non-metals?
 b What do you notice about the number of electrons in the outer shells of metals compared to non-metals?

Summary

In all atoms the electrons circle around the _____ in _____ levels or _____. Each shell only holds a maximum number of _____.

The electron _____ can be drawn as a _____ or shown using _____.

The arrangement of electrons in an atom affects the way it _____.

arrangement	diagram	electrons
energy	numbers	nucleus
reacts	shells	

Ions and ionic compounds

What are ions?

Ions are usually found in compounds of metals with non-metals. Metal atoms lose electrons to form **positive ions**. Non-metal atoms gain electrons to form **negative ions**.

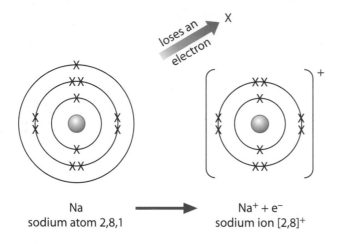

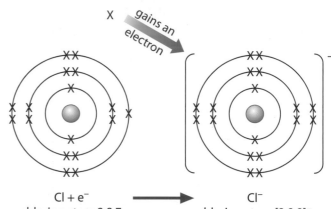

Na		Na⁺ + e⁻
sodium atom 2,8,1	→	sodium ion [2,8]⁺

Cl + e⁻		Cl⁻
chlorine atom 2,8,7	→	chlorine atom [2,8,8]⁻

A A sodium atom (proton number 11) loses one electron to form an ion. As the ion has 11 protons and 10 electrons, it has a positive charge.

B A chlorine atom (proton number 17) gains one electron to form an ion. As the ion has 17 protons and 18 electrons, it has a negative charge.

?

1 a What kind of elements form positive ions?
   b How are positive ions formed?
   c What kind of elements form negative ions?
   d How are negative ions formed?

Ionic compounds are formed between metals and non-metals. They form **crystals** with straight edges and flat surfaces that reflect light.

C Crystals of sodium chloride, a typical ionic compound.

Ionic compounds form crystals as the oppositely charged ions attract each other into a regular **lattice structure**. Each positive ion is surrounded by negative ions and each negative ion is surrounded by positive ions. The structure is held together by the attraction between the opposite charges on the ions.

?

2 a What kind of elements form ionic compounds?
  b What does a crystal look like?

3 What holds the ions together in an ionic compound?

4 What word describes a regular arrangement of ions?

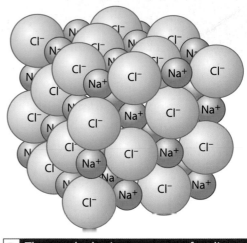

D The regular lattice structure of sodium chloride.

Electricity is the movement of charged particles. Solid ionic compounds do not conduct electricity as the charged ions are fixed in place in the lattice structure. However, if you melt an ionic compound, or dissolve it in water, the positive and negative ions break away from each other and can move around freely. This explains why ionic compounds conduct electricity when molten or in solution, and is evidence that they are made up of charged particles called ions.

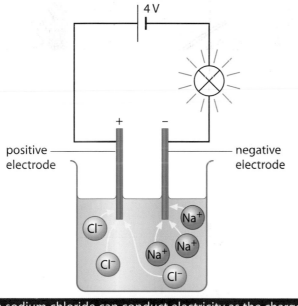

E Molten sodium chloride can conduct electricity as the charged ions can move in different directions.

When a molten ionic compound cools, or a solution evaporates, the oppositely charged ions attract each other and form solid crystals again.

?

5 Why does molten potassium bromide conduct electricity?

6 Draw diagrams like A and B to show how lithium and fluorine form ions. Your drawings should clearly show the electron arrangements of the atoms and the ions.

Summary

Compounds of metals and non-metals conduct _____ as they contain _____ particles called _____.

Metals form _____ ions by _____ electrons. Non-metals form _____ ions by _____ electrons.

Ionic compounds form solid _____ as the ions attract each other and form a regular _____ structure.

charged	crystals	electricity
gaining	ions	lattice	losing
negative	positive	

Ions and electron arrangements

What does the Periodic Table tell us about atoms?

The elements in the Periodic Table are arranged in order of increasing proton number. That is, they are ordered by the number of protons in their nucleus, which is the same as the number of electrons in their shells.

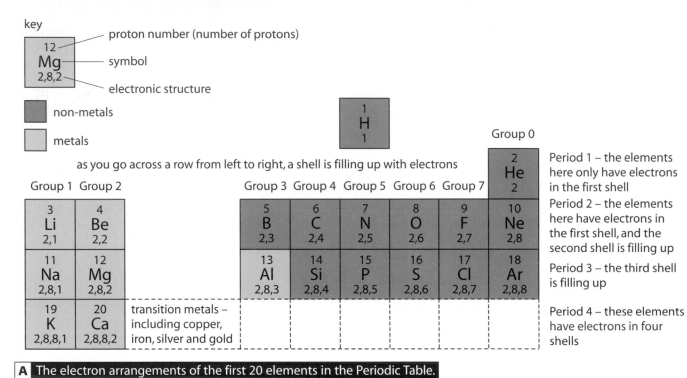

A The electron arrangements of the first 20 elements in the Periodic Table.

?

1 What two things does the proton number tell you about an atom?

2 Look at table A. What can you tell about an element's electron arrangement from:
   a the group number
   b the period number?

The simplest element, hydrogen, has just one proton and one electron. As we move along a period the number of electrons in the outer shell increases until it is full up. If more electrons are added they go in a new shell further away from the nucleus and we start a new period in the table. This means that elements in the same group have the same number of electrons in their outer shell.

The charge on the ion depends on the electron arrangement of the atom involved. The atoms gain or lose electrons to get a full outer electron shell.

B The noble gases do not form ions because their outer shells are full. They are useful for airships, advertising signs and filling light bulbs because they are unreactive.

helium 2   neon 2,8   Ar 2,8,8

The examples of atoms and ions in table C show that:
• all Group 1 elements form 1+ ions (as they lose 1 electron)
• all Group 7 elements form 1– ions (as they gain 1 electron).

Element	Group in Periodic Table	Proton number	Atom symbol	Electron arrangement of atom	Ion symbol	Electron arrangement of ion
lithium	1	3	Li	2, 1	Li^+	$[2]^+$
sodium	1	11	Na	2, 8, 1	Na^+	$[2, 8]^+$
fluorine	7	9	F	2, 7	F^-	$[2, 8]^-$
chlorine	7	17	Cl	2, 8, 7	Cl^-	$[2, 8, 8]^-$

C

?

3 Write the symbols for the following ions:
  a sodium   **c** chlorine
  b potassium   **d** iodine.

The general change in properties across a period can also be explained by electron arrangements. In any period, metals are found on the left as they usually have just a few outer electrons (often 1, 2 or 3). Non-metals are found on the right as they usually have lots of outer electrons (often 5, 6 or 7). So there is a trend across the whole Periodic Table, with metals on the left and non-metals on the right.

?

4 Why do some groups of elements always form ions with the same charge?

5 If you were drawing up a Periodic Table, there are several places you could put hydrogen.
  a Explain why you might put it at the top of Group 7.
  b Explain why you might put it at the top of Group 1.
  c Why do you think it is usually shown on its own?

Summary

The _____ in the Periodic Table are arranged in order of their _____ number. The charge on an ion depends on the atom's electron _____ . The _____ metals (Group 1) form _____ ions. The _____ (Group 7) form _____ ions.

Chemical properties _____ change across a _____ . For example _____ are found on the left and _____ are found on the right.

alkali	arrangement	elements
gradually	halogens	metals
non-metals	period	proton	1+	1–

Flame tests and spectroscopy

How can chemists identify elements?

A Fireworks can produce many different colours.

Fireworks contain a mixture of chemicals to send them up into the air or to make them explode. They also include small amounts of certain elements that produce coloured flames, to give them their different colours.

Flame tests were one of the first techniques used to analyse unknown substances. If a clean piece of wire is dipped in a solution of a compound and then held in the hot part of a Bunsen flame, the colour produced gives a clue to the elements it contains.

? **1** Why do different fireworks produce different colours?

Element	Flame colour
lithium	crimson
sodium	yellow
potassium	lilac
calcium	brick red
strontium	crimson
copper	green

B

? **2** What do the following flame colours tell you about the elements present:
a i yellow **ii** crimson?
b What element produces the flame colour in photo C?

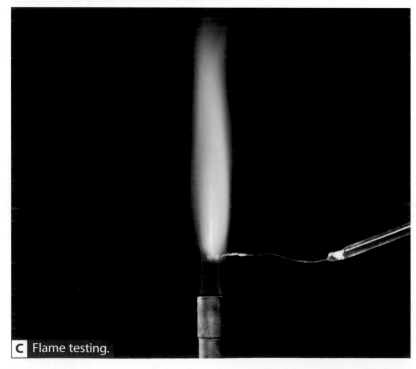

C Flame testing.

The colours emitted can be analysed using **spectroscopy**. This technique splits the light up into its different colours and produces a **spectrum** showing the bands of light given out.

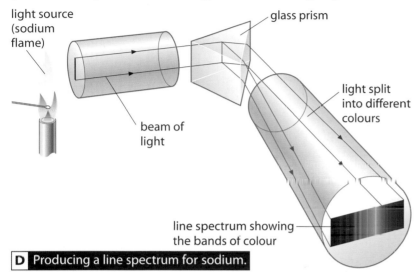

light source (sodium flame)

glass prism

beam of light

light split into different colours

line spectrum showing the bands of colour

D Producing a line spectrum for sodium.

Each element produces a unique set of lines and so the elements present in an unknown sample can be identified from the bands of light.

Owing to the development of new practical techniques, like spectroscopy, the number of known elements greatly increased during the 19th century. In 1800 there were just 33 known elements. Fifty more were identified in the next 100 years. Spectroscopy is still used today to identify the elements present in an unknown sample.

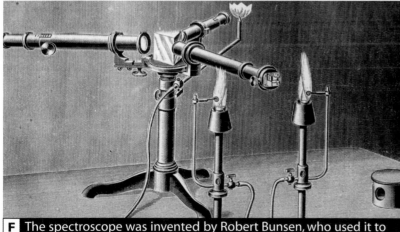

F The spectroscope was invented by Robert Bunsen, who used it to discover the elements caesium and rubidium.

? 5 How many elements were known in: **a** 1800 **b** 1900?

6 Explain how spectroscopy can be used to identify the elements present in a sample.

7 What are the seven main colours in the spectrum of sunlight? (The initial letters of the colours are *roygbiv*.)

? 3 What is the name of the apparatus used to look at spectra?

4 Use drawing D to help you answer the following questions.
  a What splits up the light into different colours?
  b What do you call the picture showing the bands of light?

E A rainbow is a spectrum formed when sunlight passes through droplets of water.

Summary

Some elements produce distinctive _____ in a flame. For example sodium/yellow, lithium/_____ and _____/lilac. Spectroscopy studies the _____ of light produced and uses them to identify the _____ present.

The discovery of new elements sometimes depends on the _____ of new techniques like _____.

colours	crimson	development
elements	potassium	spectra
	spectroscopy	

The alkaline earth metals

What patterns are there in other groups of elements?

The elements in Group 2 of the Periodic Table are called the alkaline earth metals. These elements, which have several important uses, show patterns in their chemical and physical properties.

Alkaline earth metal	Symbol	Proton number	Relative atomic mass	Density (g/cm³)
beryllium	Be	4	9	1.85
magnesium	Mg	12	24	1.74
calcium	Ca	20	40	1.54
strontium	Sr	38	88	2.60
barium	Ba	56	137	3.51

A

The elements of this group have many similarities. They are all fairly soft, silvery-coloured metals. They are all shiny when polished. They are fairly reactive elements and tarnish quickly in moist air.

1 The elements in Group 2 are all metals. List four common properties of metals.

2 **a** Draw a graph of density against proton number for the alkaline earth metals using axes like these.

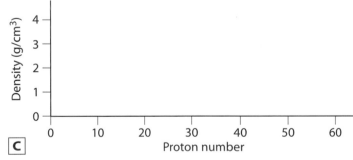

C

b How does the density change as you go down the group?

3 **a** Copy and complete this table.

Metal	Protons	Electrons	Electron arrangement
beryllium			
magnesium			
calcium			

b How are the electron arrangements these metals:
i different **ii** similar?

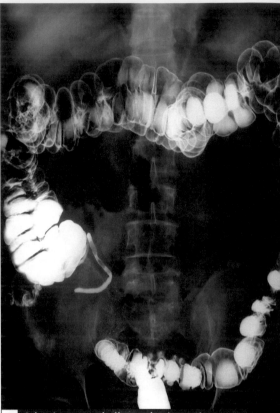

B A barium meal allows the intestines to show up on X-ray images.

4 Draw a labelled diagram showing the structure of a beryllium atom. Include the following labels.

electrons protons neutron nucleus first electron shell second electron shell

5 Why do elements in the same group have similar chemical properties?

Barium is the most reactive metal in Group 2. Like sodium and potassium, it is stored under oil. Barium and calcium both react quickly with water to form hydrogen gas and an alkaline solution.

$$Ca\,(s) + 2H_2O\,(l) \rightarrow Ca(OH)_2\,(aq) + H_2\,(g)$$
calcium + water → calcium hydroxide + hydrogen

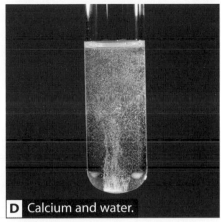

D Calcium and water.

Magnesium reacts slowly with water but reacts violently with chlorine gas, forming white crystals of magnesium chloride.

$$Mg\,(s) + Cl_2\,(g) \rightarrow MgCl_2\,(s)$$
magnesium + chlorine → magnesium chloride

Beryllium is the least reactive alkaline earth metal, with slightly different properties from the others. However, all Group 2 metals, including beryllium, react with halogens to produce metal halides. These crystalline solids contain ions with similar charges. For example, magnesium chloride contains Mg^{2+} and Cl^- ions and barium bromide contains Ba^{2+} and Br^- ions.

6 Describe the trend in reactivity in the Group 2 metals.

7 The general formula for alkaline earth metal halides is MX_2, where M stands for the symbol of the metal and X stands for the symbol of the non-metal. Write the formula for:
   a barium fluoride
   b beryllium chloride
   c magnesium iodide.

8 Copy and complete the word and symbol equations for the reaction of barium with water.

   _____ + _____ → _____ + hydrogen
   _____ + $2H_2O\,(l)$ → $Ba(OH)_2\,(aq)$ + _____

9 Copy and complete the word and symbol equations for the reaction of calcium with bromine.

   _____ + bromine → _____ _____
   _____ + _____ → $CaBr_2\,(s)$

10 Barium has some similar properties to sodium metal.
   a Why is it stored under oil?
   b What safety precautions should be observed when handling the metal?

11 a What are ions and how are they formed?
   b Write down the electron arrangements of a chlorine atom (Cl) and a chloride ion (Cl^-).
   c Explain why chlorine forms a Cl^- ion.

12 Care has to be take when handling certain compounds of alkaline earth metals as they can be dangerous. Explain the safety precautions required when handling chemicals which show the following hazard symbols.
   a

   b

   c

13 The flame test for barium produces green flashes of colour.
   a What other element produces a green colour in a flame?
   b What is the name of the technique that can be used to produce a spectrum for an element?
   c What does a spectrum show?
   d How can this be used to confirm the identity of an element?

Explaining motion

What is the link between force, speed and sports day?

Sports Day Report

The day started off bright and sunny, but dark clouds soon appeared. It wasn't long before the heavens opened, making life very difficult for the participants. Nonetheless, there were some outstanding performances from Year 11 students.

Heide Muller may well have broken the school record for the 100 metres if the damp grass had not been so slippery, and Farouk Khan threw the javelin an amazing 28.25 metres when throwing against the wind. Sports Person of the Day was Toby Ulm, who cleared the high jump bar at a record-breaking 1.74 metres. He could jump over my head and still have a few centimetres to spare!

Well done to all those who took part.

Jane Callender
(Year 11 Team Captain)

? 1 Explain why Heide Muller and Farouk Khan might have done better in better weather conditions.

Year 11 girls 100 metres

A Science in action on sports day.

Name	Time (seconds)
Jane Callender	13.2
Roushka Munt	13.5
Samra Naveed	14.1
Shona Drummond	13.8
Heide Muller	12.9
Charlotte Bannister	13.6
Nuria Castro	13.9
Victoria Jones	13.2

B

E Calculating speed

Speed can be calculated if you know:
- the distance travelled
- the time taken to travel that distance.

speed = distance ÷ time
(metres per second, m/s) (metres, m) (seconds, s)

Year 11 boys cross country

Diagram C shows a map of the cross country course. During the race the boys' speed changed a lot. Their **average speed** can be calculated from the total distance run and the total time taken. Their speed at any one time is called the **instantaneous speed**.

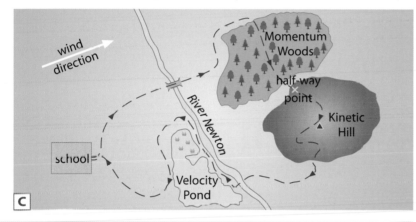

C

?

2 Look at table B.
  a Who won the race?
  b Explain how you know who won.

3 **a** Which two girls had the same average speed?
  b How did you work out your answer?

4 Shona Drummond ran the 100 metres in 13.8 seconds. Calculate her average speed.

?

5 At the half-way point Ben's speed was 6 m/s. He took 20 minutes to run the whole 5000 m course.
  a What was his average speed for the race?
  b Suggest three reasons why this was slower than his speed at the half-way point.
  c Explain the difference between average speed and instantaneous speed.

6 Diagram D shows the forces acting on a boy running through the woods.

D

  a What will be happening to his speed? Explain your answer.
  b Why might he slow down when running over some wet leaves?
  c Draw a diagram with force arrows to show the boy running against the wind at a steady speed.

Summary

When running a race the fastest person covers the same distance in the shortest _____ . We calculate speed using the equation speed = _____ ÷ time. Running against the wind slows us down because the wind exerts a _____ against us.

distance   force   time

Distance–time graphs

How can we use a graph to show movement?

It is often useful to show the motion of moving objects using distance–time graphs. Diagram A shows a distance–time graph for a fox running across a field.

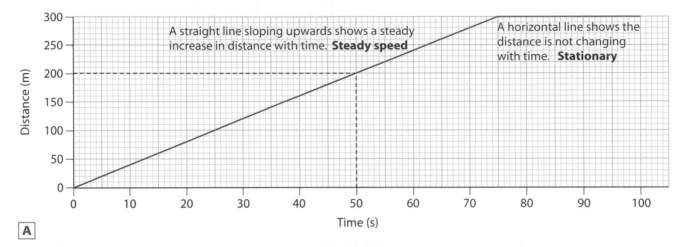

A straight line sloping upwards shows a steady increase in distance with time. **Steady speed**

A horizontal line shows the distance is not changing with time. **Stationary**

A

B

We can indicate the direction something is travelling in by using **positive distance** and **negative distance**. Diagram C shows the graph for someone who dropped her pencil case in the corridor. The graph shows her travelling a negative distance when she went back to fetch it.

?

3 Look at diagram C.
  a How far did Emma have to go back to get her pencil case?
  b How long did it take Emma to get back to where she turned round?

4 a Suggest two sports that involve people going backwards and forwards along a straight line.
  b Draw a distance–time graph for one of the sports.

?

1 How far had the fox travelled after:
  a 50 seconds
  b 70 seconds
  c 90 seconds?

2 How long did it take the fox to cover the first 100 metres?

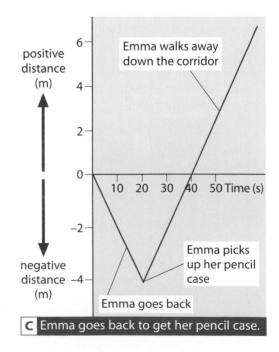

positive distance (m)

Emma walks away down the corridor

Emma picks up her pencil case

Emma goes back

negative distance (m)

C Emma goes back to get her pencil case.

What do distance–time graphs tell us about speed?

The gradient of a distance–time graph tells us the speed. A faster speed gives a steeper graph.

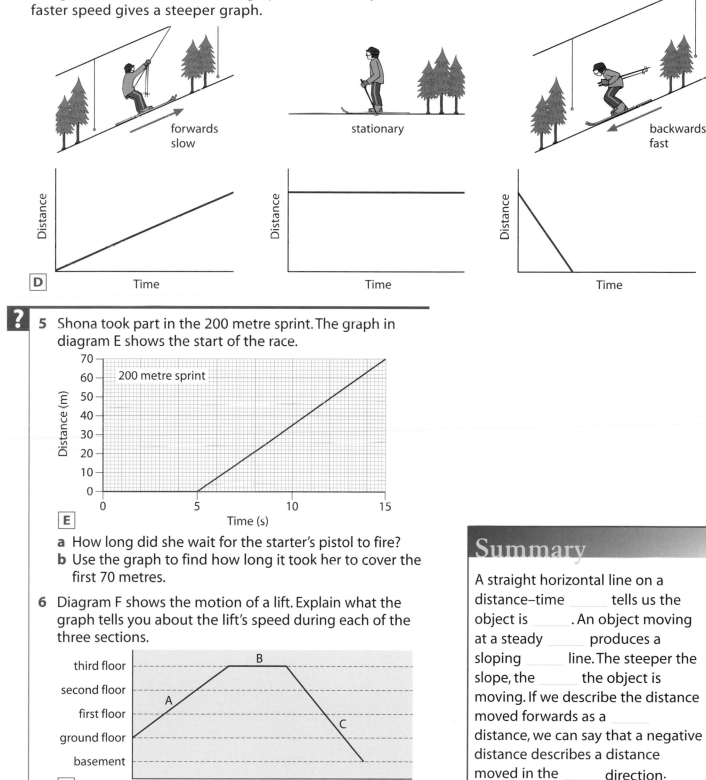

forwards
slow

stationary

backwards
fast

Distance

Distance

Distance

D Time

Time

Time

5 Shona took part in the 200 metre sprint. The graph in diagram E shows the start of the race.

200 metre sprint

Distance (m)

Time (s)

E

a How long did she wait for the starter's pistol to fire?

b Use the graph to find how long it took her to cover the first 70 metres.

6 Diagram F shows the motion of a lift. Explain what the graph tells you about the lift's speed during each of the three sections.

third floor

second floor

first floor

ground floor

basement

A

B

C

F Time

7 Suggest a reason why the lift does not travel upwards at the same speed that it travels downwards.

Summary

A straight horizontal line on a distance–time _____ tells us the object is _____. An object moving at a steady _____ produces a sloping _____ line. The steeper the slope, the _____ the object is moving. If we describe the distance moved forwards as a _____ distance, we can say that a negative distance describes a distance moved in the _____ direction.

faster   graph   opposite   positive
speed   stationary   straight

Velocity–time graphs

How can we show the change in speed of an object on a graph?

Speed tells us how fast something is travelling. **Velocity** not only tells how fast something is travelling, but also tells us which direction it is travelling in.

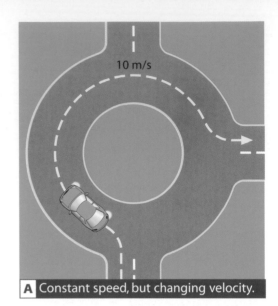

A Constant speed, but changing velocity.

? **1** Explain the difference between speed and velocity.

Velocity–time graphs show how velocity changes with time. Diagram B shows the changing velocity of a horse and rider.

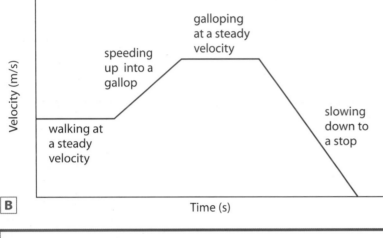

galloping at a steady velocity

speeding up into a gallop

walking at a steady velocity

slowing down to a stop

Velocity (m/s)

Time (s)

B

? **2** Look at diagram B. Describe the shape of the graph when the horse and rider are:
 a walking at a steady velocity
 b speeding up
 c slowing down.

? **3** Look at diagram C. How long after leaving the depot did the lorry driver:
 a first reach the motorway
 b take a break at a motorway service station
 c stop in a lay-by for a cup of tea
 d reach his destination?

Government regulations limit the time that coach and lorry drivers can spend driving their vehicles. To keep a record of their journey times and speeds, each vehicle is fitted with a **tachograph**. The graph produced by a tachograph will look something like diagram C.

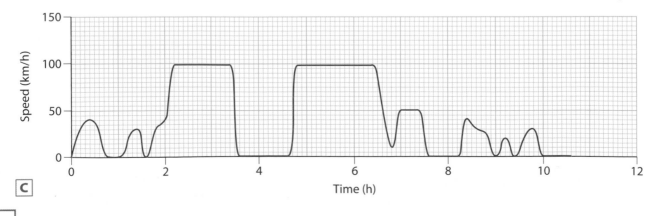

Speed (km/h)

Time (h)

C

Positive and negative velocity

If we say that an object moving away from the starting point has **positive velocity**, we can then say it has **negative velocity** when it travels back towards the starting point.

Diagram D shows the velocity–time graph for a girl swimming up and down a pool. If we say her velocity for the first length is positive, then she has negative velocity when she swims the second length in the *opposite* direction.

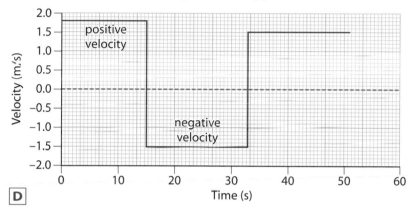

D

Photo E shows a tennis ball bouncing after it is dropped. The ball is moving fastest just before it hits the ground at X. As it bounces up again it slows down steadily until it stops at Y. Then it gains speed again until it hits the ground at Z.

The motion of the ball is shown on graph F.

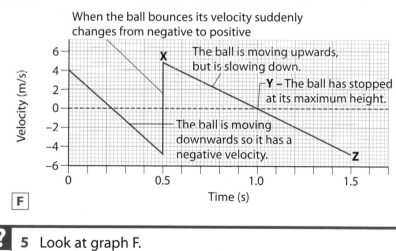

F

? 5 Look at graph F.
   a What was the ball's velocity when it left the thrower's hand?
   b For how long was the ball in the air between points X and Z?

6 Look at diagram D.
   a Sketch a second graph for the same girl swimming in a longer pool.
   b Explain the changes you have made.

? 4 Look at diagram D. Which is the odd one out from this list: +1.8 m/s, −1.5 m/s, +1.5 m/s? Explain your answers.

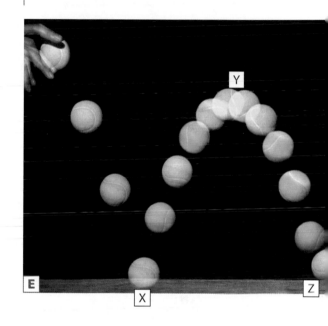

E

Summary

_____–time graphs show both the speed and _____ of moving objects. A flat straight line shows a _____ velocity. A positive slope shows an _____ velocity. A negative _____ shows a decreasing velocity.

If _____ motion has a positive value for velocity, backward motion will have a _____ value for velocity.

| direction forward increasing |
| negative slope steady velocity |

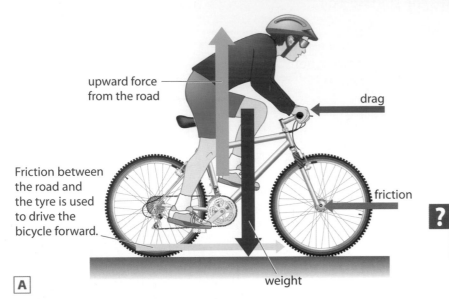

A

Diagram A shows the some of the forces acting on a cyclist and his bike. Forces arise when objects **interact** with each other and they are measured in **newtons**. The size and direction of a force can be shown using force arrows. Some of these forces act in opposite directions to each other.

If you lean against a wall, the wall stops you from falling over. By leaning against it you apply a force to the wall. The wall applies an equal force on you but in the opposite direction. This force is called the **reaction**.

Forces always act in pairs like this. Interactions between objects produce two forces that are equal in size but opposite in direction. The forces act on different objects.

? **1** Look at diagram A. What forces act in the opposite direction to:
a the upward force from the road
b the forward force on the bike?

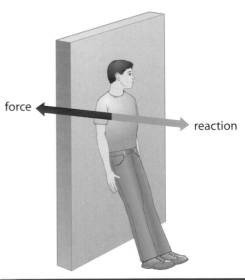

B The forces in a pair are equal and opposite. They act on *different* objects.

? **2** Diagram C shows the forces acting on a girl standing on a gymnastics beam.
   a Explain why the girl does not move downwards.
   b The girl pushes on the beam with a downward force of 520 N. How big is the upward force from the beam?
   c What name is given to the upward force from the beam?

weight of the girl 520 N

upward force from beam

C

How can you find out how much a spring stretches when you add weights to it?
- What apparatus will you need?
- How will you present your results?

? 3 Mrs Walters laid her hosepipe out on the lawn and then turned the tap on. The hosepipe snaked about all over the lawn and sprayed her with water before she managed to get hold of it. Explain why this happened.

Friction

Friction is a force that opposes motion. It is caused by the interaction between two surfaces. When a person tries to push an object across the floor, the object will only move if the pushing force is greater than the force of friction. **Lubricants** such as oil are often used to reduce friction.

When a rugby player slides along friction means that he applies a force to the ground. Friction also applies a force to the rugby player in a direction that tends to prevent his motion.

D A large force is needed to push the water forward. This **action** force produces an equal and opposite reaction force that the firefighters need to control.

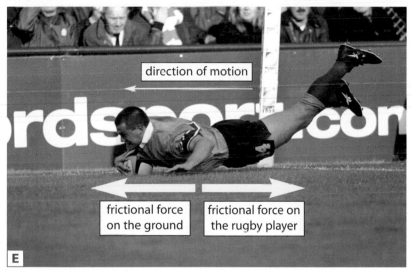

direction of motion

frictional force on the ground   frictional force on the rugby player

E

? 4 What is friction?

5 Give two examples of where:
   a friction is useful
   b lubricants are used to reduce friction.

6 Think of a plus, a minus and an interesting point about this statement: Cars would work better in a world without friction.

7 Explain how the following conditions might affect how far a rugby player slides:
   a wet grass rather than dry grass
   b long grass rather than short grass.

Summary

Forces are measured in _____ and they always act in pairs. The size and _____ of a force can be shown using an _____. When you stand on the ground the upward force that stops you _____ downwards is called the _____.

Friction is caused by the interaction between _____ and can be reduced using _____.

arrow   direction   lubricants   moving   newtons   reaction   surfaces

Forces and motion

Is there a link between force and motion?

Force can change the motion of an object. A force may make the object start to move, change its speed or change the direction the object is moving in.

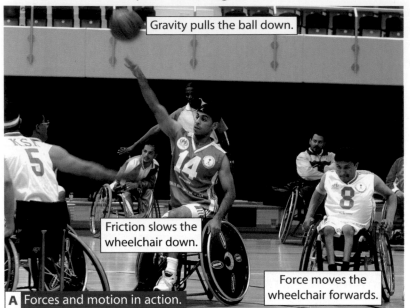

Gravity pulls the ball down.

Friction slows the wheelchair down.

Force moves the wheelchair forwards.

A Forces and motion in action.

There is usually more than one force on an object. We need to think about all the forces and their directions. The 'overall' force, which is the sum of all the forces, is called the **resultant force**. The change in motion of the object will be the same as if the resultant force was the only force acting upon it.

?

1 A hockey ball is travelling across a grass pitch. Name the force that is:
   a reducing the velocity of the ball
   b acting downwards on the ball
   c acting upwards on the ball.

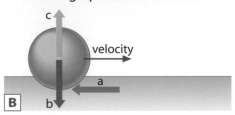

c

velocity

a

B b

2 Andy is playing football. Write down three different things he could do to the ball by applying a force to it.

3 Samantha is playing ice hockey. She hits the puck across the ice. Explain why the puck takes a long time to slow down.

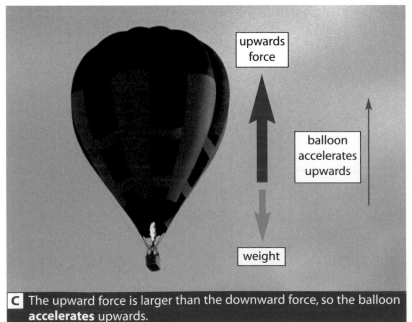

upwards force

balloon accelerates upwards

weight

C The upward force is larger than the downward force, so the balloon **accelerates** upwards.

4 A motorbike is accelerating forwards. What does this tell you about the forward force created by the engine compared to the backward forces from friction and air resistance?

5 Danny pushes a book across the desk. Friction opposes the force he applies.

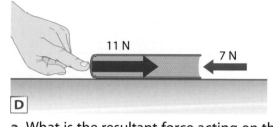

11 N   7 N

D

a What is the resultant force acting on the book?
b Describe the motion of the book.

When you throw a heavy object away from you, you feel a force pushing you back. This reaction force is equal to the force you applied to the heavy object, but in the opposite direction.

Rockets and jet engines work in a similar way. They push large amounts of gas in the opposite direction to which they are travelling. This causes a reaction force on the engine which pushes it forward.

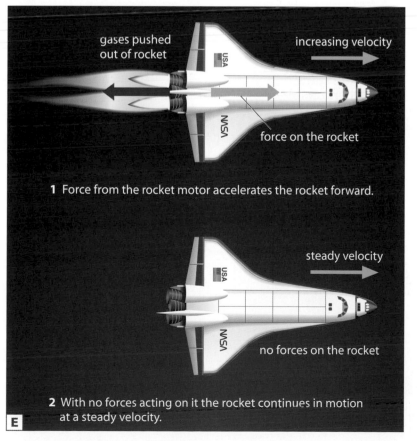

gases pushed out of rocket   increasing velocity

force on the rocket

1 Force from the rocket motor accelerates the rocket forward.

steady velocity

no forces on the rocket

2 With no forces acting on it the rocket continues in motion at a steady velocity.

E

6 Explain why you might fall over if you threw a very heavy object.

7 Rockets burn fuel to produce large amounts of gas. Explain how this gas is used to drive the rocket forward.

Summary

Forces can cause objects to increase _____ or slow down. When the _____ on an object are equal but in opposite _____ the object remains _____ or continues to move at a _____ velocity.

If there is a _____ force on an object, the object will _____ to move, change its direction or change its velocity.

directions forces resultant start
stationary steady velocity

Momentum

How do we account for both mass and velocity?

When we are thinking about moving objects we need to think about their mass and their velocity. These combine in a quantity called **momentum**. The unit for momentum is kilogram metres per second (**kg m/s**).

In photo A the car is moving faster than the lorry. The momentum of each vehicle depends on its mass and its velocity. Although the car is travelling at a higher velocity than the lorry, it has less momentum because it has a much smaller mass.

If two objects are travelling at the same velocity, the one with the larger mass will have the greater momentum.

A

?

1 Sam has a mass of 50 kg and Nadeem has a mass of 60 kg. They are both running along the track at 5 m/s.
  a Who has the greater momentum?
  b Explain your answer.

E **Calculating momentum**

Momentum can be calculated if you know:
• the mass of the object
• the velocity of the object.

momentum	=	mass	×	velocity
(kilogram metres per second, kg m/s)		(kilograms, kg)		(metres per second, m/s)

A dog has a mass of 15 kg. Calculate the dog's momentum when it is running at 10 m/s.
momentum = mass × velocity
       = 5 kg × 10 m/s
       = 150 kg m/s

B Using momentum to knock down the pins.

?

2 Use the information given in question **1** to calculate:
  a Sam's momentum.
  b Nadeem's momentum.

3 A 6 kg bowling ball is travelling down the lane at 3 m/s. Calculate the ball's momentum.

4 A car of mass 1200 kg is travelling at 15 m/s along a straight road. Calculate the momentum of the car.

Changing momentum

Forces can change the velocity of an object. When the velocity of an object either increases or decreases its momentum has changed – the force applied has changed the momentum. The change in momentum will be in the same direction as the force causing the change. The larger the force applied, the greater the momentum change will be.

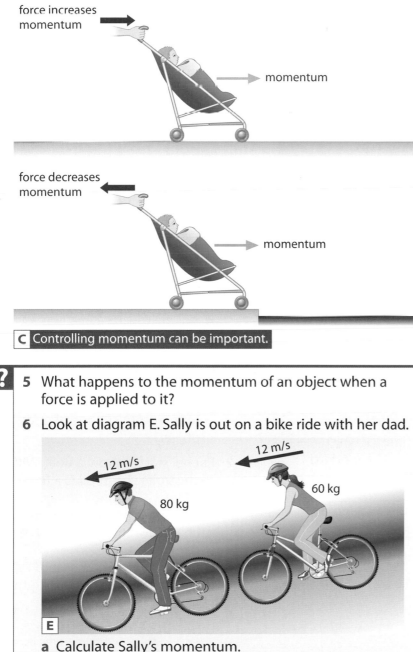

force increases momentum

momentum

force decreases momentum

momentum

C Controlling momentum can be important.

D The tennis ball changes velocity when it is hit by the racket. The racket changes the momentum of the ball.

?

5 What happens to the momentum of an object when a force is applied to it?

6 Look at diagram E. Sally is out on a bike ride with her dad.

12 m/s

12 m/s

80 kg

60 kg

E

a Calculate Sally's momentum.
b Calculate her dad's momentum.
c What would Sally have to do to increase her momentum?
d By how much would Sally have to increase her momentum to have the same momentum as her dad?

Summary

The _____ of an object depends on its mass and its velocity. The unit for momentum is _____.

momentum = _____ × _____

Applying a _____ to an object can increase or _____ the object's momentum.

| decrease | force | kg m/s | mass |
| momentum | velocity |

Force and momentum

How do forces change momentum?

A The force from the rocket engine changes the momentum of the rocket.

If there is no resultant force acting on an object, then its momentum does not change. If it is not moving, it stays still. If it is moving, it continues at a steady speed in a straight line.

If there is a resultant force, then the **change in momentum** depends on the size of the force and also how long the force is applied for.

E **Calculating a change in momentum**

We can calculate a change in momentum if we know:
• the resultant force applied to the object
• the time for which that force acts on the object.

change of momentum = resultant force × time for which it acts
(kilogram metres per (newtons, N) (seconds, s)
second, kg m/s)

Luke starts to push his younger brother on a swing. He pushes with a force of 60 N for 0.5 seconds.

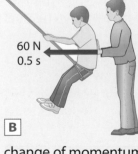

60 N
0.5 s

B

change of momentum = resultant force × time for which it acts
= 60 N × 0.5 s
= 30 kg m/s

? 1 **a** How can you change the momentum of an object?
   b What two things affect the momentum change of an object?

2 Rachel starts to row a boat. With each stroke she applies a force of 50 N for 1.5 seconds.
   a Calculate the momentum change of the boat during each stroke.
   b Calculate the momentum change of the boat during the first four strokes.

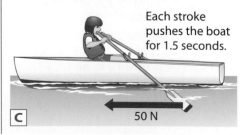

Each stroke pushes the boat for 1.5 seconds.

C

50 N

Decreasing momentum

The same equation is used when a force is reducing the momentum of an object.

> A fully loaded van has a momentum of 55 000 kg m/s when the driver applies the brakes. The brakes exert a stopping force of 10 000 N for 4 seconds.
>
> **A** Calculate the momentum change caused by applying the brakes.
>
> momentum change = resultant force × time for which it acts
> $$= 10\,000\,N \times 4\,s$$
> $$= 40\,000\,kg\,m/s$$
>
> **B** Calculate the new momentum of the van.
> new momentum $= 55\,000\,kg\,m/s - 40\,000\,kg\,m/s$
> $$= 15\,000\,kg\,m/s$$

D The force shown by the yellow arrow is decreasing the momentum of the rugby player.

?

3 A skier travels uphill for 6 seconds. The resultant of the forces on the skier is a force of 50 N that slows the skier down. Calculate the momentum change of the skier.

E

4 The momentum of a fire engine is decreasing. Write down as many different explanations for this statement as you can.

5 Anna is riding her bike at a velocity of 6.0 m/s when she applies the brakes for 1.5 seconds. Anna and her bike have a combined mass of 80 kg and the braking force is 320 N.
   a Calculate the initial momentum of Anna and her bike.
   b Calculate the momentum change achieved by braking.
   c What is Anna's new momentum after braking?

Summary

Change in momentum depends on the _____ of the force and also how long the force is _____ for.

change of _____ = resultant _____ × _____ for which it acts

This equation can be used when the force is increasing or _____ the momentum of an object.

applied	decreasing	force
momentum	size	time

Road safety

How can we reduce injuries in an accident?

When a car crashes, its momentum changes very suddenly. The force that causes the rapid change of momentum is what damages the car and its occupants. The faster a car is travelling, the more momentum it has.

?

1 In a crash test two identical cars hit a brick wall. One is travelling at 30 km/h and the other at 60 km/h.
   a Which car will experience the greater force?
   b Explain your answer.

Diagram B shows an egg on a trolley moving towards a wall. The egg represents passengers in a car. When the trolley hits the buffers, the trolley will stop but the egg will continue to move forwards until it hits the wall. This is what happens to passengers inside a car that stops rapidly. The passengers continue to move forward until they experience a force that stops them.

A The damage caused by a rapid momentum change.

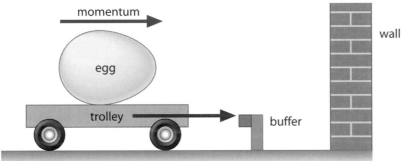

Both the trolley and the egg have momentum.

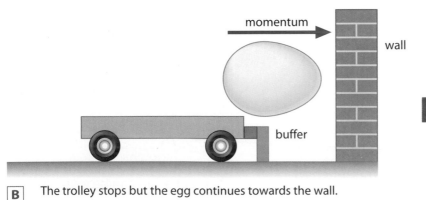

B The trolley stops but the egg continues towards the wall.

?

2 Look at diagram B.
   a Why doesn't the egg stop when the trolley stops?
   b Why might the egg break when it hits the wall?

A How can you find out the minimum drop height needed to break an egg?
• What apparatus will you need?
• How will you present your results?

Slowing down the momentum change

Injuries to people involved in car accidents can be reduced if the forces acting upon them are reduced. This can be achieved by increasing the time taken for the person to stop moving. Photos C and D illustrate some of the methods used.

C The air bag increases the time taken for the person's head to stop moving.

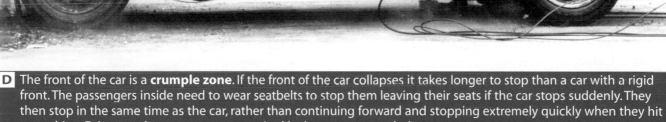

D The front of the car is a **crumple zone**. If the front of the car collapses it takes longer to stop than a car with a rigid front. The passengers inside need to wear seatbelts to stop them leaving their seats if the car stops suddenly. They then stop in the same time as the car, rather than continuing forward and stopping extremely quickly when they hit something. Drivers and passengers are required by law to wear seatbelts.

?

3 Explain how each of the following can reduce injuries during accidents:
  a air bags
  b car crumple zones
  c seatbelts.

4 Motorcycle helmets have a hard outer surface with a soft lining inside the helmet. How will the soft lining reduce the risk of head injuries if the rider falls off?

5 Which is the odd one out from this list: crumple zone, motorcycle helmet, seatbelt? Explain your answers.

6 The front and back of a car are designed to crumple in an accident but the roof is rigid. Explain why a rigid roof is needed to protect passengers.

Summary

The _____ acting on a person during an accident depends on the time taken for the _____ change to occur. The risk of injury can be reduced if the stopping _____ can be increased. Crumple _____, air bags and _____ are designed to _____ the stopping time during an accident.

force	increase	momentum
seatbelts	time	zones

Motion and energy transfer

What is work?

A

Moving objects have **kinetic energy**. To make an object move we apply a force to it. The force does **work** that is transferred to kinetic energy.

Photo A shows someone pushing a curling stone over the ice. The kinetic energy gained by the stone is equal to the work done on it. The kinetic energy is measured in joules. The work done is also measured in joules.

? 1 Look at photo A.
   a What are the units for work done?
   b What happens to the work done on the stone?

E **Calculating work done**

We can calculate work done if we know:
• the force used to move an object
• the distance the object moves while the force is applied to it.

work done   =   force   ×   distance
 (joules, J)   (newtons, N)   (metres, m)

Susie pulls a case with a steady force of 20 N for a distance of 40 m. Calculate the work Susie does in pulling the case.

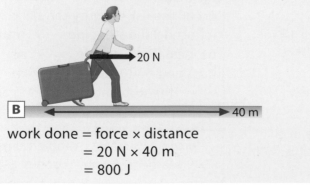

→20 N

B   → 40 m

work done = force × distance
        = 20 N × 40 m
        = 800 J

? 2 Matt pushes an armchair 3 m with a steady force of 40 N. Calculate the work Matt does.

3 Miah uses a force of 15 N to lift a large bottle of drink 0.80 m from the floor and onto her kitchen worktop. Calculate the work Miah does in moving the bottle of drink.

Changes in energy

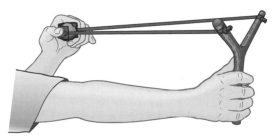

1 Work is done to stretch the elastic.

2 When the elastic is released it does work on the stone and the stone gains kinetic energy.

C

When work is done, energy is transferred from one object to another. Look at diagram C.

- The catapult loses energy because *it does work* on the stone.
- Work is done *on* the stone, so the stone gains energy.

E | change in energy = work done
     (joules, J)   (joules, J)

?

4 What happens to the energy of an object when work is done:
  a *on* the object
  b *by* the object?

5 Ruth uses a catapult to fire a stone that gains 125 J of energy.
  a How much work did the catapult do to fire the stone?
  b How much work did Ruth do to stretch the elastic of the catapult?

6 Before firing an arrow, Marie applies an average force of 150 N to pull the string of a bow back 0.60 m. Calculate the kinetic energy gained by the arrow when it is fired.

D

Summary

Work is _____ when a force moves an object through a _____.

work done = _____ × distance
   (_____)   (newtons)   (_____)

When work is done on an object, the _____ of the object increases. When work is done by an _____, the energy of the object _____.

decreases   distance   done   energy
force   joules   metres   object

Doing work against gravity

How much energy does an object gain when we lift it?

A When rising at a steady velocity, lift = weight.

When an object is lifted at a steady velocity the two forces acting upon it are equal in size but opposite in direction. The force required to lift an object is equal to its weight.

Work is done on the object to lift it so it gains energy. The type of energy an object has due to its height is called **gravitational potential energy (GPE)**. The gravitational potential energy gained by the object is equal to the work done in lifting it. When an object falls its gravitational potential energy decreases.

E | **Calculating the change in gravitational potential energy.**

The change in gravitational potential energy can be calculated if we know:
- the weight of the object
- the vertical height distance between the starting and finishing points.

change in GPE = weight × vertical height difference
(joules, J)   (newtons, N)   (metres, m)

A cat that weighs 40 N climbs 3 m up a tree. Calculate the cat's gain in gravitational potential energy.

change in GPE = weight × vertical height difference
= 40 N × 3 m
= 120 J

? **1** A girl lifts a book onto a shelf at a steady velocity. The book weighs 4.2 N. What force does the girl use to lift the book?

? **2** A woman who weighs 60 N walks up some stairs. If she increases her height above the ground by 4 m, calculate the woman's gain in gravitational potential energy.

3 A squirrel weighing 8 N climbs 2.6 m down a tree. Calculate the decrease in GPE of the squirrel.

B

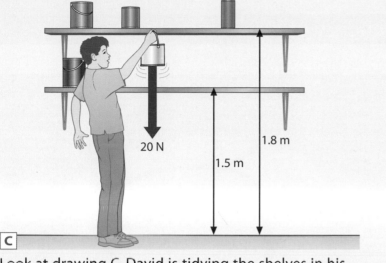

C

Look at drawing C. David is tidying the shelves in his garage. How much gravitational potential energy does the pot of paint gain when David moves it from the bottom shelf to the top one?

vertical height difference = 1.8 m – 1.5 m

= 0.3 m

change in GPE = weight × vertical height difference

= 20 N × 0.3 m

= 6 J

?

4 A window cleaner lifts a 50 N bucket of water further up his ladder. The bucket moves from 2.2 m above the ground to 4.9 m above the ground. Calculate the GPE gained by the bucket.

D Gaining gravitational potential energy.

5 A lift takes 25 washing machines between two floors in a department store. The two floors are 7 m apart. Each washing machine weighs 900 N. Calculate:

a the gravitational potential energy gained by each washing machine

b the total work done by the lift.

Summary

The force needed to lift an object is equal to its _____. As the object is lifted it gains gravitational _____ energy (GPE) equal to the _____ done in lifting it.

change   =   weight   × vertical
in GPE   (_____, N)   _____
(_____, J)   difference
                               (metres, m)

height   joules   newtons   potential
          weight   work

Kinetic energy

How do we calculate the energy of a moving object?

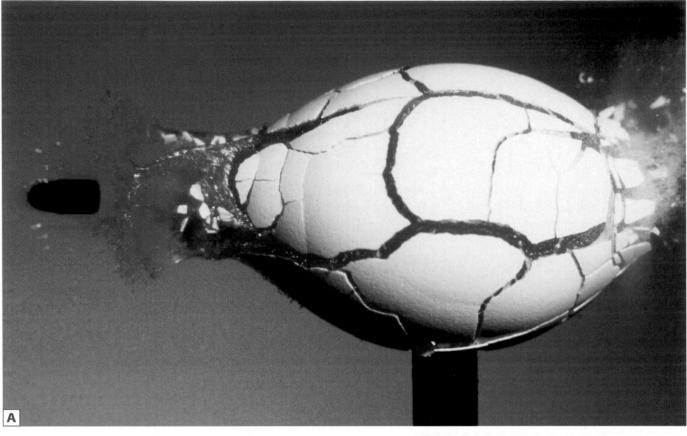

A

Moving objects have kinetic energy. Their kinetic energy depends on their mass and their speed. The faster they are moving or the greater their mass, the more kinetic energy they have.

E **Calculating kinetic energy**

Kinetic energy can be calculated if we know:
• the mass of the object
• the velocity of the object.

kinetic energy = ½ ×   mass   ×   (velocity)²
  (joules, J)   (kilograms, kg) (metres per second, m/s)²

Joe dropped his school bag. The bag had a mass of 3 kg and hit the floor at 4 m/s. Calculate the kinetic energy of the bag as it hit the floor.

kinetic energy = ½ × mass × (speed)²
             = ½ × 3 kg × (4 m/s)²
             = ½ × 3 kg × 16 (m/s)²
             = 24 J

?

1 How could you increase the kinetic energy of a moving object?

2 A 6 kg fox chases a 2 kg rabbit. Both run at 10 m/s.
   a Which animal has more kinetic energy? Explain how you know this without calculating their energies.
   b Calculate the kinetic energies of the fox and the rabbit.

3 A 20 kg suitcase travels on a conveyor belt at 2 m/s.
   a Calculate the kinetic energy of the suitcase.
   b Calculate its kinetic energy if the velocity of the conveyor belt doubles.

What happens when kinetic energy is reduced?

When a car stops in a hurry, friction from the brakes converts its kinetic energy into heat energy. The tyres may also skid on the road surface, transferring kinetic energy to heat energy and sound energy. Friction does work against the motion, converting kinetic energy to other forms of energy.

B

? **4 a** What form of energy does a moving car have?
  b What force does work to stop a car?

The amount of work needed to stop a moving object is equal to the kinetic energy of the moving object. When an object stops moving, all of its kinetic energy has been converted to other forms of energy.

? **5** A racing greyhound crosses the finishing line with a kinetic energy of 1200 J.
  a How much work must the greyhound do to stop itself?
  b What will have happened to the 1200 J of kinetic energy the greyhound had when it crossed the finishing line?

C

6 Use ideas about kinetic energy to explain the following road safety statement:
Pedestrians are almost four times more likely to be killed by a car travelling at 40 miles per hour than by one travelling at 30 miles per hour.

Summary

The greater the _____ of an object and the _____ its velocity the more kinetic _____ it has. The _____ done to stop a moving object is equal to the object's _____ energy.

kinetic energy = ½ × mass × (_____)²
(joules, _____)   (_____ , kg)   (metres per second, m/s)²

energy   higher   J   kilograms   kinetic   mass   velocity   work

Conservation of energy

What happens to the energy when a force does work?

When a force does work some of the energy will be transferred to kinetic energy. Opposing forces like friction and air resistance will cause some of the energy to be transferred into heat and sound energy.

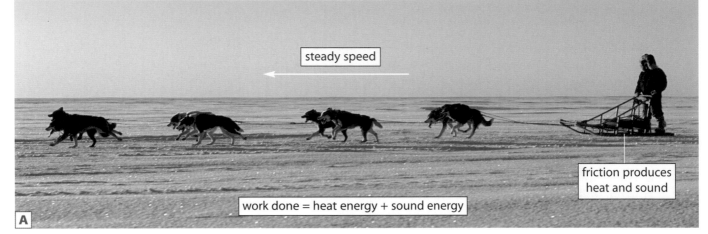

steady speed

friction produces heat and sound

work done = heat energy + sound energy

A

The sledge is moving at a steady velocity. It is not gaining kinetic energy, so the work the dogs are doing is all being transferred to heat and sound energy.

Law of conservation of energy

Energy cannot be created or destroyed – it can only be transferred from one form to another.

? 1 Look at photo A.
  a What is happening to the work the dogs are doing?
  b Why would the dogs do more work pulling the sledge at a steady speed over grass than they would pulling it at the same speed over ice?

When a moving object stops or slows down, its kinetic energy is transferred to heat and sound energy. The brakes on vehicles push pads against a disc attached to the wheel. Friction between the brake pad and the disc transfers the vehicle's kinetic energy to heat and a little bit of sound energy.

? 2 A motorbike had 400 kJ of kinetic energy before it stopped.
  a How much kinetic energy did it have by the time it stopped?
  b How much of the motorbike's kinetic energy was transferred to heat and sound energy?

B Friction in the brakes transfers kinetic energy to heat and sound energy.

Energy conservation and falling objects

Falling objects convert gravitational potential energy to kinetic energy. They usually experience an opposing force such as air resistance or friction. This causes some of the potential energy to be transferred to heat and sound.

C Converting gravitational potential energy to kinetic energy.

E gravitational potential energy lost = kinetic energy gained
weight × change in height = ½ × mass × (velocity)²

weight = mass × gravitational field strength

On Earth, weight (N) = mass (kg) × 10 N/kg

? 5 A girl weighing 450 N fell 2 m out of a tree.
  a Calculate her gravitational potential energy before the fall.
  b How much kinetic energy did she gain during the fall?

6 A 60 kg boy on a trampoline reaches a maximum height of 2.5 m.
  a Calculate the boy's weight.
  b Calculate his gravitational potential energy at a height of 2.5 m.
  c What will be the maximum kinetic energy achieved by the boy?

? 3 A boy loses 900 J of gravitational potential energy falling out of a tree. If we ignore air resistance, how much kinetic energy does he gain during the fall?

4 Why is the gravitational potential energy of a roller coaster not all converted to kinetic energy?

Summary

Energy cannot be _____ or destroyed – it can only be _____ from one form to another. Moving objects usually convert _____ energy to heat and sound energy because of _____ and air resistance. Falling objects convert _____ potential energy to kinetic energy. Air resistance will also convert some of the energy to heat and _____ energy.

| created | friction | gravitational |
| kinetic | sound | transferred |

A cycle ride around the wildlife park

How can we explain the way things move?

Tariq and Nancy went for a cycle ride around a wildlife park.

1 Diagram A shows the graph for part of Tariq's journey.

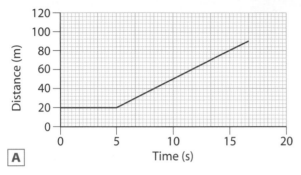

A

a For how long was Tariq stationary?
b i use the graph to find how far he travelled between 5 and 15 seconds.
ii Calculate Tariq's speed during this time.

2 Nancy and Tariq stopped to watch a lion inside an enclosure. Diagram B shows the motion of the lion.

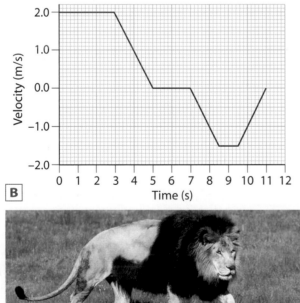

B

C

a Use the graph to find:
i the time for which the lion was stationary
ii the lion's maximum velocity
iii the lion's maximum *negative velocity*.
b Explain the term negative velocity.

3 Inside the monkey house a monkey was sitting on a branch.

D   265 N

a What name is given to the downward force on the monkey?
b What size force does the monkey apply to the branch?
c What size force does the branch apply to the monkey?

4 Another monkey weighing 40 N climbed 2.5 m up a tree.
a Calculate the change in gravitational potential energy of the monkey.
b The monkey then dropped to the ground. How much kinetic energy did the monkey have just before it reached the ground?

5 Tariq noticed a keeper chasing a rabbit that had escaped across a field. The keeper and the rabbit were both running at 5 m/s.

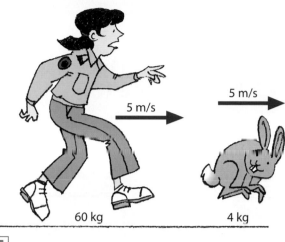

5 m/s

5 m/s

60 kg

4 kg

E

Calculate:

a the rabbit's momentum

b the keeper's momentum

c the rabbit's kinetic energy

d the keeper's kinetic energy.

6 On the way home Tariq and Nancy cycled past the scene of a minor car accident. The front of one car had crumpled completely but the driver and passengers did not seem to be injured.

a Explain how the crumpled front of the car would have helped to reduce injuries to passengers during this collision.

b Name another car safety feature that may have helped prevent injury in this accident.

7 For the last kilometre of the journey home Nancy rode her bike at a steady speed of 6 m/s. The total mass of Nancy and her bike was 80 kg. She applied a driving force of 20 N to the bike.

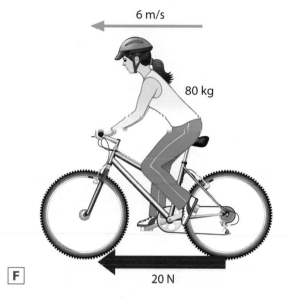

6 m/s

80 kg

F

20 N

Write down the equations you used and show your working in your answers to these questions.

a What is the resultant of the air resistance and friction forces on Nancy and her bike?

b Calculate the work done by Nancy when she cycles 100 metres.

c Calculate the kinetic energy of Nancy and her bike.

d Show that the momentum of Nancy and her bike is 480 kg m/s.

8 As she approached her house Nancy slowed the bike down by applying a 40 N braking force for 7 seconds.

a Calculate the momentum change Nancy achieved by braking.

b Calculate the new momentum.

Growth and development

What is DNA and how was it discovered?

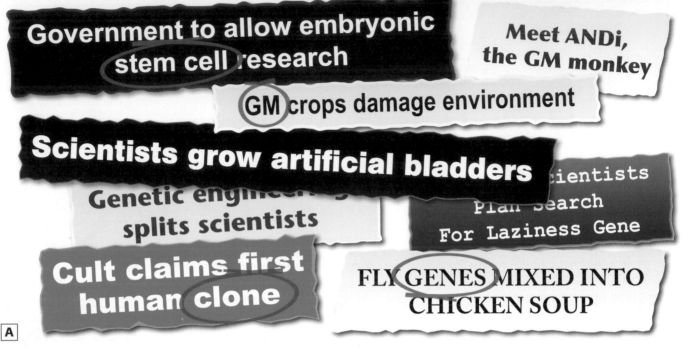

Government to allow embryonic stem cell research

Meet ANDi, the GM monkey

GM crops damage environment

Scientists grow artificial bladders

Genetic engineering splits scientists

Scientists Plan Search For Laziness Gene

Cult claims first human clone

FLY GENES MIXED INTO CHICKEN SOUP

A

Newspapers are full of stories about how new biological technologies will affect our lives.

Cells

All living things are made up of **cells** and each cell has a **nucleus** that controls it. A nucleus contains molecules of **DNA**, and these form long threads called **chromosomes**, which are divided into sections called **genes**. Genes control our **characteristics**. Although we can't see individual genes, we can use special dyes to find them.

? 1 Many people don't know what the circled words mean. Write out the meanings of any words that you know.

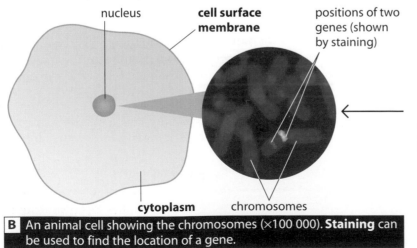

nucleus

cell surface membrane

positions of two genes (shown by staining)

cytoplasm

chromosomes

B An animal cell showing the chromosomes (×100 000). **Staining** can be used to find the location of a gene.

? 2 Write these things in order of their sizes, starting with the largest.
cell chromosome gene nucleus

3 What process is used to find out where a certain gene is?

The secret of life

At lunchtime on 28 February 1953, two men burst into The Eagle pub in Cambridge and one of them announced: 'We have discovered the secret of life.' Their names were James Watson (1928–) and Francis Crick (1916–2004). They had made a cardboard model of DNA.

They had used other scientists' results (**data**) to build their model. Their first attempts were so bad that their boss told them to stop working on DNA. Ignoring this instruction, they finally came up with another idea (**theory**) after seeing photo C, taken by Rosalind Franklin (1920–1958). Although it looks like a blurry X, it helped Watson and Crick to work out that DNA was shaped like two spirals joined together – a **double helix**. However, the photograph had been shown to them without Franklin's permission.

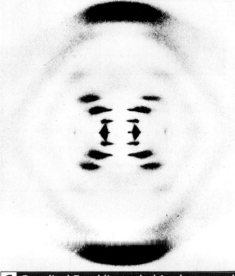

C Rosalind Franklin took this photograph of DNA using X rays. Cross-shapes are formed by spiral molecules.

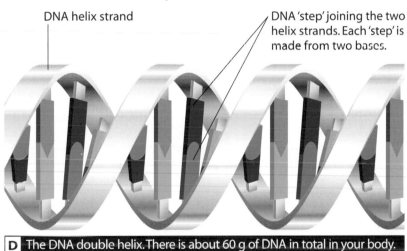

DNA helix strand

DNA 'step' joining the two helix strands. Each 'step' is made from two bases.

D The DNA double helix. There is about 60 g of DNA in total in your body.

Watson and Crick published their work as a **paper** in a **scientific journal**, called *Nature*, on 25 April 1953. Scientists publish papers in journals so that other scientists can see their results and repeat their experiments.

E The journal *Nature*.

4 a What theory did Watson and Crick come up with?
　b Name one piece of data that helped them come up with their theory.

5 Watson and Crick called their paper *A Structure for Deoxyribose Nucleic Acid*.
　a What is deoxyribose nucleic acid commonly called today?
　b Make up a newspaper headline announcing this discovery.
　c In what ways are newspaper headlines different from scientific paper titles?
　d Why do you think they are different?

6 a Write a list of all the ways in which scientists can share information.
　b How do you think this is different today than it was in 1953?

Summary

The _____ of a cell contains _____ made from DNA molecules. Chromosomes are divided into sections called _____, which control our _____.

characteristics　chromosomes
genes　nucleus

Copying DNA

How does DNA copy itself?

For organisms to grow, their cells need to make new cells. Each new cell must contain an *exact* copy of the DNA from the original cell. If this doesn't happen, the new cells will not work properly.

? 1 How can cancer be caused?

The main process used to make new cells is called **mitosis**. In this process, a **parent cell** splits or **divides** to form two **daughter cells**, which are identical to the parent cell.

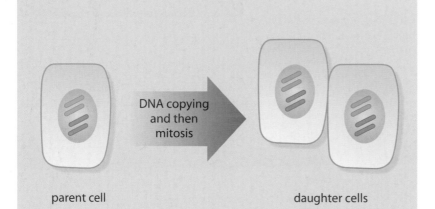

DNA copying and then mitosis

parent cell   daughter cells

B During mitosis, a parent cell forms two daughter cells.

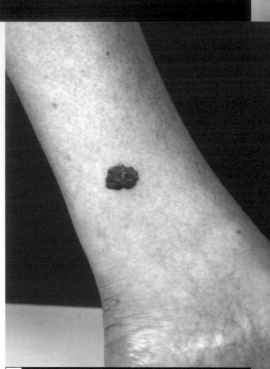

A Cancer is caused when the DNA of cells is damaged. This is skin cancer.

? 2 a Copy the parent cell from diagram B. Label its nucleus and chromosomes.
  b What happens during mitosis?
  c Before mitosis occurs, what must happen to the amount of DNA in a parent cell?

Before mitosis, the chromosomes in the parent cell all need to be copied, so that each new cell ends up with the same number of chromosomes as the parent cell. In humans this takes about 8 hours.

The structure of DNA allows accurate copies to be made. The two strands in a DNA molecule are joined together by four different chemicals called **bases** (G, C, A and T).

? 3 Look at diagram C.
  a Which letters are used to show the different bases?
  b What do you notice about which bases join together?

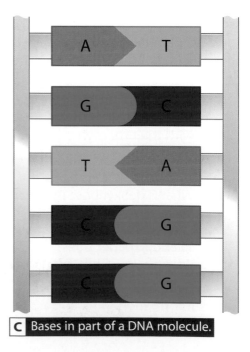

C Bases in part of a DNA molecule.

When a DNA molecule makes a copy of itself, it starts to split apart. New bases inside the nucleus of the cell join onto the old strands of DNA and so copies are made. This is shown in diagram D.

The DNA strands split apart.

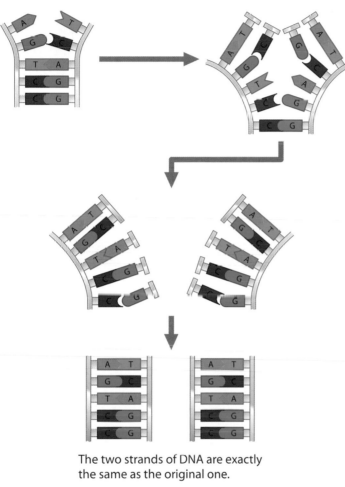

The two strands of DNA are exactly the same as the original one.

D

This process occurs along the whole length of each chromosome. The identical copies remain joined together and we say that each chromosome now consists of two **chromatids**. The chromatids form an X-shape and that's why chromosomes can be drawn as straight lines or as Xs.

?

4 Why are chromosomes only sometimes X-shaped?

5 Here is a single strand of a DNA molecule. Copy it and add the other strand of the DNA molecule.

C A T G G G C T T A A T A C A

F

6 Using your knowledge of DNA, suggest a way in which a cancer cell might be formed.

DNA copying

E A chromosome becomes X-shaped when all its DNA has been copied.

Summary

DNA contains four different _____ called G, C, A and T. G only joins up with _____ and A only joins up with _____. _____ copies itself by splitting apart, and new _____ then join onto the old ones on each _____. Just after a _____ has copied itself, it is made of two joined _____. Chromosomes are copied before _____, which is when a _____ cell divides into two identical _____ cells.

| bases C chromatids chromosome |
| daughter DNA mitosis parent |
| strand T |

The cell cycle

How are new cells for growth made?

About half a million older people in the UK have Alzheimer's disease. These people have trouble remembering things.

The disease is caused by nerve cells dying in the brain. During the 1990s scientists came up with a theory to explain why. Nerve cells cannot normally copy themselves but in Alzheimer's disease they try to. The cells copy their chromosomes but then cannot divide into two, so the cells have too many chromosomes, which causes them to die.

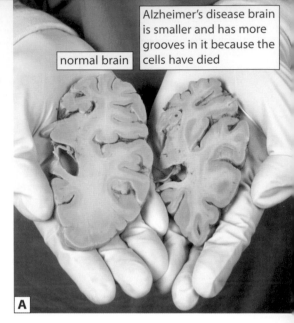

Alzheimer's disease brain is smaller and has more grooves in it because the cells have died

normal brain

A

?
1 What is Alzheimer's disease?

2 What theory did scientists come up with in the 1990s?

In cells that *can* make copies of themselves, there are two main stages: **cell growth** and mitosis. Together these stages are known as the **cell cycle**.

Cell growth

The cytoplasm of cells contains many small parts called **organelles**. Some of the most important organelles are **mitochondria** which release energy for cells.

During the cell growth stage of the cell cycle:
• more organelles are made
• every chromosome is copied so there are two chromatids.

?
3 Name one organelle inside an animal cell.

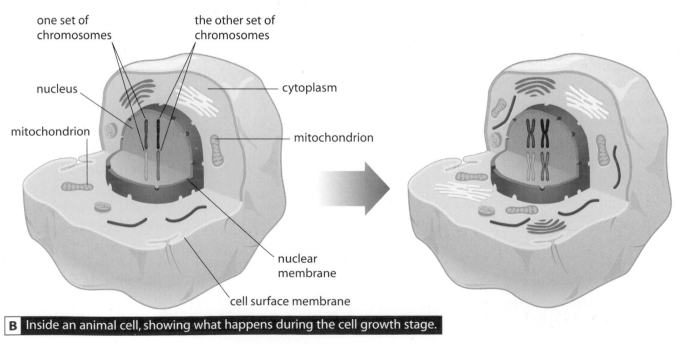

one set of chromosomes

the other set of chromosomes

nucleus

cytoplasm

mitochondrion

mitochondrion

nuclear membrane

cell surface membrane

B Inside an animal cell, showing what happens during the cell growth stage.

Mitosis

Next the membrane around the nucleus (the **nuclear membrane**) breaks apart. The chromosomes line up in the middle of the cell and each chromatid is pulled away from its copy.

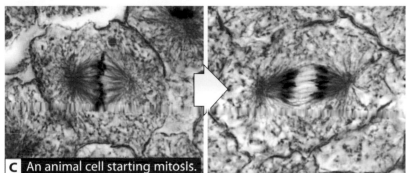

C An animal cell starting mitosis.

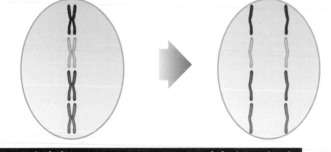

D The copied chromosomes are separated during mitosis.

A new nuclear membrane forms around each new set of chromosomes to make two nuclei. Then the cytoplasm divides in two and a cell surface membrane forms between the two areas of cytoplasm. The cell cycle can then happen again in each of the new daughter cells.

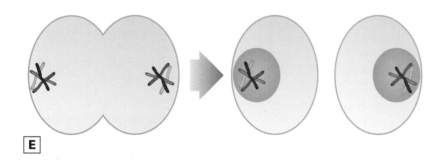

E

?
6 a In which stage of the cell cycle are new organelles made?
  b Why are new organelles needed?

7 Make a bullet list of the things that happen in the cell cycle. List the steps in order.

8 Draw a diagram to compare a normal dividing cell with an Alzheimer's nerve cell.

?
4 a What is the membrane around the nucleus called?
  b In which stage of the cell cycle does it break down?

5 Why do the chromosomes become X shaped in the cell growth stage?

A How would you compare the numbers of cells that are dividing in different areas of a plant root?
- What apparatus will you use?
- How will you know a cell is dividing?
- How will you present your results?

Summary

Some cells copy themselves during the cell _____ . First comes the cell _____ stage in which the _____ and _____ are copied. Then there is the cell _____ stage (or _____) in which the chromatids separate and the cytoplasm divides into two. New _____ are made and two cells are formed, which are _____ to the original cell.

division   growth   chromosomes
cycle   identical   mitosis
membranes   organelles

Making proteins
What does DNA actually do?

Rhinoceroses have thick horns that are made out of hair! Cells in their skin make a **protein** called **keratin** and this forms fibres that stick together to make the horn. Cells in our skin also make keratin, which forms strands of hair.

?
1 What type of substance is keratin?

2 Name two things made out of keratin.

The genetic code

The instructions for making proteins are found in genes. Each gene carries the instructions for one protein. In humans, the gene for keratin is found on chromosome 12.

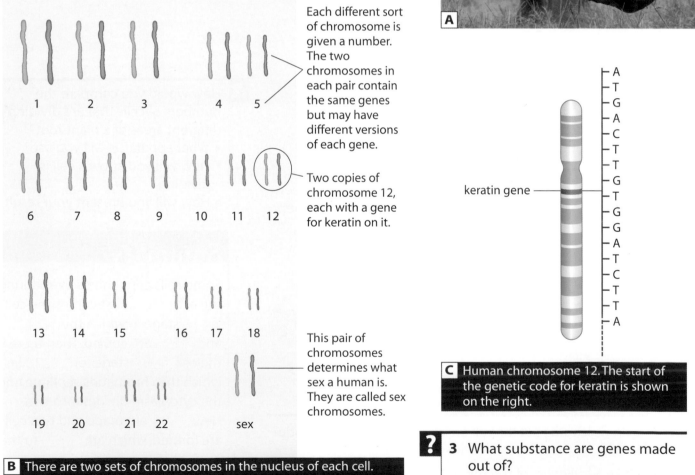

Each different sort of chromosome is given a number. The two chromosomes in each pair contain the same genes but may have different versions of each gene.

Two copies of chromosome 12, each with a gene for keratin on it.

This pair of chromosomes determines what sex a human is. They are called sex chromosomes.

B There are two sets of chromosomes in the nucleus of each cell. Each set contains 23 chromosomes.

keratin gene

A
T
G
A
C
T
T
T
G
T
G
G
A
T
C
T
T
A

C Human chromosome 12. The start of the genetic code for keratin is shown on the right.

The instructions for a protein are found in the precise sequence of DNA bases (G, C, A and T) along the length of a gene. This sequence of bases is called the **genetic code**.

?
3 What substance are genes made out of?

4 How many pairs of chromosomes are there in a normal human cell?

5 What is the genetic code?

Protein manufacture

Although genes are found inside the nucleus of a cell, proteins are made in the cytoplasm. The genetic code from one DNA strand in a gene is copied. The copy travels into the cytoplasm and the code is then used to make a protein by linking **amino acids** together. The genetic code controls the order in which the amino acids are added.

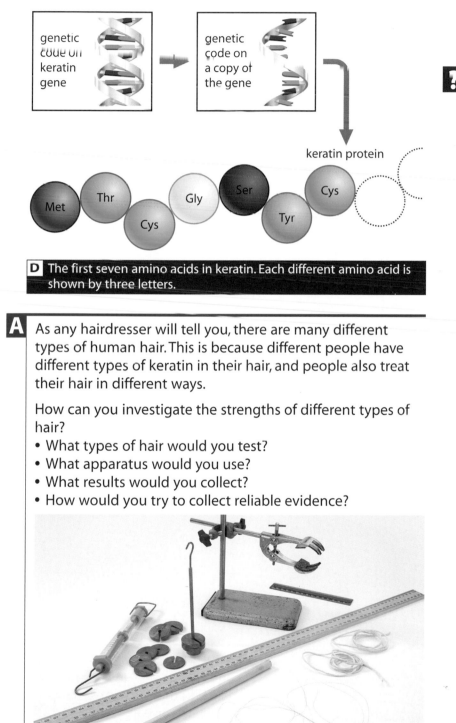

genetic code on keratin gene

genetic code on a copy of the gene

keratin protein

Met — Thr — Cys — Gly — Ser — Tyr — Cys

D The first seven amino acids in keratin. Each different amino acid is shown by three letters.

A As any hairdresser will tell you, there are many different types of human hair. This is because different people have different types of keratin in their hair, and people also treat their hair in different ways.

How can you investigate the strengths of different types of hair?
• What types of hair would you test?
• What apparatus would you use?
• What results would you collect?
• How would you try to collect reliable evidence?

F

? 6 How many different amino acids are shown in diagram D?

7 The next three amino acids to be added to this chain are Gly, Gly and Arg. Make a copy of the amino acids in diagram D and add the next three amino acids to the chain.

8 Photo E shows a hairless rat. Suggest all the possible reasons why it is hairless.

E

Summary

Genes are found on _____ inside the _____ of a cell. Each gene carries the instructions or _____ code for one _____. A copy of the genetic code is made from a gene and this travels to the _____. Here it is used to join _____ acids together in a specific way to make a _____. An example of a protein is _____, found in hair.

amino   chromosomes   cytoplasm
genetic   keratin   nucleus   protein

Different sorts of proteins

What do proteins do?

Some proteins are found in most cells, like those used in cell surface membranes. Other proteins are only made by certain kinds of cell. For example, hair cells produce keratin. Cells only make the proteins they need and the genes for other proteins are 'switched off'.

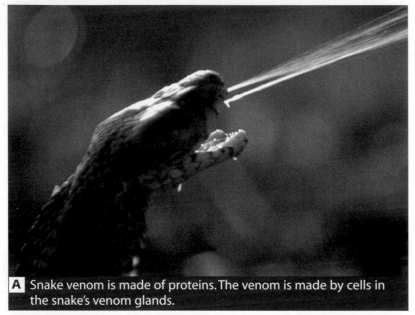

A Snake venom is made of proteins. The venom is made by cells in the snake's venom glands.

Enzymes are also proteins. Enzymes are 'biological **catalysts**', which means that they are molecules made by living things that speed up (**catalyse**) chemical reactions. Catalysts only help reactions, they do not get used up themselves.

B Flashlight fish have pouches that glow in the dark. The light is produced by a chemical reaction speeded up by an enzyme. In some parts of the world shoals of these fish are sometimes bombed or shot at when mistaken for enemy divers with diving lamps!

? 1 There are about 22 000 different human genes. How many proteins do you think humans make? Explain your answer.

2 What are enzymes?

Biological catalysts

All living things need enzymes to help the chemical reactions needed for life to occur. Cells could not stay alive without enzymes.

? **3** Look at diagram C. Some of the 'units' used to make amylase are coloured blue. What sort of molecule are these 'units'?

Humans produce thousands of different enzymes. Some digest your food and one of these is called **amylase**. It is produced by cells in your salivary glands and catalyses this reaction:

starch → maltose (a sugar)

If you mix 1 kg of starch with some water, about 0.00002 g of the starch will change into maltose each year. If you add amylase, about 0.5 g of the starch will be converted each minute. The amylase makes the reaction happen over 13 *billion* times faster.

Uses of enzymes

Enzymes are used in things like washing powders to help digest stains. They are even starting to be used in display screens. Display screens made of organic light-emitting diodes (OLEDs) use enzymes found in animals like the flashlight fish.

D An OLED display screen.

? **5** What makes enzymes found in the flashlight fish useful for OLEDs?

6 A cell does not produce keratin. Think of as many explanations for this as you can.

7 Human enzymes do not work so well if it is cold. What do you think happens to the activity of cells deep inside your body on a cold day? Explain your answer.

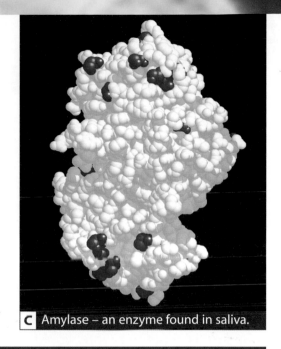

C Amylase – an enzyme found in saliva.

? **4** Is salivary amylase produced in all your cells or just some? Explain your answer.

Summary

Some proteins are made by most _____, other _____ are only made by certain kinds of cell. For example, _____ cells produce keratin and _____ cells produce an enzyme called _____. _____ speed up (_____) chemical _____ in the body.

amylase   catalyse   cells
enzymes   hair   proteins
reactions   salivary gland

How does cell division produce new organisms?

Many organisms start life as single fertilised egg cells, called **zygotes**. A zygote grows bigger by producing new cells by mitosis and an adult human body contains about 1000 million million cells.

You started off life this size.

? 1 a What is a zygote?
b How does it grow?

To make a zygote, two cells join together during **fertilisation**. Most human cells contain two sets of 23 chromosomes, making 46 in all. If two of these cells joined in fertilisation the zygote would have 92 chromosomes. So a zygote is formed from special cells, each containing just one set of chromosomes. These are called **sex cells** or **gametes**.

? 2 How many chromosomes do these have?
a human sperm cell
b human gamete
c human zygote

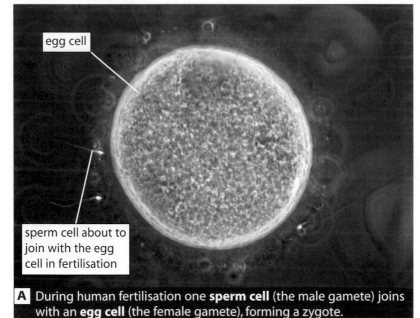

egg cell

sperm cell about to join with the egg cell in fertilisation

A During human fertilisation one **sperm cell** (the male gamete) joins with an **egg cell** (the female gamete), forming a zygote.

Gamete production

Mitosis produces new cells containing two sets of chromosomes. A different process is needed to produce gametes with only one set of chromosomes. This process is called **meiosis**.

Before meiosis starts, each chromosome is copied to form two identical, joined chromatids. Then the nuclear membrane breaks down and meiosis occurs in two stages.

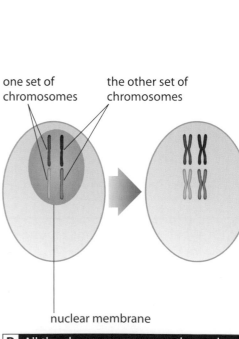

one set of chromosomes

the other set of chromosomes

nuclear membrane

B All the chromosomes copy themselves before meiosis starts.

? 3 Why are chromosomes X-shaped just before meiosis begins?

Meiosis in detail

First the *chromosomes* pair up. So, for example, both copies of chromosome 12 move next to each other. The pairs then separate to make two nuclei, each containing one chromosome from each pair.

Next, the two new nuclei each split into two when the *chromatids* are pulled away from their copies and become chromosomes. Nuclear and cell membranes form and four new cells have been created from one cell. The nucleus of each new cell contains only one set of chromosomes.

? 4 How many sets of chromosomes does each nucleus contain at the end of meiosis?

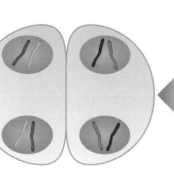

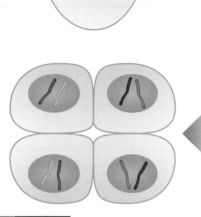

C Meiosis.

Male and female gametes are made by meiosis. When the gametes join in fertilisation, the zygote gets two sets of chromosomes – one from the father and one from the mother.

? 5 Look back at diagram D on page 91. Write down two ways in which meiosis is different from mitosis.

6 When human sperm cells are made, what is the total number of *chromatids* in the nucleus of each cell at:
  a the start of meiosis
  b the end of meiosis?

7 The egg cell in photo A is the same size as the dot at the top of the page, which is 0.1 mm in diameter. Work out the magnification of photo A.

Summary

_____ (e.g. sperm cells and egg cells) are made by _____. This form of _____ division starts with the _____ being copied and then the nucleus dividing into two. This leaves each nucleus with _____ set of _____. The _____ from each chromosome are then separated and form chromosomes. Each new nucleus ends up with _____ copy of each chromosome. _____ surface membranes form, making _____ cells from the original one.

| cell | chromosomes | chromatids | four |
| gametes | meiosis | nuclear | one |

Embryo development 1

What are embryonic stem cells?

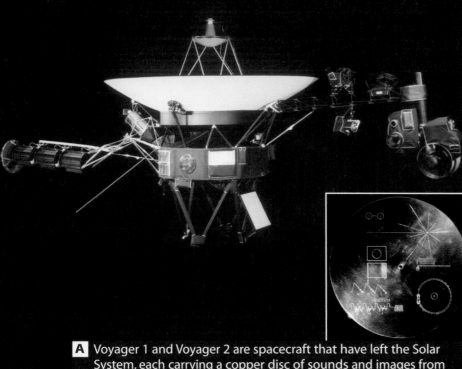

A Voyager 1 and Voyager 2 are spacecraft that have left the Solar System, each carrying a copper disc of sounds and images from Earth. The covers of the discs, designed by artist Jon Lomberg, contain instructions on how to play them.

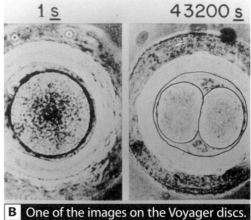

B One of the images on the Voyager discs. On the left is a zygote. On the right is what happens to it after 12 hours.

Photo B is one of 116 images being carried into outer space by the two Voyager spacecraft, in case aliens find one of them. The images are stored on discs that can be played like vinyl records but store information like CD-ROMs.

? 1 Look at photo B. What has happened to the zygote?

Forming an embryo

After 12 hours a zygote divides into two cells by mitosis, and becomes an **embryo**. After another 24 hours both these cells divide, forming four cells altogether. The cells continue dividing once every 24 hours.

? 2 If the cells were to divide by meiosis they could make four cells out of one, instead of only two. Why don't the cells use meiosis?

3 How many cells will an embryo have after 4 days?

C A 3-day-old human embryo containing eight cells (×900).

Embryonic stem cells

Up to the eight-cell stage, all the cells in an embryo are identical and each cell is capable of developing into any type of cell (e.g. muscle cell, nerve cell). A cell that can change into other types of cell is called a **stem cell**.

? 4 Why are cells in an eight-cell embryo called **embryonic stem cells**?

Genetic screening

If you remove an embryonic stem cell from an eight-cell embryo, it does not affect the embryo. In **genetic screening**, one cell is removed and its DNA is examined to find out if that embryo will become a boy or a girl, or if the baby will have a harmful genetic disease.

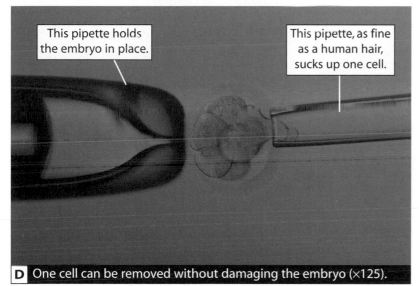

This pipette holds the embryo in place.

This pipette, as fine as a human hair, sucks up one cell.

D One cell can be removed without damaging the embryo (×125).

?
5 How many cells are there in the embryo in photo D before one is removed?

Embryo splitting

If embryonic stem cells are separated, each one can grow into a new embryo. Each of these embryos can then be placed into a female to grow and be born. This process is called **embryo splitting** and is often used with farm animals.

E Embryo splitting could be used to quickly increase the numbers of useful or endangered animals.

?
6 Why do you think farmers use embryo splitting?

7 a Do you think that genetic screening is a good idea? Explain your reasons.
  b Have you previously had a different view to your answer in part **a**? If so, explain what has made you change your mind.

Summary

A _____ divides in two after about _____ hours and forms an _____. The type of cell division used is _____. The cells divide again about every _____ hours. Up to the _____-cell stage, all the embryo cells can become any type of cell – they are _____ cells. Stem cells are used in _____ screening and _____ splitting.

| 12 | 24 | eight | embryo | genetic |
| mitosis | stem | zygote |

Embryo development 2

How do stem cells become other types of cells?

The cells in an embryo continue to divide as it travels down the oviduct, forming a ball of cells. The cells on the inside of this ball remain as embryonic stem cells and will develop into all the different types of cells in a baby.

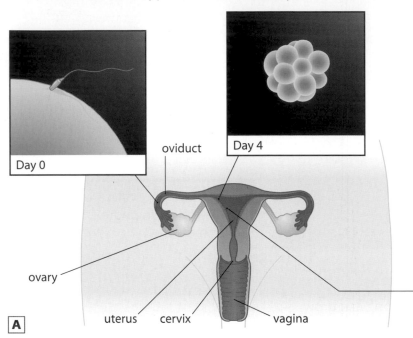

Day 0

oviduct

Day 4

ovary

uterus   cervix   vagina

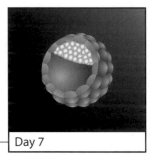

Day 7

A

? 1 **a** What is happening at Day 0 in diagram A?
  b How many cells are there in the Day 4 embryo?

2 **a** After 7 days, where in the female reproductive system is the hollow ball of cells?
  b What is inside the hollow ball of cells?

On about Day 8, the hollow ball of cells buries itself in the lining of the uterus (**implantation**). The embryonic stem cells divide quickly and start to specialise.

? 3 For each different cell in picture B, write down one place where it might be found.

4 A group of cells of the same type working together is called a **tissue**. Which of these tissues would you find in the brain?
muscle tissue   nerve tissue
ciliated epithelial tissue

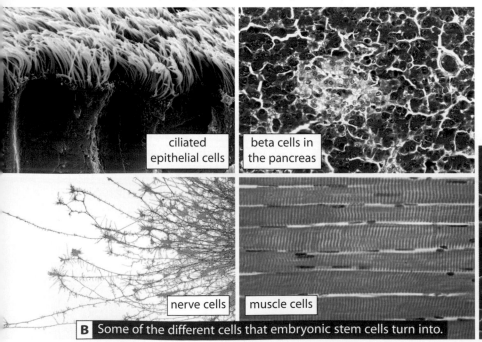

ciliated epithelial cells

beta cells in the pancreas

nerve cells   muscle cells

B Some of the different cells that embryonic stem cells turn into.

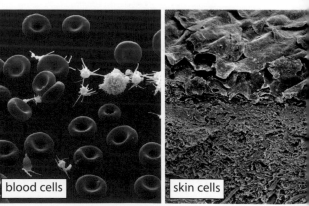

blood cells

skin cells

Getting organised

Some cells organise other cells and 'tell' them what to turn into. However, sometimes things go wrong and extra body parts are formed, or body parts do not form properly.

Cell specialisation

All of an organism's body cells contain the same chromosomes and so they contain the same genes. When a stem cell specialises and becomes another type of cell, certain genes are switched on and others are switched off. This means that an individual cell only makes the proteins that it needs to.

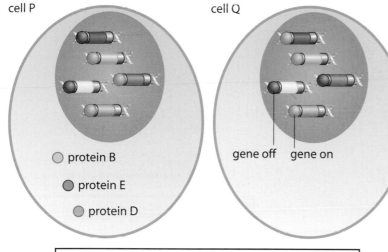

key to gene symbols			
	gene A		gene D
	gene B		gene E
	gene C		

D Different types of cells have different genes switched on and off.

? 5 a What are genes found on?
   b In diagram D, which genes are switched off in cell P?
   c Which proteins is cell Q producing?

Hair cells, nail cells and skin cells all produce keratin but other cells do not make it. The beta cells in the pancreas make a protein called insulin but no other cells make this.

? 6 What happens to the insulin gene in hair cells?

7 Where in a cell are proteins made?

8 Write a newspaper report on Lilly's birth, explaining how she got four ears. Give your report a catchy headline.

Summary

The embryo turns into a hollow ball of _____ that contains a clump of _____ stem cells. These divide to form all the cells in the _____ of the baby's body. _____ cells become other sorts of cells when some of their genes are switched _____ or off. All body cells contain the same _____ but different types of cells produce different _____ (e.g. insulin, _____) because certain genes are switched off and certain genes are switched on.

| cells | embryonic | genes | keratin |
| on | proteins | stem | tissues |

Plant cell specialisation

What tissues do plant cells form?

The rather unpleasant looking green stuff in photo A is a mass of unspecialised plant cells growing on a jelly. Just like embryonic stem cells from humans, these cells can become specialised and form all the different types of cell found in a plant.

The mass of unspecialised cells is a type of tissue – a group of cells that are all the same. When tissues of more than one type are grouped together to do a job it is called an organ. Plants have four main types of **organs** – roots, stems, leaves and flowers. Of course, not all plants have all of these organs.

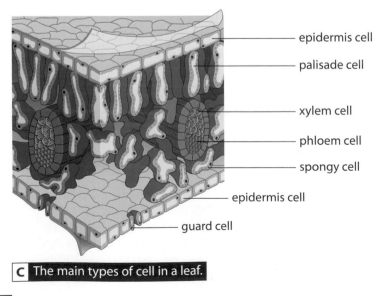

Some plants use **flowers** to reproduce.

Plants use **leaves** to make their food.

Plants use **stems** for support and to carry water and other substances to and from the leaves and roots.

Roots are used to take in water and mineral salts, and to anchor a plant in the ground.

B The main organs found in plants.

Organs contain many different types of cells but all the cells originally came from unspecialised cells. For example, diagram C shows the different cells found in a leaf.

growth jelly

A A mass of unspecialised plant cells.

? 1 Why do plants need specialised cells?

2 Why is the green growth in photo A not an organ?

3 Draw a table to show the jobs of different plant organs.

epidermis cell

palisade cell

xylem cell

phloem cell

spongy cell

epidermis cell

guard cell

C The main types of cell in a leaf.

? 4 Name three different tissues found in a leaf.

Some plants have cells that other plants do not have. For example, stinging nettles have cells that produce fine needles that break off and cut the skin if touched. Other cells, at the bottom of the needle cell, make a poison that squirts into the cut.

In the genes

Plants of different types will have different genes and so the cells of one plant may be different to the cells of another type of plant. Like animal cells, plant cells become specialised when certain genes are switched on or off.

? **5** As cells become specialised they start to produce different substances. Why?

Meristem cells

Unlike animals, plants contain large numbers of unspecialised cells throughout their lives. These cells are called **meristem cells** and are found in areas called **meristems**. Meristem cells are constantly dividing by mitosis to provide new cells, some of which will become specialised.

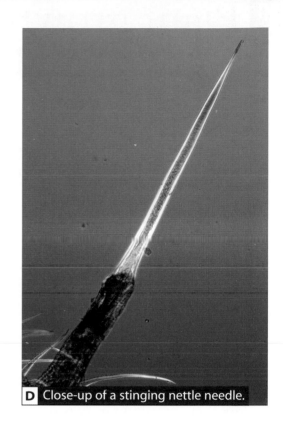
D Close-up of a stinging nettle needle.

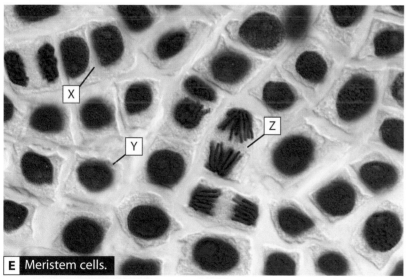
E Meristem cells.

? **6** Look at photo E.
a Which cell has just completed mitosis?
b What are the red strands in cell Z?

7 Suggest one way in which meristem cells are:
a like embryonic stem cells
b unlike embryonic stem cells.

8 Explain how a single meristem cell can become a whole leaf.

Summary

Some _____ in plants are not specialised and these are called _____ cells. They are mainly found in areas called _____. These unspecialised cells constantly use _____ to produce new cells. Some of the new cells become _____ and form _____ in new plant organs. Examples of plant organs are stems, _____, _____ and _____.

cells   flowers   leaves   meristem
meristems   mitosis   roots
specialised   tissues

Plant growth

Why do plants grow throughout their lives?

You will probably stop growing taller in your early 20s although your skull may continue to grow slightly until you are about 30. Bone growth is caused by quickly dividing cells at the ends of bones. These cells produce a substance called cartilage that is then turned into bone.

Bone growth is controlled by chemicals called hormones. One hormone increases bone growth and another, produced in high amounts in your late teens, stops growth and causes the cartilage-producing cells to die off. Sometimes this hormone control goes wrong.

Plants

Plants, on the other hand, continue to grow in height and width throughout their lives.

The reason for this continual growth is that plants do not lose their meristems as they get older, since some cells made in a meristem remain as meristem cells. Meristems stay as areas of actively dividing unspecialised cells for the whole of a plant's life.

Other cells made in a meristem specialise and become cells needed in roots, stems, leaves and flowers. These include the important cells in veins – **xylem** cells (which carry water) and **phloem** cells (which carry dissolved materials like sugars that are needed for growth).

A The tallest person ever was Robert Wadlow. He was 2.72 m tall when he died in 1940.

?

1 What process do the cells at the end of a growing bone use to divide?

2 Suggest one result of the hormones controlling growth going wrong.

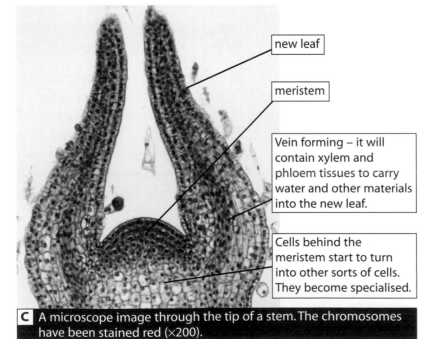

new leaf

meristem

Vein forming – it will contain xylem and phloem tissues to carry water and other materials into the new leaf.

Cells behind the meristem start to turn into other sorts of cells. They become specialised.

C A microscope image through the tip of a stem. The chromosomes have been stained red (×200).

B Some trees can reach heights of 100 m and they continue to grow until they die. These are giant sequoia trees in California.

A How would you find out which parts of a plant contain meristems?
- What would your prediction be?
- What apparatus will you use?
- What will you look for?

The meristem tissue at the edges of a tree trunk produces cells that make the tree trunk wider. If the growing conditions are good, these new cells are large and form a thick ring of new wood. If the growing conditions are not good, the new cells are small and form a thin ring.

meristem

large cells formed in spring

small cells formed in autumn

one year's growth

D

Not all plants have meristems in the same places. Bamboo plants have meristems at regular intervals in their stems, which cause them to grow taller extremely quickly – up to a metre a day in some types.

?
5 Why does a tree trunk need to grow wider?

6 How old was the tree in photo D?

7 Look back at photo C. Explain why there is more red staining in the meristem tissue than in the other tissues.

?
3 Describe two features of meristem cells.

4 Why can plants grow throughout their lives?

meristems

E Bamboo stems.

Summary

Plants _____ throughout their lives because they always contain _____ cells, which divide by _____.
Meristems allow roots and stems to grow _____ and _____.

grow	longer	meristem
	mitosis	wider

Plant cloning

How are plants cloned using tissue culture?

If you have a plant that is very pretty or produces lots of nice fruit you may wish to grow more copies of that plant. Unfortunately, the plant's seeds will not grow into plants that are identical to the one you started with.

Seeds are formed using egg cells from one plant and pollen grains from another. The pollen grains contain genes that are slightly different to those in the egg cell. Plants grown from seeds have a mixture of genes from two different plants and so are not identical to either parent plant.

? **1** Why are the flowers in photo A different colours?

Cloning

This problem can be overcome using cloning. A **clone** is an identical copy of an organism, and contains exactly the same genes. You can make plant clones by taking cuttings or using **tissue culture**.

? **2** What is a clone?

3 What method could you use to produce clones from a plant?

To start with, some meristem tissue is taken and placed into a growing jelly in a flask. The meristem cells divide and form a large clump of unspecialised cells. Once this clump has grown, it can be split into many smaller pieces. The lumps of unspecialised cells can then be treated to make them grow new shoots and roots.

A These flowers were all grown from the seeds of one plant!

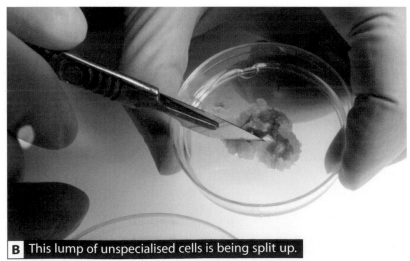

B This lump of unspecialised cells is being split up.

? **4** What is the point of splitting up a lump of unspecialised plant cells?

Plant hormones

In our bodies, chemical hormones change what our cells do. Plants have **plant hormones** (sometimes called plant growth substances) that change the way their cells work.

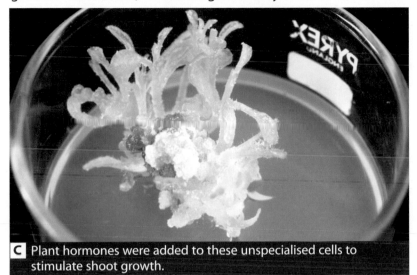

C Plant hormones were added to these unspecialised cells to stimulate shoot growth.

Different plant hormones have different effects. Some cause unspecialised cells to turn into cells found in stems and leaves. Other plant hormones cause root growth. By carefully applying different plant hormones to a lump of unspecialised cells, a whole new plant will start to grow.

A White cauliflower heads contain lots of meristem tissue. You can often use a small piece to get a new plant to grow.
- How would you grow a new cauliflower plant using tissue culture?
- How would you stop microbes growing in the jelly and ruining the experiment?

D One oil palm that produced a lot of oil was used to make thousands of clones using tissue culture.

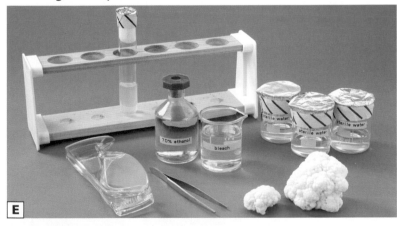

E

?

5 What characteristic do all the oil palms in photo D have?

6 Write a list of advantages and disadvantages of growing new plants using tissue culture rather than using seeds.

Summary

An identical copy (or _____) of a plant can be grown using _____ culture. Some _____ tissue is placed on a _____ jelly so that a lump of unspecialised cells forms. The jelly contains plant _____ that cause the cells to _____ and form the cells in roots, shoots and _____ .

clone   growth   hormones   leaves
meristem   specialise   tissue

More plant hormones

How are plants cloned using cuttings?

A Water hyacinths blocking a river in China.

Water hyacinth plants can choke rivers. They spread very quickly because parts of the plants break off and each part grows into a new plant. In a summer up to 60 000 clones can be produced from one plant.

Taking cuttings

A part of a water hyacinth can grow into a new plant because it contains unspecialised meristem tissue. Some of these cells specialise to form all the different cells needed. This specialisation is caused by plant hormones.

? 3 Name two types of cells that are needed in plants to transport water and other substances. (*Hint*: look back at page 104.)

The same thing happens when gardeners take **cuttings**. A cutting is often a leaf that is taken from the main plant and planted in some water or soil to grow roots. Cuttings allow gardeners to grow clones of plants with the features they want.

Hormones travel from the leaf tip to the cut point. Here they cause meristem cells to specialise to form the cells needed in new roots and leaves. Gardeners often use 'rooting powder' to give the cut points extra plant hormones.

? 4 What tissue must be in the cut end of a leaf for it to be able to grow roots?

5 What does rooting powder contain?

? 1 Suggest one problem caused by water hyacinths.

2 Why are the new plants produced by a water hyacinth called 'clones'?

B

How would you find out if it is only leaves that can be used for cuttings or whether other parts of plants will work just as well?

Other effects of plant hormones

There are lots of plant hormones in the growing parts of a plant. These control how quickly cells grow and divide, and can make some cells grow faster than others.

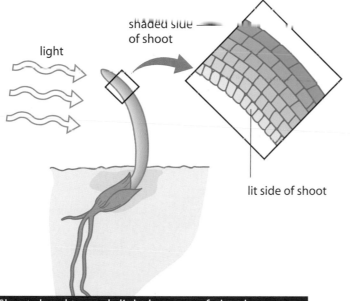

light

shaded side of shoot

lit side of shoot

C Shoots bend towards light because of plant hormones.

For instance, plant hormones cause cells on the shady side of the shoot to get bigger more quickly than cells in the light. This means that the shoot bends, growing towards the light.

? **6 a** What chemicals cause plants to grow towards light?
  b What affect do these chemicals have on cells in the shady part of a shoot?

Growing towards light is called **phototropism**. It is important because it allows the plant to get more light for photosynthesis. The more light the leaves get, the more a plant can photosynthesise, the more food it makes and the more likely it is to survive.

? **7** What is phototropism?

8 How does phototropism help a plant to survive?

9 Using rooting powder on a cutting makes roots grow faster than they would otherwise. Suggest two reasons why this is.

D Phototropism.

Summary

A plant cutting contains _____ tissue that allows it to regrow into a whole plant. Plant _____ help unspecialised cells to _____. Plant _____ also help plants survive by making them grow towards _____ - a process called _____.

hormones   light   meristem
phototropism   specialise

The Tissue Store

What do you know about growth and development?

All our treatments are made from human cells!

Stem cell treatments. Embryonic stem cells used to reduce the signs of ageing.

Cell treatments. We'll take some of your cells that aren't working and allow them to copy. We reprogram these cells, switching some genes on and others off, and re-inject them.

Genetic screening. We'll fertilise your egg cells and screen the embryos, only implanting those that don't have genetic diseases.

Henry (78) had embryonic stem cells implanted into his face. He had a cell treatment for his diabetes.

A *Vanessa (35) had an embryo screened for genetic disease.*

1 For animals and plants to grow and develop, cells need to copy themselves.
   a Write these sentences in the correct order to explain how cells do this.
   - The cell splits into two.
   - Exact copies are made of all 46 chromosomes.
   - There are now two cells, each with a nucleus containing a full set of chromosomes.
   - The nucleus splits into two.
   b What is this process called?
   c Name one organism that has 46 chromosomes in the nucleus of each cell.

2 The drawing shows a cell that is in the middle of the growing stage of the cell cycle.

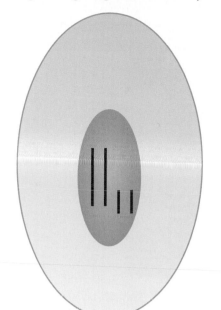

B

a Draw what the cell would look like *just before* it goes into mitosis.
b Draw the cell or cells that would be produced by this cell in mitosis.

3 Put the following into size order, starting with the smallest.

chromosome embryo gamete gene nucleus organism

The advert says that The Tissue Store can reprogram cells by turning genes on and off. This will change what proteins a cell makes.

4 The code for making proteins is found in DNA molecules.
a Where is DNA found?
b What shape are DNA molecules?
c What chemicals are used to make this code?
d Where in a cell are proteins made?
e What are proteins made up of?

5 Insulin is a hormone that helps to control the amount of sugar in the blood. In people with diabetes, insulin is not made.
a Write down a list of possible reasons why diabetics do not make insulin.
b Choose one of your reasons and then explain how you think modern science might cure this problem in the future.

The Tissue Store says that it can screen embryos for genetic diseases.

6 In genetic screening, one cell is removed from an embryo and its DNA is examined. Why doesn't this cause harm to a baby that develops from this embryo?

The Tissue Store does not offer plant services, but plants also have cells that can turn into other cells. These cells are found in meristems.

7 The photograph shows the tip of a root from a lily plant.

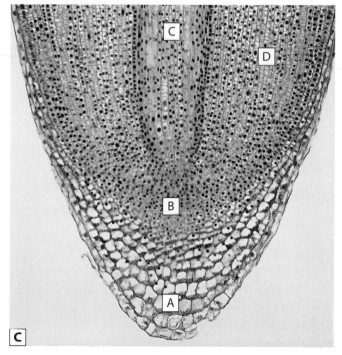

C

a Which letter shows where meristem cells are?
b Explain how you worked out your answer to part **a**.
c What chemicals cause meristem cells to specialise?
d Name two specialised cells found in a leaf.
e What do your chosen cells do?

8 a Which of the following methods can produce identical copies of a plant?

growing from seeds   taking cuttings tissue culture

b Why can the method(s) you have chosen produce identical copies of a plant?
c What name is given to a plant that is an identical copy of another?

Chemicals around us

What kinds of chemicals are found in our environment?

A Chemicals don't just exist in laboratories.

Our whole **environment** – the land, sea, sky and all the living things that live in them – is made up of millions of different chemicals.

Our Earth was formed about 4500 million years ago. Most scientists think that the whole solar system was formed from the remains of an exploded star. This means that most of the atoms of all the elements on Earth today originated in a star billions of years ago.

The Earth formed from a churning cloud of gases. Over millions of years, the Earth took on its present form.

B The glow represents the formation of new solar systems.

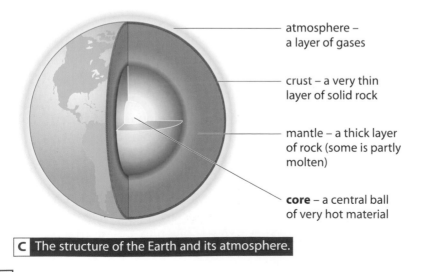

atmosphere – a layer of gases

crust – a very thin layer of solid rock

mantle – a thick layer of rock (some is partly molten)

core – a central ball of very hot material

C The structure of the Earth and its atmosphere.

?

1 How old is the Earth?

2 What is the solid outer layer of the Earth called?

The Earth's environment can be split into four different areas or 'spheres'.
- The **atmosphere** is the mixture of gases that surrounds the Earth. It includes the oxygen we need to survive and water vapour.
- The **lithosphere** is the solid **crust** and part of the **mantle**. It contains the rocks and minerals we use as raw materials.
- The **hydrosphere** includes all the water on the surface of the Earth (oceans, seas, rivers and lakes) and the chemicals dissolved in them.
- The **biosphere** includes all living things.

D Human activities can change the chemicals in our environment.

? **3** In which of the four spheres would you find:
   a humans
   b most minerals
   c oxygen gas?

The **elements** and **compounds** that make up our environment are constantly moving between the 'spheres'. Water and carbon dioxide are absorbed by plants for photosynthesis and become part of the biosphere. Minerals and salts in the soil dissolve in rainwater and are washed into the hydrosphere. Fuels are burned and the gases produced are released into our atmosphere. Therefore elements and compounds are found in more than one sphere.

Where chemicals are found depends on their properties, and their properties depend on how their atoms are joined together. Chemical **bonds** are the forces that join atoms together. We need to understand how atoms join together to form compounds to help us understand our material world. This module looks at the chemicals in our environment and tries to explain their properties in terms of their structure and bonding.

? **4** Explain the difference between an element and a compound.

5 Choose your answers to this question from the words below:
   atmosphere biosphere hydrosphere lithosphere
   a Which 'sphere' does seawater go into when it evaporates?
   b Which 'sphere' does the carbon in coal go into when it burns?
   c Which sphere is mainly water?

Summary

Our _____ is made up of four spheres. The _____ is made up of gases. The _____ contains solids like rocks and minerals. The _____ is made up of water and dissolved chemicals. The _____ contains all living things.

The properties of all chemicals depend on their _____ and _____.

| atmosphere biosphere bonding environment hydrosphere lithosphere structure |

The chemicals in the atmosphere

What types of chemicals make up the atmosphere?

A Our atmosphere.

The atmosphere is the mixture of gases (called **air**) which surrounds the Earth. Our atmosphere is about 1100 km deep, but as the air gets thinner the further you go from the Earth's surface it is difficult to say exactly where it stops. Almost half the mass of our atmosphere is concentrated in the lowest 5.6 km.

Air is made up of a mixture of elements and compounds. Table B shows the composition of dry air, which stays almost the same throughout the atmosphere.

Traces of other chemicals found in air include ozone (O_3), carbon monoxide (CO), helium (He) and variable amounts of water vapour (H_2O).

Gas	% in dry air
nitrogen	78
oxygen	21
argon	0.9
carbon dioxide	0.04
other gases	traces

B

?

1 a Which gas makes up most of the air?
  b Which gas do we need to stay alive?

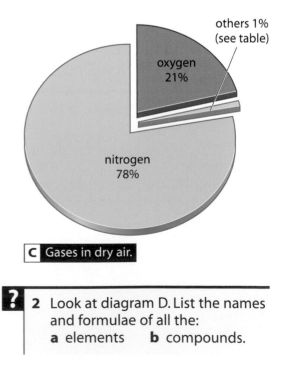

C Gases in dry air.

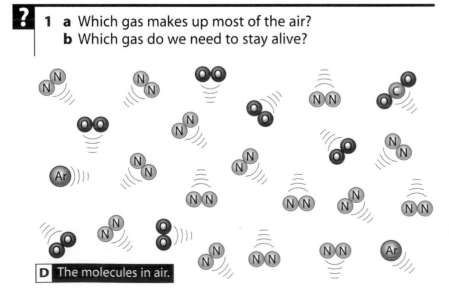

D The molecules in air.

?

2 Look at diagram D. List the names and formulae of all the:
  a elements   **b** compounds.

The elements and compounds in air are similar in several ways. They are all:
- gases with low boiling points
- non-metal elements or compounds
- made up of small molecules or single atoms.

Most non-metal elements and compounds have a **molecular structure**. Strong forces called **covalent bonds** hold the atoms together in **molecules**. However, there are only weak forces between the molecules.

When a molecular solid is heated, the energy given to its molecules makes them vibrate faster. As the temperature rises, the energy of the vibrations increases and eventually overcomes the weak forces between the molecules. The solid melts and its molecules move about more freely. If the heating is continued and the molecules get more energy, they can escape the weaker forces between them and turn into a gas.

When a molecular substance changes state the strong covalent bonds between the atoms are not broken, only the weak bonds between the molecules. These weak bonds only need a little energy to break them, which explains why covalent molecular substances usually have low melting points and boiling points and are often gases or liquids at room temperature.

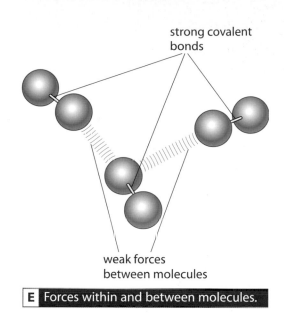

strong covalent bonds

weak forces between molecules

E Forces within and between molecules.

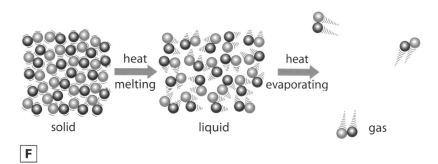

solid   heat / melting   liquid   heat / evaporating   gas

F

?

3 What do you call the type of bond that holds atoms together in molecules?

4 Think of a plus, a minus and an interesting point about this statement: Our atmosphere should contain 78% oxygen and 20% nitrogen.

5 Copy and complete this diagram to show what happens to molecules of oxygen when it changes from a liquid to a gas.

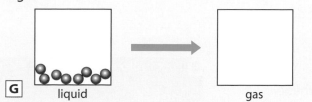

G liquid   gas

Summary

The main elements in air are _____ , _____ and _____ . Carbon dioxide is a _____ in air. Molecular compounds have _____ forces, called _____ bonds, between the atoms in each _____ , but only _____ forces holding the molecules together. Compounds like this usually have _____ melting and _____ points.

argon	boiling	compound
covalent	low	molecule	nitrogen
oxygen	strong	weak

115

The atoms of many non-metals have nearly full outer electron shells. That is, they only need to gain one or two more electrons to complete the outer shell. In non-metal elements and compounds the atoms are held together by covalent bonds. To form these bonds the non-metal atoms share pairs of electrons so that they each have a full outer shell.

For example, chlorine is made up of **diatomic molecules** which contain two chlorine atoms. The atoms are held together with a covalent bond formed by sharing two electrons, one from each atom.

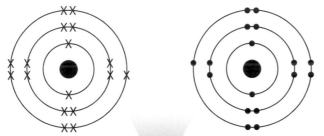

chlorine atoms – they both need one extra electron to fill their outer shells

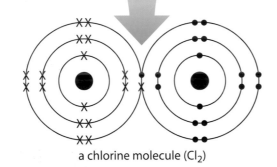

A a chlorine molecule (Cl_2)

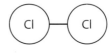

This is a simpler way of drawing a chlorine molecule. The line between the atoms represents a shared pair of electrons.

 1 a What is covalent bonding?
   b What are molecules?

The elements hydrogen, nitrogen, oxygen, fluorine, bromine and iodine also form diatomic molecules. The only non-metal elements that do not form molecules are the noble gases in Group 0. They exist as single atoms as they already have a full outer shell of electrons and do not need to share electrons.

Covalent bonds can also be formed between atoms of different non-metal elements. Diagram B shows how a methane molecule is formed.

2 Which Group contains non-metal elements that don't form bonds or molecules?

3 Look at diagram B.
   a What is the formula of methane?
   b How many covalent bonds are formed in methane?

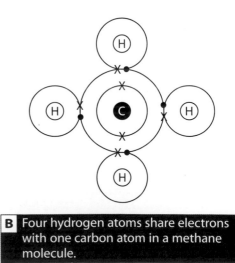

B Four hydrogen atoms share electrons with one carbon atom in a methane molecule.

We can represent covalent molecules using **molecular formulae**, three-dimensional models, or **structural formulae** with the molecules 'flattened out' and the covalent bonds shown as lines.

3D model				

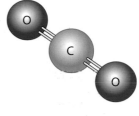

structural formula	F — F	$\begin{matrix} H \\ | \\ || \ \ C \ \ || \\ | \\ H \end{matrix}$	H O H	O=C=O
molecular formula	F_2	CH_4	H_2O	CO_2

C

The atoms in a covalent molecule are held together by the attraction between the positive nuclei and the shared negatively charged electrons. Positive and negative charges always attract each other. These powerful **electrostatic forces** explain why covalent bonds are strong.

Understanding bonding and structure helps us to explain the properties of substances. Covalent molecular substances cannot conduct electricity as there are no free electrons or ions to carry the current.

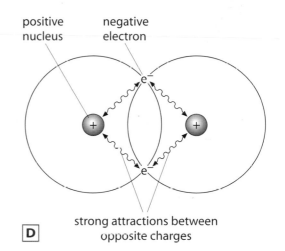

positive nucleus   negative electron

strong attractions between opposite charges

D

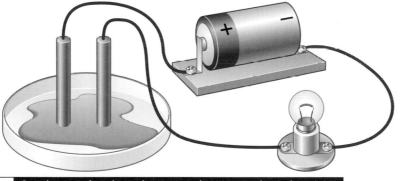

E Covalent molecular substances do not conduct electricity.

?

4 What holds the atoms together in a covalent bond?

5 Write the names and formulae of the substances shown in diagram C.

6 Which is the odd one out from this list: carbon dioxide, oxygen, argon? Explain your answers.

7 Part of the symbol equation for the formation of hydrogen chloride gas (HCl) is shown below.
   $$H_2 + Cl_2 \rightarrow$$
   a Copy and complete the symbol equation.
   b Draw a diagram of a hydrogen chloride molecule.

Summary

Non-metal elements and compounds form strong _____ bonds by _____ pairs of _____. The atoms in a _____ are held together because the _____ attract the shared electrons. Covalent substances have _____ melting points as the forces of attraction between molecules are _____. They do not _____ electricity.

conduct	covalent	electrons	low
molecule	nuclei	sharing	weak

The chemicals in the hydrosphere

What types of chemical make up the hydrosphere?

A Ari Afrizal was washed out to sea by a tsunami in 2004, and survived for 15 days. The sea is too salty to drink, but he found coconuts floating on the water and drank the liquid inside them.

The main chemical in the hydrosphere is water. However, almost all water contains some dissolved chemicals. The seas are 'salty' as they contain many different soluble compounds called **salts**.

? **1** What is the main chemical in the hydrosphere?

Some of these dissolved salts have come from the **weathering** of rocks in the lithosphere. Rain, wind and temperature changes gradually break up rocks into smaller pieces. Acids in the rain and soil attack certain rocks, forming a range of soluble compounds. These compounds dissolve in the rainwater, get washed into the rivers, and eventually find their way to the sea. Salts from the weathering of rocks contain a high proportion of the elements calcium, magnesium, silicon and carbon.

Other chemicals in the seas come from the seabed itself. For example, volcanoes under the sea release compounds containing lots of chlorine, bromine and sulfur.

B As rocks weather, chemicals are formed that dissolve in rainwater and end up in the sea.

The sea contains about 3.5 g of dissolved salts in every 100 g of water. Salts are examples of **ionic compounds**. These compounds contain positively and negatively charged atoms called **ions**. When these compounds are solid, the ions are held together by **ionic bonds**. When ionic compounds are dissolved in water the ions are free to move about in all directions.

? **2** What kind of compounds are salts?

- How could you find out if seawater conducts electricity?
- How could you find the total mass of dissolved salts in seawater?

3 Describe one way dissolved substances get into the sea.

C

Seawater has a similar composition everywhere. The main salt in seawater is sodium chloride, but there are also many other salts including compounds of magnesium, calcium, potassium, bromine and iodine. Seawater probably contains some ions of every element found on Earth.

The ions in the sea are formed when atoms or groups of atoms gain or lose electrons. Seawater is a good conductor of electricity as these ions can move around.

Ion	Formula	% by mass
chloride	Cl^-	55
sodium	Na^+	30.5
sulfate	SO_4^{2-}	7.5
magnesium	Mg^{2+}	3.5
calcium	Ca^{2+}	1
potassium	K^+	1

D The main ions in seawater.

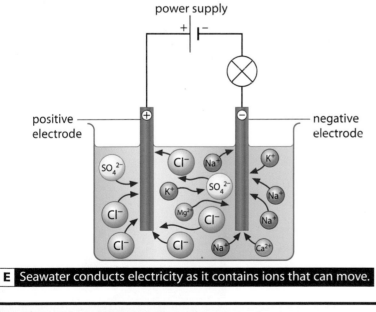

E Seawater conducts electricity as it contains ions that can move.

4 Name four elements found in the salts in seawater.

5 What are ions?

6 Think of a plus, a minus and an interesting point about this statement: Seawater should have no salts in it.

7 Look at the table showing the ions in seawater. Draw a bar graph to represent this information.

Summary

The _____ is mainly made up of water which contains dissolved _____. These are _____ compounds. Seawater conducts electricity as it contains freely moving charged _____. The main salt present in seawater is _____. Many of the salts in our _____ have come from the _____ of rocks.

hydrosphere   ionic   ions   oceans
salts   sodium chloride   weathering

Properties of ionic compounds

How are ionic and covalent compounds different?

A Salts being obtained from seawater.

B Iron sulfide is an ionic compound.

If seawater is left to evaporate, white **crystals** are formed. The crystals contain all the dissolved salts that were in the water. These salts are ionic compounds, which are usually formed between metals and non-metals. Solid ionic compounds often form crystals with a regular shape, straight edges and flat surfaces that reflect light.

Photograph C shows the crystals formed when a salt solution evaporates. These crystals are produced as billions of oppositely charged ions (positive Na^+ and negative Cl^-) attract each other and form a regular arrangement called an **ionic lattice**. The sodium chloride lattice is shown in diagram D. This ordered lattice structure explains why ionic compounds form crystals with a regular shape.

?
1 What is left if seawater is evaporated?

2 What do salt crystals look like?

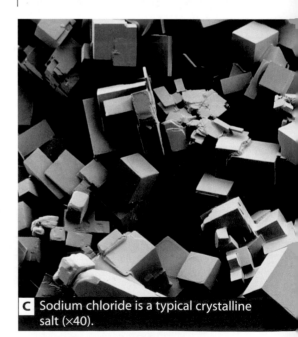

C Sodium chloride is a typical crystalline salt (×40).

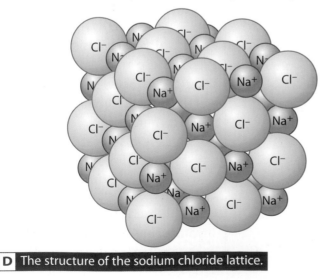

D The structure of the sodium chloride lattice.

?
3 Why do ionic compounds form regular crystals?

4 What is the formula of sodium chloride?

The forces between the ions are called ionic bonds. These bonds are very strong, so it takes a lot of energy to make the ions break away from each other. This is why ionic compounds are always solids at room temperature.

Table E compares ionic and covalent substances. The ionic compounds all have high melting points while the covalent substances have low melting points.

Covalent molecular substances	Melting point (°C)
carbon dioxide	−57
bromine	−7
oxygen	−218
nitrogen dioxide	−11

Ionic lattice compounds	Melting point (°C)
sodium chloride	800
potassium iodide	686
magnesium chloride	712
sodium sulfate	884

E

? 5 What holds the ions together in a solid ionic compound?

An ionic solid doesn't conduct electricity as it contains no free electrons, and the charged ions cannot move because they are locked in the lattice structure. However, if you melt an ionic compound or dissolve it in water, the lattice structure breaks up and the positive and negative ions can move around. A solution of an ionic compound or a molten ionic compound can therefore conduct electricity.

A How could you investigate different chemicals to find out which ones are ionic?

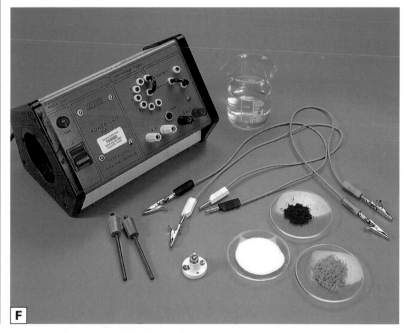

F

? 6 Think of possible explanations for this statement:
A substance does not conduct electricity.

7 **a** Would you expect solid potassium iodide to be ionic?
b Would you expect it to conduct electricity?
c Explain your answer to part **b**.

Summary

When salt solutions evaporate _____ of ionic _____ are formed.
Ionic compounds:
• are usually formed between metals and _____
• contain _____ and negative ions which _____ each other
• form an ionic _____ structure
• have _____ melting points
• are _____ at room temperature
• only conduct electricity when _____ or dissolved in _____ when the ions can move.

attract	compounds	crystals
high	lattice	molten	non-metals
positive	solids	water

Fats and oils contain fatty acids and glycerol.

The carbohydrates in these foods came from plants, and break down to glucose during digestion.

The protein molecules in meat are formed from amino acids.

A Carbohydrates, proteins, fats and oils are all biomolecules.

The biosphere contains an enormous variety of living things which are made up of similar chemicals. The chemicals in living things generally contain large complex molecules, called **biomolecules**, based on the element carbon.

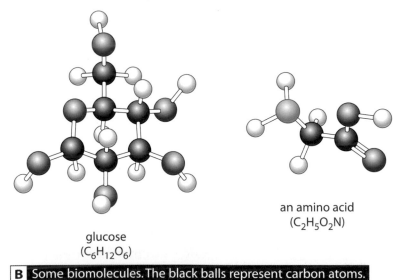

glucose
($C_6H_{12}O_6$)

an amino acid
($C_2H_5O_2N$)

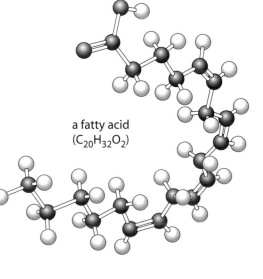

a fatty acid
($C_{20}H_{32}O_2$)

B Some biomolecules. The black balls represent carbon atoms.

Organic chemistry is the study of carbon compounds. Of the 10 million compounds known to chemists, 9.5 million are organic.

The molecules of living things contain mainly carbon, hydrogen, oxygen and nitrogen. Nearly 99% of the atoms in the human body are these four elements, which are essential for all forms of life.

?

1 What is the biosphere?

2 **a** What is the most important element in biomolecules?
  b What kind of bonding holds biomolecules together?

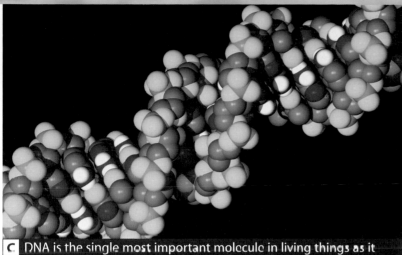

These four elements form all the most important molecules in living things. Molecules of carbohydrates, fats and oils are mainly made up of carbon, hydrogen and oxygen. Protein molecules contain these three elements plus nitrogen.

There are other elements that are essential to life, but only very small quantities of these are required. These **trace elements** include calcium, sulfur, phosphorus and potassium. These elements are often needed to make particular molecules.

The compositions of some typical biomolecules are shown in table E.

61.1% O

19.5% C

8.9% H

4.9% N

other elements

D Elements in the human body.

?
3 What are the four main elements in all living things?

4 What is the total percentage of these four elements in the human body?

	Carbon	Hydrogen	Oxygen	Nitrogen	Sulfur	Phosphorus
carbohydrates	45.6%	3.8%	50.6%			
proteins	56.4%	8.6%	18.5%	16.2%	0.3%	
fats	76.6%	12.6%	16.8%			
DNA	35.9%	3.5%	34.4%	16.7%		9.5%

E

?
5 a Which three elements make up carbohydrates and fats?
  b Which other elements can be found in proteins?

6 a Name three trace elements.
  b From table E, name the types of biomolecule which contain the highest proportion of phosphorus and nitrogen.

7 Look at diagram D.
  a What is the total percentage of other elements in the human body?
  b Draw a bar graph of the information in diagram D.

Summary

The molecules found in living things are based on the element _____. Examples of these _____ include carbohydrates, fats, _____ and DNA. The four main elements in living things are carbon, hydrogen, _____ and _____. Other trace elements like _____ and _____ are present in small amounts.

biomolecules carbon nitrogen
oxygen phosphorus proteins sulfur

Chemical cycles

Why are chemical cycles so important to life?

The elements needed by living things cycle between the lithosphere, hydrosphere, atmosphere and biosphere. There are many examples of natural cycles where the same atoms cycle through different spheres again and again. For example, the amount of water on Earth has been roughly the same for millions of years. However, the water does not stay in one place. It changes state, going from the seas into the atmosphere and back to the seas again in the natural **water cycle**.

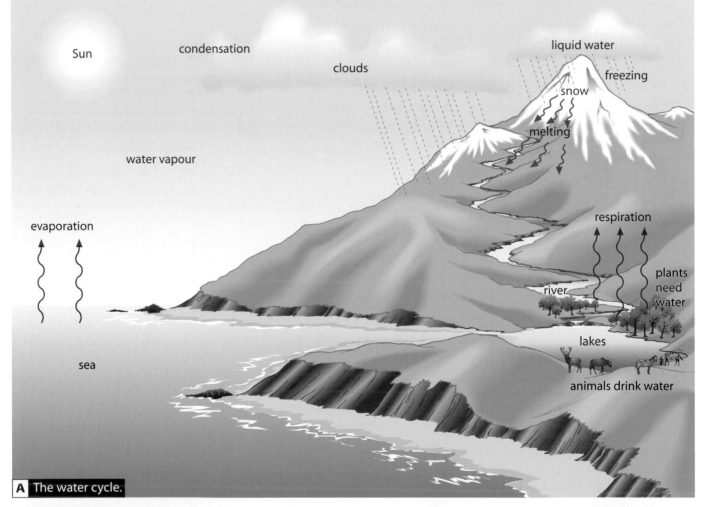

A The water cycle.

The **nitrogen cycle**, like most biological cycles, involves mostly chemical reactions. Plants and animals need nitrogen to make **proteins**, which are used to build living cells. Plants cannot use the nitrogen gas in the air to make proteins, so they have to obtain it from nitrogen compounds. These compounds come from the soil, or from bacteria which make them using nitrogen in the air.

?

1   Describe some of the main changes in the water cycle shown in diagram A. Start with:
   • The Sun evaporates the water in the sea which goes into the air.

2   Which three spheres does the water cycle through?

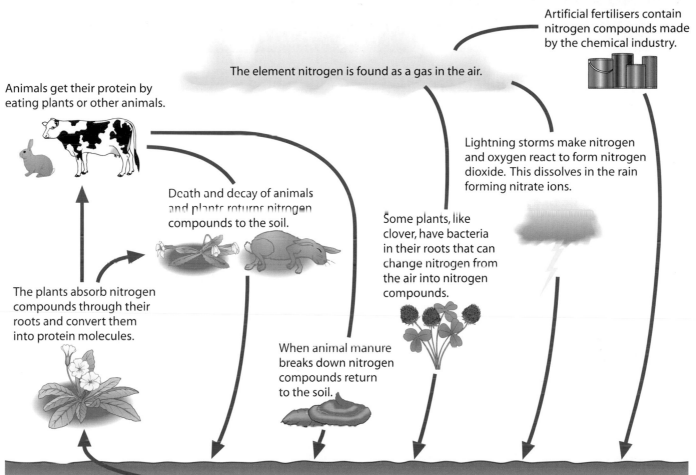

Artificial fertilisers contain nitrogen compounds made by the chemical industry.

The element nitrogen is found as a gas in the air.

Animals get their protein by eating plants or other animals.

Lightning storms make nitrogen and oxygen react to form nitrogen dioxide. This dissolves in the rain forming nitrate ions.

Death and decay of animals and plants returns nitrogen compounds to the soil.

Some plants, like clover, have bacteria in their roots that can change nitrogen from the air into nitrogen compounds.

The plants absorb nitrogen compounds through their roots and convert them into protein molecules.

When animal manure breaks down nitrogen compounds return to the soil.

B The nitrogen cycle.

Nitrogen in the soil exists as compounds containing ammonium (NH_4^+) or nitrate (NO_3^-) ions.

In nature the nitrogen cycle is in balance. However, modern farming takes crops away and doesn't allow them to rot back into the soil. We have to add fertilisers to the soil to replace the missing nitrogen. There are natural fertilisers such as compost and manure. The chemical industry also makes artificial fertilisers which often contain soluble ammonium or nitrate salts, such as potassium nitrate (KNO_3) and ammonium sulfate ($(NH_4)_2SO_4$).

3 Why do plants and animals need nitrogen?

4 Describe three ways that nitrogen is returned to the soil.

5 a Which ions are found in artificial fertilisers?
b Why are artificial fertilisers needed?

6 Neutralising sulfuric acid with ammonia forms a solution of ammonium sulfate, a compound which can be used as a fertiliser.
a Write a word equation for the manufacture of ammonium sulfate.
b Give two reasons why ammonium sulfate is a good fertiliser.

7 Which is the odd one out from this list: carbon, water, nitrogen? Explain your answers.

Summary

The elements needed by living things take part in _____. The elements take different forms and are found in different _____ as they cycle back and forth between the lithosphere, _____, hydrosphere and _____. The _____ cycle is an example of an important life cycle.

atmosphere   biosphere   compounds
cycles   nitrogen

Chemicals in the lithosphere

Which elements are found in the Earth's crust?

The lithosphere, which includes the Earth's crust and some parts of the upper mantle, is our greatest source of elements.

? 1 What is the lithosphere?

Nearly three-quarters of the Earth's crust is made up of just two elements, oxygen and silicon. The oxygen and silicon are found in compounds in the crust, not as elements. Aluminium is the most common metal, which is also found in compounds and not as lumps of metal.

B Pure silicon.

A The molten lava from some volcanoes comes from the upper mantle and is part of the lithosphere.

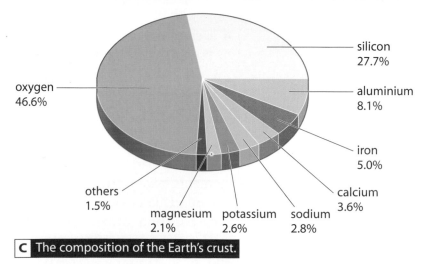

silicon 27.7%

aluminium 8.1%

oxygen 46.6%

iron 5.0%

calcium 3.6%

others 1.5%

magnesium 2.1%

potassium 2.6%

sodium 2.8%

C The composition of the Earth's crust.

? 2 a Which two elements make up 75% of the Earth's crust?
b List the five most common metals in the Earth's crust in order, starting with the most common one.

The elements in the lithosphere are found in **rocks** and **minerals**. A mineral is a solid element or compound that has been formed naturally in or on the Earth's crust. Some rocks are made up of only one mineral, but most rocks are mixtures of different minerals.

D Mica is a pure mineral.

E Granite is a rock that contains the minerals feldspar, quartz and mica.

Different minerals can have different properties and uses, depending on their structure and bonding (how their atoms are held together). Some minerals are found in the form of crystals. Crystals are solids that have regular shapes and flat surfaces that reflect the light. The crystals of some minerals, like diamond and ruby, are extremely hard and very beautiful. This makes them attractive, and if they are also rare, they are expensive. These types of minerals are called **gemstones**.

? 3 What is the difference between a rock and a mineral?

4 Look at photo E. How can you tell that granite is a mixture of minerals?

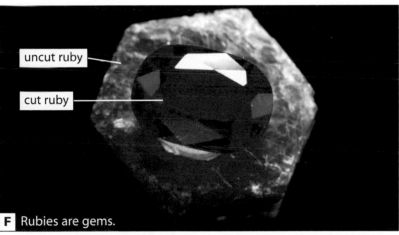

uncut ruby

cut ruby

F Rubies are gems.

? 5 Name two minerals which can be used to make jewellery.

6 A ruby is an expensive crystalline mineral.
   a What name is given to these minerals?
   b What makes them expensive?

7 Think of a plus, a minus and an interesting point about this statement: Gemstones should be cheap to buy.

8 Most minerals don't last forever. They can be changed and take part in cycles. Briefly describe how some minerals in the Earth's crust are changed over time.

Summary

The lithosphere, which is the _____ and upper _____, is made up of a mixture of _____. Minerals are solid _____ or _____ found naturally. The most common elements in the Earth's crust are _____, oxygen and _____. Some rare minerals, which form _____, are very beautiful and expensive. They are called _____.

aluminium compounds crust crystals elements gemstones mantle minerals silicon

Giant covalent structures

How can we explain the properties of certain minerals?

quartz

sand is small grains of quartz

A Two forms of silicon dioxide.

The silicon and oxygen that make up 75% of the Earth's crust are mainly found as silicon dioxide. This can exist as the mineral **quartz**, which is found in rocks such as granite and sandstone.

Most compounds formed from non-metals contain small molecules held together by covalent bonds. They usually have low melting points and boiling points as there are only very weak forces between the molecules. The atoms in silicon dioxide are held together by covalent bonds but they form a **giant covalent structure**, sometimes called a lattice structure, as shown in diagram B.

A single grain of sand contains billions of silicon and oxygen atoms, all held together in one giant covalent structure. This structure explains the properties of silicon dioxide. Because there are many strong covalent bonds holding the atoms together, it is very difficult to break them apart. This makes silicon dioxide very hard, with a high melting point. It also means that silicon dioxide does not dissolve in water. The regular lattice structure makes it crystalline. As it has no free electrons or charged ions it does not conduct electricity.

?
1 Name three different materials that we find silicon dioxide in.

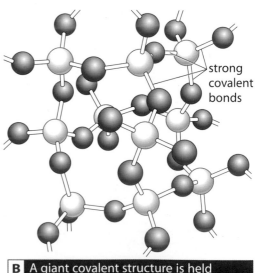

strong covalent bonds

B A giant covalent structure is held together by millions of strong covalent bonds.

?
2 Describe the structure of silicon dioxide shown in diagram B.

3 What is another name for a giant covalent structure?

4 Why does silicon dioxide not conduct electricity?

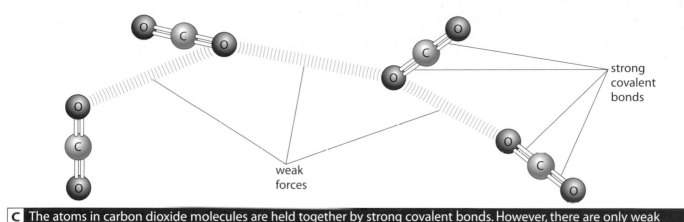

strong covalent bonds

weak forces

C The atoms in carbon dioxide molecules are held together by strong covalent bonds. However, there are only weak forces holding the molecules together.

Other elements and compounds found in the lithosphere also have giant covalent structures and these structures help explain their properties. For example there are two forms of carbon, graphite and **diamond**. Both forms have covalent bonds with giant lattice structures.

D Diamond is a rare form of carbon that is used in jewellery and for cutting glass.

E Graphite is a fairly common form of carbon and is used in pencils.

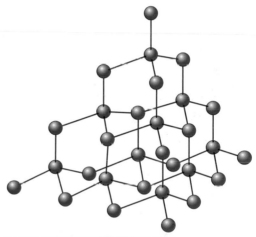

F The structure of diamond.

In the diamond lattice each carbon atom is joined to four others by strong covalent bonds. As it takes a lot of energy to break these strong bonds, diamond has a high melting point and is the hardest natural substance. Like silicon dioxide, diamond is also crystalline and doesn't conduct electricity.

?

5 a How are the structures of diamond and silicon dioxide similar?
  b Write down one difference between them.

6 Why do silicon dioxide and diamond have such high melting points?

7 Look at diagrams B and C, which show the structure of silicon dioxide and carbon dioxide.
  a What are the formulae of these compounds?
  b Explain why carbon dioxide is a gas and silicon dioxide is a solid.

Summary

Silicon dioxide is found naturally in _____ in granite and sandstone. It is hard, has a _____ melting point, does not _____ electricity and does not _____ in water. Silicon dioxide has a _____ covalent structure held together by _____ bonds.

Other elements and compounds which are _____ and have very high melting points may also have a giant covalent _____.

conduct covalent dissolve giant
hard high quartz structure

Metal ores

Where do we find metals?

Most metals are found combined in rocks, which are mixtures of minerals. **Ores** are special rocks that contain varying amounts of minerals that include metal atoms, which can be used as a source of metal. Some ores contain a very low percentage of metal. For example, large quantities of copper ore have to be mined to meet the demand for the metal.

? 1 What is an ore?

2 Name three examples of ores.

| Bauxite (aluminium) | Cinnabar (mercury) | Galena (lead) | Haematite (iron) | Malachite (copper) |

A Examples of metal ores.

The production and use of metals can cause pollution that affects the environment for a long time. Ores have to be dug out of the ground, and the waste from the mines looks ugly. Dust from mining can pollute the atmosphere.

To extract metals from their ores we need large amounts of heat and electricity. These are obtained by burning fossil fuels. This produces air pollution and uses up non-renewable natural resources. The impurities and waste left after the metals have been extracted can also pollute the land and water.

B A copper mine producing vast amounts of copper ore.

C Extracting metals can pollute the air, land and water.

3 What kinds of energy are used when extracting a metal from its ore in industry?

4 How can the extraction of metals cause damage to the environment?

Some metals are extracted by heating their metal oxide ores with carbon. For example, lead is formed when lead oxide is heated with carbon powder.

lead oxide + carbon → lead + carbon dioxide

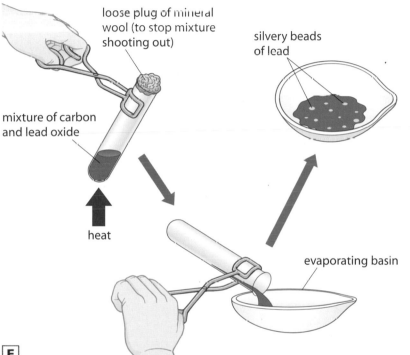

loose plug of mineral wool (to stop mixture shooting out)

silvery beads of lead

mixture of carbon and lead oxide

heat

evaporating basin

E

D The disposal of metals after use can be a problem. Scrap metal can be ugly and dangerous, so recycling is important as it reduces pollution and saves money.

During the reaction the lead oxide loses oxygen. This is called a **reduction reaction** and we say the lead oxide has been **reduced**. The carbon combines with the oxygen from the ore to form carbon dioxide. This is called an **oxidation reaction**, and we say the carbon has been **oxidised**. The ores of metals like zinc, iron, nickel, tin, lead and copper are commonly reduced by heating with carbon.

5 Iron is extracted from iron oxide by heating with carbon.
  a Write a word equation to represent this process.
  b During the extraction what is:
    i reduced   **ii** oxidised?

6 Name three other metals that are usually extracted by heating with carbon.

7 a Name three *finite* natural resources which are used up in the production of metals.
  b What does the term *finite* mean?

Summary

Ores are rocks that contain _____ from which _____ can be extracted. Vast amounts of some ores are required as they contain _____ amounts of metal. The extraction of metals causes _____.

Metals like iron, _____ and _____ can be extracted from their ores by heating them with _____. The metal ore is _____ and the carbon is _____.

carbon	lead	metals	minerals
	oxidised	pollution	reduced
		small	tin

Extracting metals using electricity

How is electricity used to extract metals?

If an ionic compound is melted or dissolved in water, the ionic lattice breaks up and the ions can move about freely, so they can conduct electricity. Substances that contain mobile ions are called **electrolytes**. They can be **decomposed** (broken up) using an electric current in a process called **electrolysis**. During electrolysis metals are formed at the negative electrode while non-metals are formed at the positive electrode.

? **1** During the electrolysis of copper chloride:
   a where is the copper formed
   b what is formed at the other electrode?

Heating with carbon cannot break down the ores of the most reactive metals like potassium, sodium, calcium, magnesium and aluminium. However, as these ores are ionic, formed between metals and non-metals, the metal can be extracted by electrolysis. Industrial electrolysis requires large quantities of expensive electricity, so electrolysis is only used when no other method will work.

Aluminium is one of our most useful metals. It is extracted industrially by passing a massive current of 150 000 amps through molten aluminium oxide in an electrolysis cell. Each cell produces 50 kg of aluminium per hour and over 250 000 tonnes of aluminium are produced in the UK each year.

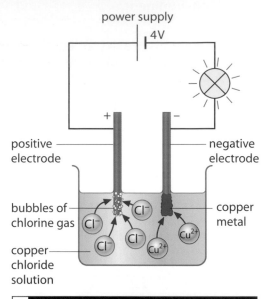

A The electrolysis of copper chloride solution forms copper at the negative electrode and chlorine at the positive electrode.

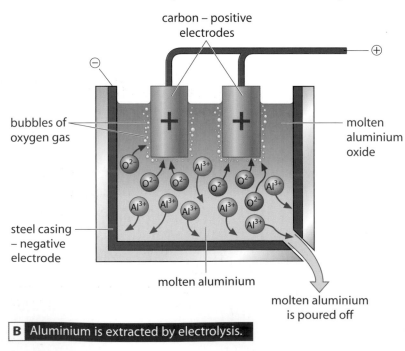

B Aluminium is extracted by electrolysis.

The reduction reaction involves breaking up the aluminium oxide.

aluminium oxide → aluminium + oxygen

The aluminium is produced at the negative electrode while oxygen is formed at the positive electrode.

? 2 Name four metals extracted by electrolysis.

3 Think about the extraction of aluminium.
   a Why must the ore be molten?
   b What elements are formed at each electrode?

We can show what happens in reactions using a **balanced symbol equation**. This has the same numbers of atoms of each element on both sides of the equation. They are more useful than word equations as they give extra information about the reaction. For example, the extraction of lead can be shown in two ways.

lead oxide + carbon → lead + carbon dioxide   *word equation*

$2PbO$ + C → $2Pb$ + CO_2 *balanced symbol equation*

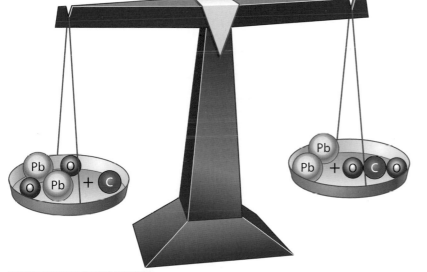

C Balancing equations.

State symbols can also be used in equations: (s) solid; (l) liquid; (g) gas and (aq) dissolved in water.

For example: $2PbO$ (s) + C (s) → $2Pb$ (s) + CO_2 (g)

? 4 Write a balanced symbol equation, including state symbols, for heating copper sulfide (CuS) in oxygen (O_2) to produce solid copper oxide (CuO) and sulfur dioxide (SO_2) gas.

5 Explain why aluminium is not produced by heating with carbon and copper is not produced by electrolysis.

Summary

Metal ores are _____ compounds. They only conduct when molten or _____ in water when the ions can _____. Metals like sodium, _____ and _____ can be extracted from their ores by _____ where the metal is produced at the _____ electrode.

| aluminium | calcium | dissolved |
| electrolysis | ionic | move | negative |

Metallic bonding

How can we explain the properties of metals?

Iron is used for bridges as it is strong.

Parts of jet engines are made using titanium because it is lightweight and has a high melting point.

Gold and silver are used to make jewellery as they are malleable and are easily shaped.

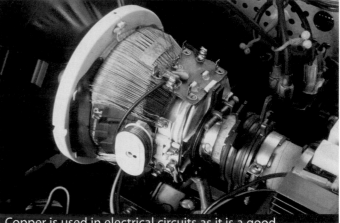

Copper is used in electrical circuits as it is a good conductor of electricity.

A

People have been using metals for thousands of years. Metals are used for construction, in cars and ships, to make tools and equipment, for electrical circuits, for jewellery, and for lots of other things. It is the valuable properties of metals that make them useful. The photos in A show some of the different uses of metals.

?

1 Write down the names of six metals.

2 Write down four properties of most metals.

Atoms in a solid metal are held together by **metallic bonds**. The metal atoms form a giant **metallic lattice** structure with a 'sea' of freely moving electrons.

?

3 What name is used to describe the structure of all solid metals?

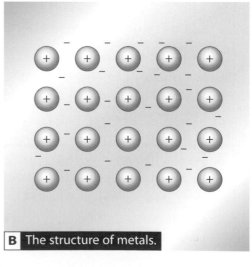

B The structure of metals.

The metallic bonds are very strong so metals are usually strong and have high melting points. Most metals are solids – mercury is the only liquid metal at room temperature. Metals are good conductors of electricity when solid or liquid, as the outer electrons are free to move. If a voltage is applied across a piece of metal, the electrons will move in one direction and carry the current.

Metals are malleable and can be hammered into shape, as the structure isn't rigid. If a metal is hit by a hammer, the layers of atoms slide over each other. The atoms are still held together by metallic bonds, so the metal bends instead of breaking.

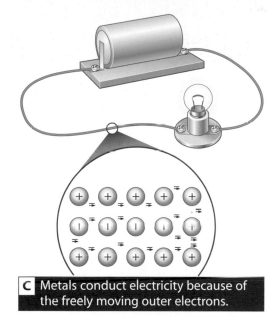

C Metals conduct electricity because of the freely moving outer electrons.

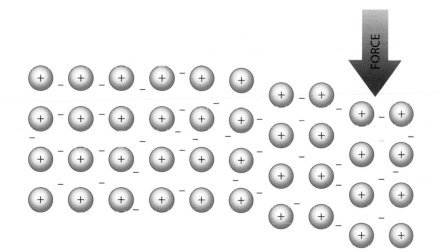

FORCE

D Metals are malleable as the layers of atoms can slip over each other.

?

4 Explain why metals are:
   a good conductors of electricity
   b malleable.

5 Copy and complete these sentences about metals.
   a Metals are strong because …
   b Copper is a good conductor of electricity so …

6 The four most used metals are iron, aluminium, copper and zinc. Find out about these metals and for each one:
   a name an ore
   b describe a use.

Summary

In metallic bonding, billions of atoms form a giant metallic _____ structure. The metallic bond is _____ so metals are generally strong solids with high _____ points. Metals are _____, as the layers of atoms can slide past each other. Metals _____ electricity, as the outer electrons can _____ freely.

| conduct | lattice | malleable |
| melting | move | strong |

Earth for sale

Where will we find all the chemicals we need?

A

1 Diagram B shows the different areas of the Earth.

Which labels best describe each area, **a** to **d**? Choose from the words in the box.

atmosphere	biosphere
hydrosphere	lithosphere

2 The Earth is a source of many useful chemicals. Some of these are listed below.

diamond	gold	iron oxide
oxygen	sodium chloride	

Which of these chemicals is:
a a gemstone
b an ore of a useful metal
c found in large quantities in the sea?

B

To understand the properties of substances, we need to understand their structure and how their atoms are held together.

C

3 The diagrams below show some different chemicals.

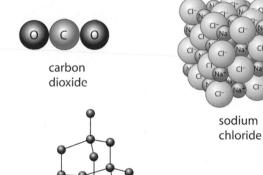

carbon dioxide

sodium chloride

D diamond

oxygen

a What kind of bonding holds the sodium chloride structure together?
b Why have diamonds such a high melting point?
c What is the formula of carbon dioxide?
d Explain why solutions of sodium chloride conduct electricity but solid sodium chloride does not.

4 Diagram E shows the forces of attraction in a sample of oxygen gas.

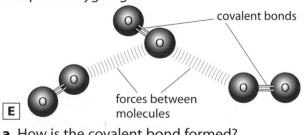

covalent bonds

forces between molecules

E

a How is the covalent bond formed?
b Explain why oxygen is a gas at room temperature.

5 Only some rocks on Earth contain a high enough concentration of metal compounds to be used as a source of the metals.
a What name is given to a rock that can be used as a source of metals?
b What method is used to extract:
   i the most reactive metals like sodium
   ii less reactive metals like iron?

6 Tin can be extracted from tin oxide (SnO_2) by heating it with carbon. This releases the metal and also produces carbon dioxide.
a Write a word equation and a balanced symbol equation, including state symbols, for the extraction of tin.
b During this reaction the tin oxide is reduced. What happens to the carbon?

7 The bonding and structure of metals is different from that of non-metals.
a Briefly describe the structure of a solid metal.
b State two properties of all metals that are the result of this structure.

There are millions of different living things in the Earth's biosphere and they can take many different forms. However, no matter where life is found on Earth or in the Universe, it will most likely be based on molecules that contain carbon atoms.

F

8 What do you call the molecules in living things?

9 Apart from carbon, name the three other most important elements in the biosphere.

Electric circuits

How do we use electricity?

A
These instruments help the skipper to navigate the yacht.

B

Electricity is a very useful way of transferring energy. Some energy transfers, such as using an electric fire to heat a room, could be achieved by burning a fuel instead. However there are some things that can only be done using electricity.

Static electricity

Static electricity was known about by the ancient Greeks. If a piece of amber was rubbed with silk cloth, it could pick up feathers or other small objects.

This effect can be explained by thinking about the structure of an atom. All atoms contain electrically charged particles called **protons** and **electrons**. Protons have a positive charge, and are found in the **nucleus** of atoms. Electrons move around the nucleus of the atom. An atom normally has no overall charge because the positive charges on the protons are balanced by the negative charges on the electrons.

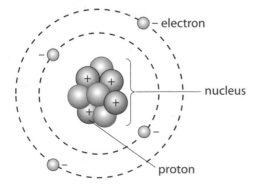

C

? 1 Write a list of things that electricity is used for, that:
  a cannot be achieved using other types of energy
  b can be achieved using other types of energy.

? 2 Where are these particles found in an atom?
  a proton
  b electron

3 An atom has 10 protons.
  a How many electrons does it normally have?
  b Explain your answer.

If you rub two insulating materials together, electrons may be transferred from one material to the other. Protons cannot be transferred, because they are fixed in the nuclei of atoms.

When you rub an acetate rod with a piece of cloth, some of the electrons in the acetate move onto the cloth.

The acetate now has more protons than electrons, so it has a positive charge. The cloth has more electrons than protons, so it has a negative charge.

When you rub a polythene rod, some of the electrons in the cloth move onto the polythene.

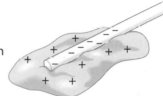

D

If two things with static charges are close to each other, they exert a force on each other. If the charges on the objects are opposite, the two objects **attract** each other. If the charges on both are the same, the two objects **repel** each other (push each other apart).

? **4 a** Which particles can be transferred when you rub an insulating material?
 b Explain your answer.

5 Explain why a polythene rod gets a negative charge when you rub it.

E The machine gives the girl a charge of static electricity. All the strands of her hair have the same charge.

? **6** Look at photo E. Why is the girl's hair standing up?

7 You rub two balloons on your jumper. Explain why the balloons will then repel each other.

8 A paint spraying machine gives the drops of paint a positive charge and a metal object a negative charge. How will this help to stop paint being wasted?

Summary

When two objects are rubbed together, _____ can be transferred from one object to the other. This gives the objects a _____ . Objects with similar charges will _____ each other, and objects with _____ charges will _____ .

attract   charge   electrons
opposite   repel

139

Current and voltage

What is electric current?

In an electrical circuit the **current** is a flow of **electric charge**. For a current to flow, we need materials that have charged particles that are free to move. These materials are called **conductors**. Metals are very good electrical conductors.

All materials contain negatively charged particles called electrons but in metals some of the electrons are free to move easily. In materials like plastics, rubber and ceramics all the electrons are bound firmly to atoms and cannot move around freely. These types of material do not conduct electricity and are called **insulators**.

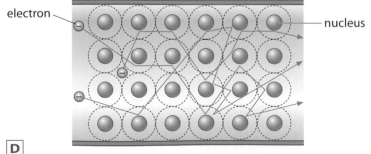

B Power cables are made of good electrical conductors. They are supported by insulators.

In a piece of metal the free electrons are moving around all the time in different directions, but they are not actually going anywhere. When we put a metal wire in a circuit, the **cell** pushes the free electrons in one direction around the electric circuit.

Moving electrons have **energy**. As they pass through **components** like lamps the electrons transfer energy to the component. The energy the electrons have is transferred, but the electrons themselves are not 'used up'.

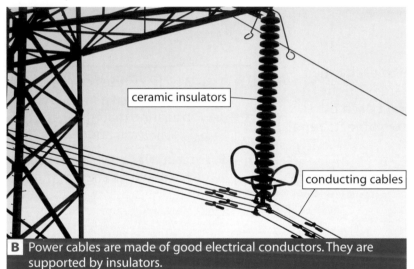

D

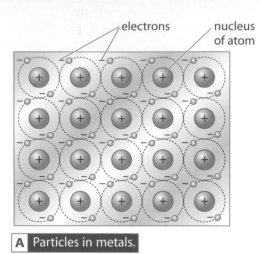

A Particles in metals.

?

1 What is an electric current?

2 What is the difference between conductors and insulators? Use the word 'electrons' in your answer.

3 Give three examples of electrical insulators.

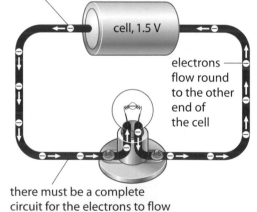

electrons are pushed out of one end of the cell

cell, 1.5 V

electrons flow round to the other end of the cell

there must be a complete circuit for the electrons to flow

C In an **electric circuit** there is a continuous path made from conducting materials.

Measuring current

We cannot see electrons moving when a current flows in a circuit so we need a measuring instrument. An **ammeter** is used to measure current and the unit of current is the **amp** (**A**). Very small currents are measured in **milliamps** (**mA**). 1000 mA = 1 A.

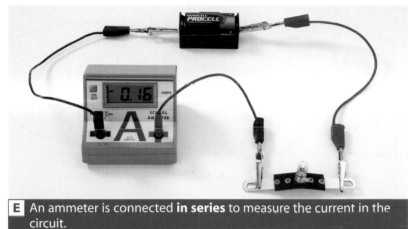

E An ammeter is connected **in series** to measure the current in the circuit.

Voltage – electrical push

One way of pumping electrons around a circuit is to use a cell. The **voltage** of a cell is a measure of how well it can push electrons around a circuit and transfer energy. We measure voltage with a **voltmeter**. Voltage is measured in **volts** (**V**).

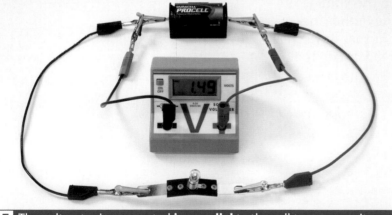

F The voltmeter is connected **in parallel** to the cell to measure its voltage.

?

4 What instrument do we use to measure:
   a current
   b voltage?

5 Which is the odd one out from this list: plastic, metal, ceramic? Explain your answers.

6 Draw a circuit diagram to show how you would measure the current through a lamp and the voltage across it.

Summary

Metals are _____ of electricity, because they have _____ which are free to move. In _____ there are no _____ particles that can move. Current can be pumped around a circuit by a _____. Current is measured in _____ and the voltage of a cell is measured in _____. Current is not _____ as it flows around a circuit.

amps	cell	charged	conductors
electrons	insulators	used up	volts

Changing the current

What affects the size of a current in a circuit?

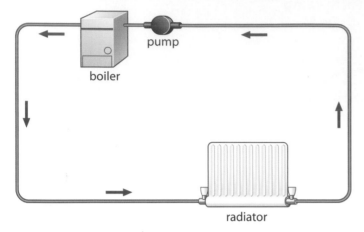

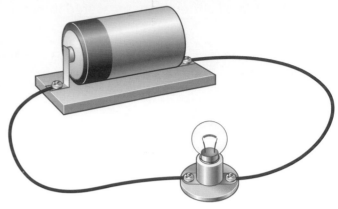

A A model for a circuit.

A central heating system pumps hot water around pipes. We can use this as a **model** to help us think about electricity. An electric current is like the flow of water through a pipe. The amount of water passing through the pipe is like the size of the current. The water is heated and pushed through the pipe by a pump just as the cells in a circuit give electrons energy and push them through the wires.

The size of an electric current depends on the voltage of the cells or power supply in the circuit. The higher the voltage, the bigger the current. The current that flows in a circuit also depends on how easy it is for electricity to flow around the circuit.

?
1 Look at diagram A. Which part of the model represents:
   a an electric current
   b the connecting wires
   c the cells?

A How do the components in a circuit affect the current?

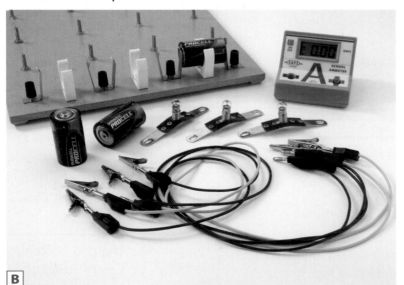

B

Photo C shows another model for electricity. In this model the number of cars passing a point on the road depends on how easy it is to travel along the road. In the same way, more current flows in a circuit when it is easy for it to flow.

The size of the current depends on the **resistance** of the circuit. The resistance depends on the number of components in the circuit, and on what they are. The greater the resistance of the circuit, the smaller the current. The resistance of the connecting wires is usually small enough to be ignored.

Transferring energy

Wherever there is resistance in an electric circuit the energy carried by the moving electrons is converted into other forms, usually heat energy and light energy. Only the energy carried by the electrons is transferred – the electrons themselves are not used up. The cell replaces the transferred energy as the electrons it is pumping pass through it.

C A motorway model of a wire.

?

2 Is the motorway in photo C showing 'high' or 'low' resistance?

3 a Which circuit do you think will have the most resistance – a circuit with two bulbs or a circuit with three bulbs?
  b Explain your answer.

D The filament in the bulb has resistance. Electrical energy is converted into heat and light energy as the electrons move through the wire.

?

4 When current passes through wires with resistance, what is transferred?

5 Should the connecting wires in a circuit have high or low resistance? Give a reason for your answer.

6 Long wires have more resistance than short wires. Try to explain this using a model.

Summary

Circuits have resistance to the flow of electric _____ ; the greater the resistance the _____ the current. Cells give electrons _____ as they push them round the circuit. The _____ carried by the electrons is converted to other _____ of energy as they pass around a _____ .

circuit   current   energy
forms   smaller

Resistors in series and parallel

What happens when we use more than one resistor?

All components have resistance. Lamps, heaters, electric motors and **resistors** all convert the energy of electrons that are pushed through them into other forms of energy. The resistance of the components in the circuit limits the size of the current. The connecting wires have a very low resistance.

Components can be connected together in different ways, as shown in diagrams A and B. The current depends on how the components are connected, as well as the resistance of the components.

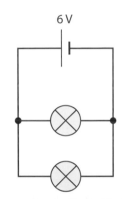

A A **series circuit**.

1 **a** Which lamps have the larger current flowing through them, those in diagram A or those in diagram B?
   b Which circuit do you think has the greater resistance to current flow?

We can use some more models to help us think about how resistance changes in series and parallel circuits.

B A **parallel circuit**. The lamps in this circuit are brighter than the ones in diagram A.

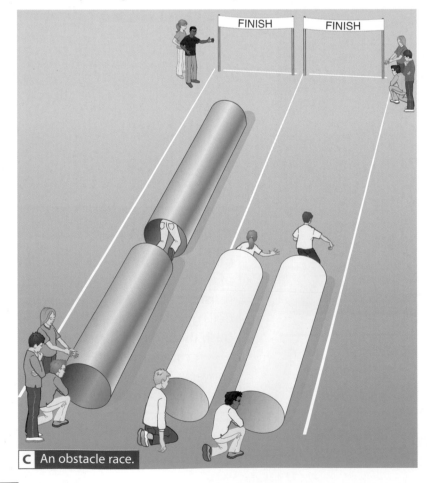

C An obstacle race.

2 Look at drawing C. Explain why the yellow team will win the race.

3 Look at diagrams A and B. Use the race model to help you to explain why there is a different current in each circuit.

When resistors are added to a circuit in series, the resistance increases because the electrons have to be pushed through each resistor, one after the other. The total current in the circuit goes down.

If resistors are added in parallel, the resistance goes down because some electrons can go through one resistor and some can go through another. The current in the main part of the circuit increases.

A How is the size of current changed by the number of components in a circuit?

?

4 Look at the circuits in diagram D.

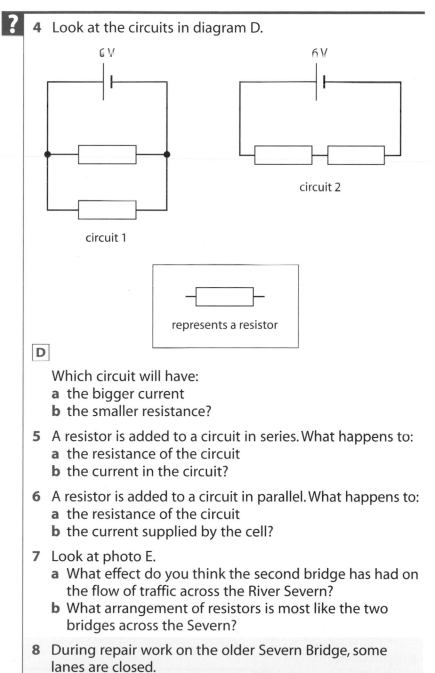

6 V

circuit 2

circuit 1

represents a resistor

D

Which circuit will have:
a the bigger current
b the smaller resistance?

5 A resistor is added to a circuit in series. What happens to:
a the resistance of the circuit
b the current in the circuit?

6 A resistor is added to a circuit in parallel. What happens to:
a the resistance of the circuit
b the current supplied by the cell?

7 Look at photo E.
a What effect do you think the second bridge has had on the flow of traffic across the River Severn?
b What arrangement of resistors is most like the two bridges across the Severn?

8 During repair work on the older Severn Bridge, some lanes are closed.
a What will happen to the flow of traffic on the old bridge?
b How would you change your answer to question **7b** to show this new situation?

E When there was just one bridge crossing the River Severn there were often traffic jams, particularly on busy days in the summer. A second bridge has been built near the first.

Summary

_____ and other components limit the flow of _____. When resistors are joined in _____ the resistance in a circuit increases and the _____ gets less. When resistors are connected in _____ there is less _____ to the current.

current parallel resistance
resistors series

Measuring resistance

How do we measure resistance?

The size of the current flowing in a circuit depends on the voltage of the cell and on the resistance of the circuit. If we use the same voltage in different circuits we can tell which circuit has the most resistance by measuring the current in the circuit The circuit with the largest resistance will have the smallest current.

? **1** Put the resistors R1, R2 and R3 in order of their size, smallest to largest.

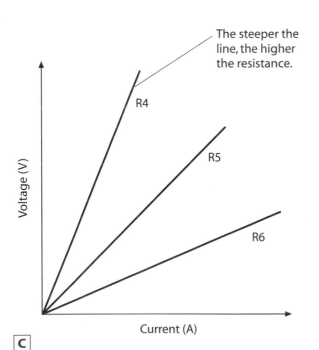

| 6 V | R1 | 6 V | R2 | 6 V | R3 |

A   0.2 A   0.1 A   0.3 A

A How can you find the relationship between voltage and current?

B

The steeper the line, the higher the resistance.

C

Voltage (V) / Current (A)

R4

R5

R6

Graph C shows the current and voltage for several different resistors. The straight lines on the graph show that the current through each resistor is **directly proportional** to the voltage across it, so if you double the voltage the current through the resistor doubles. This rule only applies if the resistor stays at a constant temperature. The steeper the line on the graph, the higher the resistance.

? **2** Put the resistors in graph C in order of their resistance, starting with the smallest.

The resistance of some circuit components can vary.

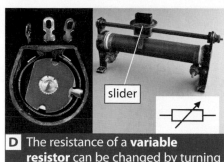

D The resistance of a **variable resistor** can be changed by turning the knob or moving the slider.

A **thermistor** is a component whose resistance is designed to decrease when the temperature increases

F The resistance of a **light-dependent resistor** (**LDR**) decreases as light intensity increases (gets brighter).

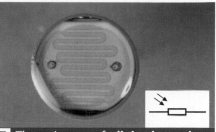

Calculating resistance

If you double the voltage across a resistor, then the current flowing through it doubles. The amount of current for a given voltage depends on the resistance. The unit of resistance is the **ohm** (Ω). A resistor with a resistance of 1 Ω lets a current of 1 A pass through it when connected to a 1 V supply.

E The resistance can be worked out using this equation:

$$\text{resistance (ohms, } \Omega) = \frac{\text{voltage (volts, V)}}{\text{current (amps, A)}}$$

There is a current of 3 A through a lamp connected to a 12 V power supply. What is the resistance of the lamp?

$$\text{resistance} = \frac{\text{voltage}}{\text{current}}$$
$$= \frac{12 \text{ V}}{3 \text{ A}}$$
$$= 4 \, \Omega$$

?

3 a A resistor is connected to a 10 V supply, and a current of 0.5 A flows. What is its resistance?
b The voltage is reduced to 5 V. What will happen to the current?

4 The following measurements were taken for different resistors. Calculate the resistance of each one.
a 12 V, 2 A
b 230 V, 10 A
c 2.5 A, 10 V

5 a A lamp has a current of 60 mA flowing through it when connected to a 6 V battery. What is its resistance in ohms?
b When a 3 V battery is connected to the lamp its resistance is 75 Ω. Why do you think this is different to your answer to part **a**?

Summary

Resistance is measured in _____ , Ω. The resistance of a component is calculated by dividing the _____ (in volts) connected across it by the _____ (in _____) passing through it.

amps   current   ohms   voltage

147

Energy in circuits

What is potential difference?

A **voltage** is needed to make electrons flow around a circuit. We can provide this by using a cell.

When a cell is connected into a circuit a chemical reaction inside it produces energy. The energy is transferred to electrons so they can move around the circuit. When we talk about electricity we often refer to 'charges' flowing, rather than electrons.

Diagram B shows a model that can help us to think about what happens inside cells.

A This clock uses a cell made from two lemons with two different metals stuck into them.

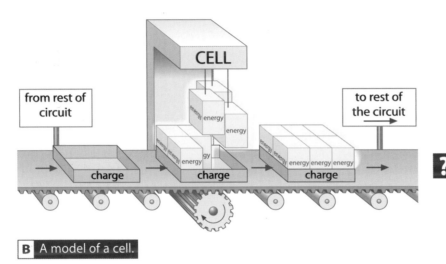

B A model of a cell.

Cell voltage

The voltage of a cell is a sometimes called the **potential difference**. It is a measure of how much energy is given to the electrons that are pumped around the circuit. A cell with a bigger voltage (or potential difference) will:

• transfer more energy to a given number of electrons passing through the cell
• push more electrons around the circuit (so the current is bigger).

We can use more than one cell together in a circuit. If the cells are connected in series (end to end), we can add up the voltages of all the cells to find the voltage of the whole **battery**.

?
1 Look at diagram B. Which part of the model represents:
  a a cell
  b the wires
  c the electrons?

?
2 What is another word for potential difference?

3 Three 2 V cells are connected together in series.
  a What is the voltage of the battery?
  b How much current will there be compared to a circuit with only one cell?

Voltage across components

The energy carried by moving electrons is transferred to other forms of energy in components such as bulbs or resistors. We can find out how much energy is transferred in each component by measuring the voltage across it, as shown in diagram C.

The voltmeter shows how much energy is transferred as electrons pass through a component.

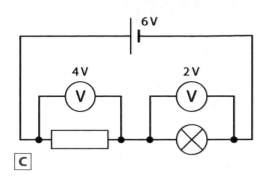

C

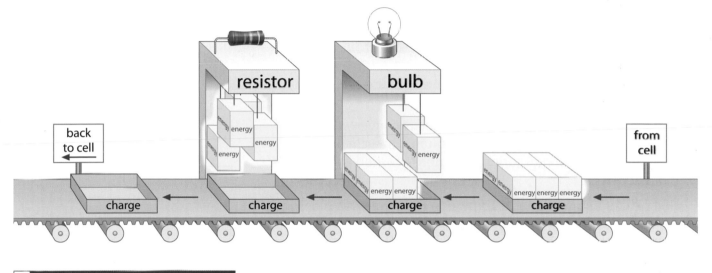

D A model of the circuit in diagram C.

In diagram C, we can see that the resistor is transferring twice as much energy as the bulb, because the potential difference across it is twice as big. Diagram D represents this circuit using a model to show what happens to the energy.

? 4 Look at diagram E.

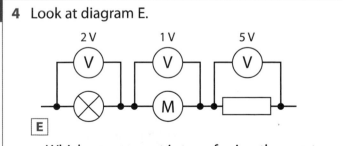

E

   a Which component is transferring the most energy?
   b Explain your answer.

5 Think of as many different explanations for this statement as you can: one bulb is brighter than another.

6 Look at the model in diagram D. How would the diagram look different if you increased the resistance of the components in the 'circuit'?

Summary

Energy is transferred to _____ as they pass through a battery. The _____ of a battery is a measure of how much _____ is transferred to a given number of electrons. The voltage across a _____ shows how much _____ is transferred to the component. The _____ is another term for voltage.

| component | electrons | energy |
| potential difference | voltage |

Current and voltage in circuits

How do current and voltage behave in circuits?

Series circuits

In a series circuit there is just one path for an electric current. The same charged particles travel through the whole circuit, so the current is the same everywhere in the circuit.

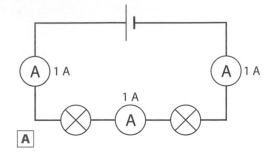

Rule 1: In a series circuit the current is the same at any point in the circuit.

? 1 The current leaving one end of a cell is 3 A. What will be the current returning to the other end of the cell?

The electrical energy provided by a cell is converted to other forms of energy by the components in a circuit. The voltage is a way of measuring the energy carried by the current.

The cell in diagram B has a voltage of 6 V. When the cell is in a circuit the energy it provides is divided between all the components in a circuit. In circuit B the bulbs are identical, so the voltage across each one is 3 V. In some circuits the components have different resistances so the voltage is not shared equally between them. The voltage is largest across the component with the greatest resistance.

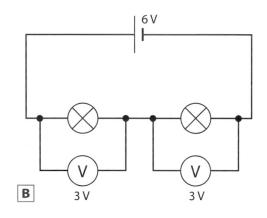

Rule 2: In a series circuit the voltage (potential difference) is shared between the components in the circuit, so the voltages across the components add up to the voltage across the cell.

Rule 3: The voltage (potential difference) is greatest across the component with the largest resistance.

? 2 What is the voltage of the cell in circuit C?

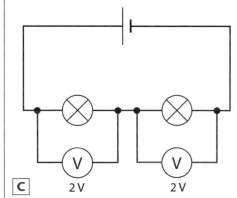

? 3 Look at circuit D.

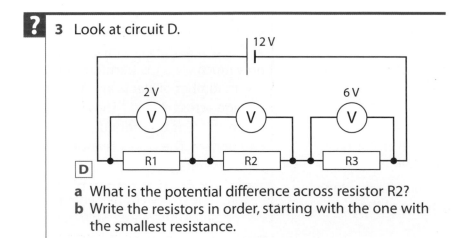

a What is the potential difference across resistor R2?
b Write the resistors in order, starting with the one with the smallest resistance.

Parallel circuits

In a parallel circuit there is more than one path for the electric current to flow through.

Rule 4: In a parallel circuit the currents through each branch add up to the total current from (and back to) the cell.

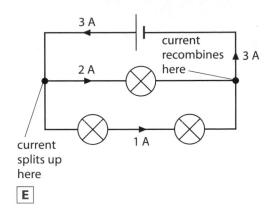

E

? **4** Look at circuit F.

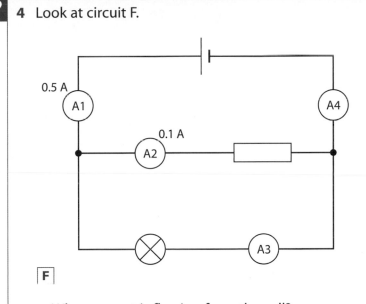

F

   a What current is flowing from the cell?
   b How much current flows through the lamp?
   c What is the reading on ammeter A4?

The current in each branch depends on the resistance of the components in each branch. The branch with the lowest total resistance will have the highest current.

Rule 5: In a parallel circuit the current in each branch depends on the resistances of the components in the branch. The branch of the circuit with the highest resistance will have the lowest current flowing through it.

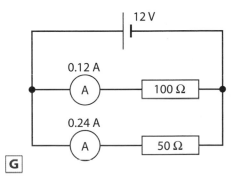

G

? **5** Look at circuit G.
   a What is the total current through the cell?
   b Why is the current highest through the 50 Ω resistor?

  6 Look back at the circuit model in Topic P5.6. Choose two of the circuit rules on this page, and use this model to explain them. You can draw diagrams or pictures to help you to explain.

Summary

When components are connected in _____ the current through them is the same and the _____ across them add up to the voltage of the _____ in the circuit. The voltage across a component depends on its _____.

When _____ are connected in parallel the total current flowing to and from the _____ is always the same.

> cell   components   resistance
>   series   voltages

Making electricity
How is electricity generated?

Batteries provide the energy for portable electrical items like torches and MP3 players. The current they produce always flows in the same direction – it is called **direct current** (**d.c.**). However, batteries run down and cannot be used for devices like heaters which transfer a lot more energy. For most of our electricity needs we simply plug into the 230 V mains supply. Mains electricity is generated in power stations.

Generators in a power station make the voltage needed to push current around a circuit by rotating a coil of wire in a magnetic field. This process is called **electromagnetic induction**.

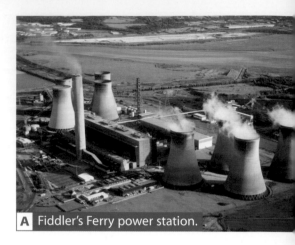

A Fiddler's Ferry power station.

? 1 What is the name of the process that produces a voltage in a generator?

Diagram B shows how you can demonstrate the process of electromagnetic induction. When the magnet is moved quickly into the coil of wire the voltmeter shows that there is a voltage in the coil. We say that a voltage has been **induced** in the coil. This only happens while the magnet is moving. This induced voltage will make a current flow if there is a complete circuit.

? 2 How could we use an induced voltage to make a current?

3 Is a voltage induced in the coil if the magnet is held stationary in the coil?

B

C Michael Faraday (1791–1867) demonstrated how to induce voltages in 1831.

The direction of the voltage that is induced depends on which way the magnet is moving, and which end of the magnet is pushed into the coil of wire.

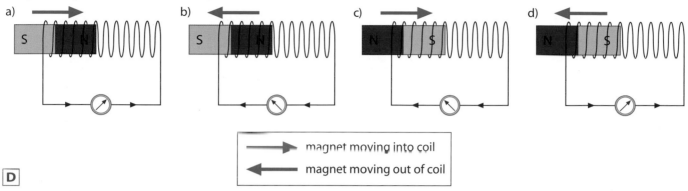

a) b) c) d)

magnet moving into coil

magnet moving out of coil

D

To create a continuous current we must keep the magnet moving *relative to* the coil of wire. It does not matter if it is the coil that moves or the magnet. In generators this is done by spinning a coil in a magnetic field. When we do this the current keeps changing direction, flowing backwards and forwards as the direction of the induced voltage changes. This kind of current is called **alternating current** (a.c.).

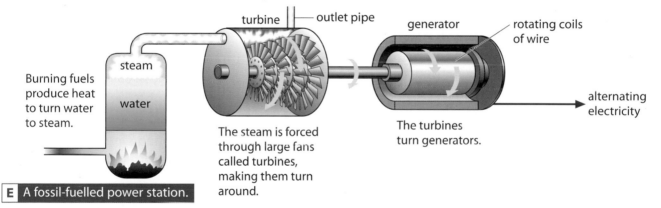

turbine — outlet pipe

generator — rotating coils of wire

steam

water

Burning fuels produce heat to turn water to steam.

The steam is forced through large fans called turbines, making them turn around.

The turbines turn generators.

alternating electricity

E A fossil-fuelled power station.

?

4 a What is the difference between a.c. and d.c.?
  b What can be used to produce each kind of current?

5 How is a generator in a power station different to the apparatus shown in diagram B?

6 a If you move a magnet into and out of a coil continuously, what happens to the direction of the voltage induced?
  b At which points will the induced voltage be zero as you move the magnet in and out of the coil?

Summary

Mains electricity is produced by _____ which move a _____ of wire in a _____ field to induce a voltage. If there is a complete circuit the voltage will make _____ flow around the circuit. The _____ of the induced current depends on the direction of movement of the magnet and also on which way round the N and S _____ of the magnet are.

coil   current   direction   generators
magnetic   poles

More about generators

How can the voltage from a generator be increased?

motion of wheel

iron core
spinning magnet
coil of wire
to bicycle lights

A The movement of the wheel drives the dynamo. The faster the bicycle is going, the brighter the lights.

B

Some bicycles have dynamos to produce electricity for the lights. Dynamos are simple generators where a magnet spins inside a coil.

A bicycle dynamo demonstrates that we can increase the voltage produced by a generator by spinning it faster. The design of a generator can be changed to increase the induced voltage by:
• putting more turns of wire on the coil
• using stronger magnets
• using an iron core inside the coil.

?
1 a Would the bicycle's lights be brighter when you were going up a hill or down it?
  b Explain your answer.

2 Why do you think that most bicycles have batteries to power their lights, rather than dynamos?

3 Write down four ways to increase the voltage induced by a generator.

A How can you show that the size of the voltage induced by a magnet moving into a coil depends on the number of turns on the coil?

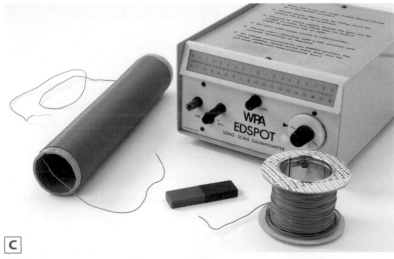

C
• What apparatus will you need?
• How would you make this a fair test?

Generator design

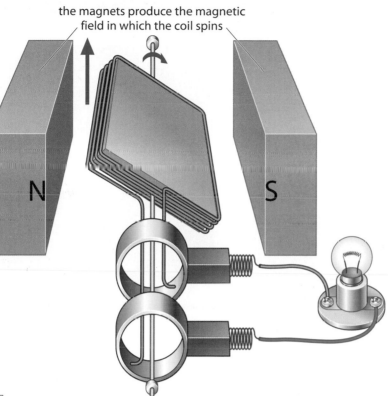

the magnets produce the magnetic field in which the coil spins

N   S

D

Diagram D shows a simple a.c. generator, similar to one you could use in a school laboratory. A generator works whether a magnet spins inside or coil, or if a coil spins between magnets.

The generators in power stations need to induce a very high voltage. Strong permanent magnets are very expensive, so generators often use electromagnets instead. The electromagnet spins 3000 times per minute inside coils of copper wire. These generators can induce voltages of 20 000 V or more.

E A generator in a power station.

?

4 Look at diagram D.
   a How could you change the design to make the generator induce a higher voltage?
   b What would happen to the output of the generator if fewer turns of wire were used on the coil?

5 Why are electromagnets used in power stations instead of permanent magnets?

6 Why does the generator in diagram D produce a.c. not d.c.? (*Hint*: look carefully at diagram D, and you may need to look back at diagram D on page 153.)

Summary

The size of the _____ voltage in a generator is increased by _____ the speed the coil rotates and by having _____ turns of wire on the coil. The voltage can also be increased by using _____ magnets and putting _____ inside the coil.

increasing   induced   iron
more   stronger

Transformers

How do transformers work?

Most appliances such as cookers, washing machines and heaters in homes and offices use the mains electricity supply directly. However, some electrical equipment needs a higher voltage than this, and other equipment only needs a much lower voltage.

?
1 a What is the voltage of the mains supply to homes?
   b Is the mains supply alternating or direct current?

A This furnace needs high voltage electricity to work.

B Laptops and cameras need a low voltage supply.

The size of an alternating voltage can be changed using a **transformer**. Transformers are also used to increase the voltage of the electricity generated by power stations.

C Electricity is sent round the country at 400 000 V. The high voltage helps to stop energy being wasted heating the wires.

?
2 A power station generates electricity at about 20 000 V. Why are there large transformers outside the power station?

A transformer consists of two coils of wire wound onto an iron core. The primary coil acts like an electromagnet, and magnetises the iron core. Because the direction of the current in an alternating supply keeps changing, the magnetic field produced by the coil keeps changing.

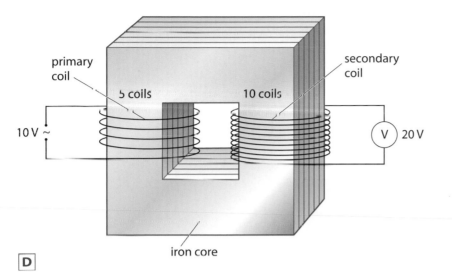

D

The iron core concentrates the magnetic field. The changing magnetic field in the iron core has the same effect on the secondary coil as moving a magnet in and out of the coil. A voltage is induced in the secondary coil, and a current will flow if this coil is connected to a circuit.

?

3 a Why does the direction of the magnetic field in the core keep changing?
  b What effect does this changing field have on the secondary coil?

A transformer can be used to increase or decrease the voltage of the electricity supply. A step-up transformer increases the voltage and a step-down transformer decreases it.

?

4 Look at photo B.
  a Is the transformer for the laptop computer a step-up or step-down transformer?
  b Explain your answer.

5 a What is the voltage across the primary coil in the laptop's transformer?
  b Explain your answer.

6 A radio runs off the mains supply, but only needs a 23 V supply. The transformer has 100 turns of wire in the primary coil. How many turns do you think there are in the secondary coil?

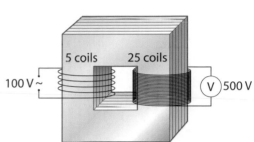

A step-up transformer has more turns in the secondary coil than in the primary coil.

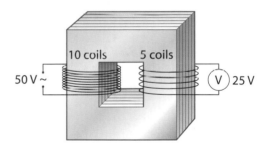

A step-down transformer has fewer turns in the secondary coil than in the primary coil.

E

Summary

A _____ can change the size of an _____ voltage. It consists of two coils of wire on an _____ core. The changing _____ field in one coil induces a _____ in the other one.

alternating   iron   magnetic
transformer   voltage

Electrical energy and power

How much energy do we get from electricity?

Batteries and generators give electrons the energy needed to flow around an electric circuit. Their energy is transferred to components like resistors, lamps, heaters and motors as the electrons flow through them.

Energy is measured in **joules** (**J**). The rate at which energy is transferred to an electrical component is called **power**. Power is measured in **watts** (**W**). One watt is one joule of energy being transferred every second. As many electrical appliances use a lot of power, we sometimes have to work in **kilowatts** (**kW**). 1 kW = 1000 W.

A The more powerful lamp gives out more light energy each second.

?

1 Look at photo A.
 a Which lamp is the more powerful?
 b Explain your answer.

E The power of an electrical device can be worked out using this equation:

power = potential difference (voltage) × current
(watts, W)   (volts, V)   (amps, A)

A car headlamp needs a current of 4 A from a 12 V battery. What is its power?

power = voltage × current
= 12 V × 4 A
= 48 W

This means that the headlamp transfers 48 J of energy every second.

?

2 Calculate the power of these items:
 a an electric iron which uses a current of 4 A from the 230 V mains supply
 b a torch bulb which uses a current of 0.1 A from a 6 V battery.

Measuring electrical energy

E The energy used can be calculated using this equation:

energy transferred = power × time
(joules, J)   (watts, W)   (seconds, s)

The electricity companies use a much larger unit for electrical energy called the **kilowatt-hour** (**kWh**). This is the amount of energy that is transferred by a 1 kW device in one hour.

The equation to calculate energy transferred in kilowatt-hours is the same, but the units are different.

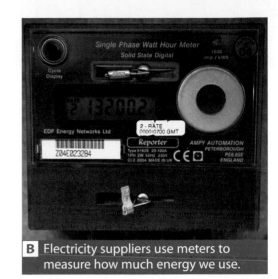

B Electricity suppliers use meters to measure how much energy we use.

E
energy transferred = power × time
(kilowatt-hours, kWh) (kilowatts, kW) (hours, h)

A 10 kW electric shower is used for a total of 1.5 hours during a week. How many kilowatt-hours of energy does it transfer?

energy transferred = power × time
= 10 kW × 1.5 h
= 15 kWh

C

?

3 How much energy, in joules, is transferred to a 40 W car headlamp that is turned on for 5 minutes (300 seconds)?

4 How much energy, in kilowatt-hours, is transferred to a 3 kW electrical heater that is turned on for 2 hours and 30 minutes (2.5 hours)?

5 The kWh is a large unit of energy. What is a kWh in joules?

Summary

Power is measured in _____.
Electrical power is calculated by multiplying the _____ by the _____.
The energy used is calculated by multiplying the power by the _____ the current is flowing. A _____ is the energy used by a 1 kW appliance in one _____.

| current | hour | kilowatt-hour | time |
| voltage | watts |

Cost and efficiency

How much does electricity cost?

We have to pay electricity companies for the amount of energy we use. The price is usually given in pence per kWh. We can work out the cost of electricity by multiplying the energy used by the cost per kWh.

> An electric heater has a power rating of 2 kW. What is the cost of using the fire for 3 hours if a kWh of electricity costs 5 p?
>
> energy in kWh = 2 kW × 3 h
> = 6 kWh
> cost in pence = 6 kWh × 5 pence
> = 30 p

Product Code: 30110   Volts: 230a.c.
Model: 32LGB   Watts: 2000
Serial No: 2004.07/294/   2076

Duallt   **CE**

Email: Info@duallt.com
Made in England

A

?

1 An electric lawnmower has a power rating of 1.2 kW.

   a It takes 30 minutes (0.5 h) to mow a lawn. How many kWh of electricity does it use?

   b If a kWh costs 6 p, how much does it cost to mow the lawn?

B

2 Each bar of an electric fire uses 1 kW of electricity. If electricity costs 5 p per kWh, how much does it cost to use:

   a one bar of the fire for 3 hours

   b two bars of the fire for 5 hours?

Efficiency

Most electrical appliances waste some energy by transferring it to a form we do not want. We can keep down the cost of electricity by making electrical appliances more efficient. Efficient electrical appliances waste less energy.

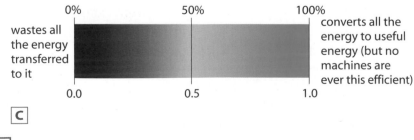

0%   50%   100%

wastes all the energy transferred to it

converts all the energy to useful energy (but no machines are ever this efficient)

0.0   0.5   1.0

C

E The **efficiency** of an appliance is calculated using this equation:

$$\text{efficiency} = \frac{\text{energy usefully transferred}}{\text{total energy supplied}} \times 100\%$$

The units for energy can be J or kJ, as long as both numbers are in the same units.

What is the efficiency of an electric kettle if it uses 500 kJ of electrical energy and transfers only 400 kJ of energy to the water in the kettle?

$$\begin{aligned}
\text{efficiency} &= \frac{\text{energy usefully transferred}}{\text{total energy supplied}} \times 100\% \\
&= \frac{400 \text{ kJ}}{500 \text{ kJ}} \times 100\% \\
&= 80\%
\end{aligned}$$

So the kettle only wastes 20% of the energy that is transferred to it.

?

3 An electric immersion heater uses 50 kJ of electrical energy and transfers 40 kJ of heat to the water. How efficient is it?

4 a A 100 W light bulb uses 100 J of electricity every second. It gives out 9 J of light energy. How efficient is it?
   b An 'energy-saving' bulb gives out the same amount of light, but only uses 12 J of energy per second. How efficient is this bulb?

D

5 Think of a plus, a minus and an interesting point about this statement: Electricity should cost more.

6 A room in a house has a total of five lamps each rated at 60 W. If these lamps are on for 30 hours a week, how many units of electricity do they use?

Summary

To calculate electricity costs you must know the _____ of an appliance, how long it is used for (in _____) and the cost per _____ of electricity. Efficiency is how much _____ energy an appliance transfers divided by the _____ energy supplied to it.

| hours | kWh | power | total | useful |

Making toys

What do you know about electricity and circuits?

Ella and David are designing toys to give to their local nursery school. The first toy they build is a doll's house. They want to put electric lights in the rooms.

A

1 Are these statements true or false? If you think a statement is false, explain why.
   a An electric current is the movement of charged particles.
   b A cell is needed in a circuit to make the charged particles.
   c All materials have lots of charged particles in them.
   d In metals there are electrons that can move freely.

2 Ella has some bulbs that need 3 V to light brightly. She wants to use two bulbs in the doll's house. She arranges the bulbs as shown.

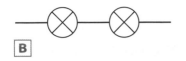

B

   a What voltage should Ella's battery provide to give the bulbs 3 V each?
   b How can she use 1.5 V cells to give her this voltage? Draw a diagram to show how she should arrange the cells.

3 Why does a light bulb glow when it is connected into a circuit? Explain in as much detail as you can.

The lights in the technology room run off the mains supply.

4 a What is the voltage of the mains supply?
   b The lights are 100 W light bulbs. How much energy (in kWh) does each light use in 8 hours?
   c If electricity costs 8 p per kWh, how much does it cost to run 3 lamps for 8 hours?

5 The mains supply is alternating current.
   a What does this mean?
   b What kind of current is supplied by cells?

6 a What can be used to change the voltage of the mains supply?
   b Draw a sketch of this component and label its parts.

David has found some resistors that he can use to make a circuit for a toy windmill.

C

7 David tests the resistors to find out what the resistance of each one is.

a Copy this circuit and draw an ammeter and voltmeter on it in the correct places so that David can measure the current and voltage.

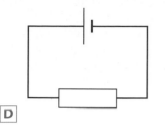

D

b He finds that the voltage across one resistor is 4 V and the current is 0.5 A. What is its resistance?

c David tests some of the resistors at several different voltages, and draws graphs of his results.

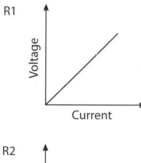

R1

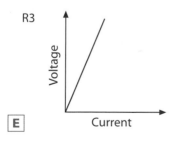

R2

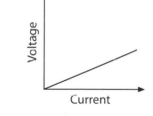

R3

E

Which resistor has the smallest resistance? Explain your answer.

8 David uses a circuit like this to make the windmill sails turn. He tests his circuit using two voltmeters and an ammeter.

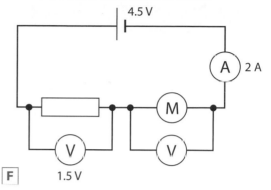

F   1.5 V

a What is the voltage across the motor? Explain your answer.

b Which is transferring more energy, the motor or the resistor? Explain your answer.

9 a What is the power of the motor in David's windmill? Show all your working.

b How much energy will the motor transfer if it is switched on for 10 minutes?

Ella is making a game that tests how fast you can move your hand. She has made a model generator and connected it to a voltmeter.

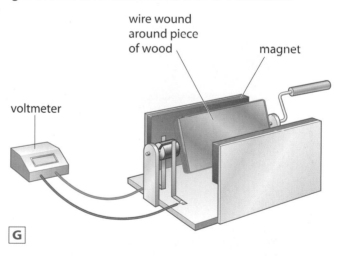

wire wound around piece of wood

magnet

voltmeter

G

10 When Ella tests the game, it does not produce enough voltage to show up on the voltmeter. Write down three ways she could change the design to make it produce more voltage for the same turning speed.

Brain and mind

How has knowledge about the brain changed over the centuries?

In April 1995, the House of Lords debated whether to ban professional boxing. They decided that boxing should be allowed.

?
1 Why do you think some people want to ban boxing?

2 Do you think boxing should be banned? Explain your reasons.

Old ideas about the brain

It might seem obvious that our **brains** control what we do and allow us to think, but in ancient Egypt people thought that the **heart** was the **organ** that did these things. In fact, when someone was buried the heart was left in the body but the brain was thrown away.

A Gerald McClellan (left) suffered brain damage in a boxing match in 1995 and has been blind and deaf since. Greg Page (right) is paralysed on his left side due to brain damage he received during a match in 2001.

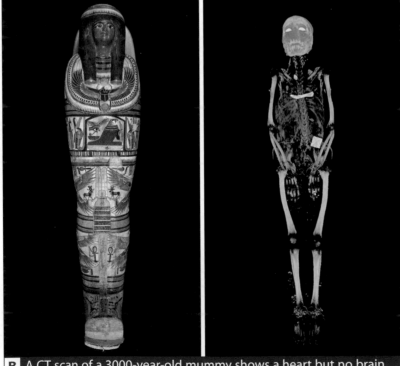

B A CT scan of a 3000-year-old mummy shows a heart but no brain.

The Greek thinker Aristotle (384–322 BC) dissected many animals. He could not find brains in small animals like insects but always found heart-like organs. He also knew that chickens could run around without heads. This convinced him that people's hearts controlled what they did. He suggested that the brain cooled the blood.

?
3 a What was Aristotle's theory?
 b What evidence supported his theory?

Galen (c.130–201) was a doctor who looked after Roman gladiators. He suggested that the brain controlled the body and contained four 'vital liquids' (blood, phlegm, choler and black bile). The amount of each liquid altered how a person felt and acted.

Gradually it became accepted that the brain controlled the body, but how it worked remained a mystery. For instance, during the Middle Ages, barbers treated mentally ill people by cutting holes in their **skulls** to release demons.

4 How did barbers think cutting a hole into the skull would help someone?

In 1543, Andreas Vesalius (1514–1564) published drawings of the brain and **nerves** attached to it. In 1791 Luigi Galvani (1737–1798) showed that electricity flowed through nerves. People soon began to wonder what different parts of the brain did.

Franz Gall (1758–1828) claimed that the brain was divided into various areas that controlled personality. These areas could cause lumps in the skull. For instance, someone with a lump in the 'cautiousness' part of the skull was very cautious.

C Hieronymus Bosch (c. 1450–1516) painted this scene showing a hole being made in someone's skull.

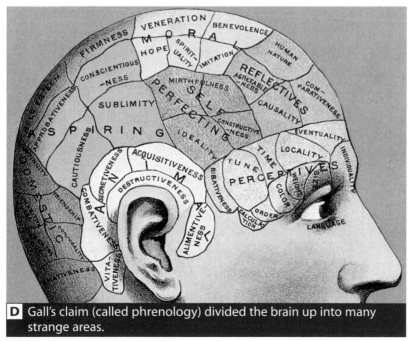

D Gall's claim (called phrenology) divided the brain up into many strange areas.

During the 20th century scientists found out how nerve cells work and discovered much more about the brain.

5 What evidence is there in everyday life that the brain controls the body?

6 Why do Valentine's cards often have hearts on them?

Summary

The _____ (found inside the _____) is made up of nerve cells. It is the _____ that controls our bodies and how we think.

brain   organ   skull

165

Responses to stimuli

What simple responses do organisms make?

A This man drank too much alcohol and collapsed on a cold street. He now has hypothermia.

This man is being treated for hypothermia, a dangerous condition caused by the body temperature getting too low (below 35 °C). It can cause death. People get hypothermia when they are exposed to the cold for a long time and their bodies lose heat faster than it can be produced.

In a house, a thermostat controls the temperature. If the house gets too cold, the thermostat switches on the heating, and then switches it off again when the house is at the right temperature.

Your brain acts like a thermostat. If your body temperature goes above 37 °C, your brain detects this and sends signals to your skin to make you sweat and so cool you down. If your body temperature starts to go below 37 °C, your brain sends signals to muscles which make you shiver and warm you up. If your body can't make enough heat to warm you up, you are in danger of getting hypothermia.

Keeping things in your body at constant levels is called **homeostasis**. When something inside your body changes, your body reacts. The thing that is changing is called the **stimulus** and your body's reaction is called the **response**.

Responses of small animals

Small animals often respond to stimuli in their environment by moving, which helps them to get things they need and to avoid danger. A movement towards a stimulus is described as a positive movement and a movement away from a stimulus is negative.

? **1** What is hypothermia?

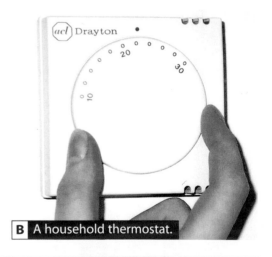

B A household thermostat.

? **2 a** Give one example of homeostasis in a human body.
b What is the stimulus in your example?

C This burning coil gives off a substance that is poisonous to mosquitoes, which avoid it.

D *Euglena* are swimming algae. They need light for photosynthesis.

E Bees are attracted to flowers by scent and by colour. They feed on nectar inside the flowers.

A How would you investigate the way brine shrimps respond to light, temperature and chemicals?
- How would you make sure your results are reliable?

F

?

3 Look at photos C, D and E. For each one, write down:
  a what the stimulus is
  b whether the response is positive or negative
  c how the response helps the organism.

4 Some arum flowers smell like rotting flesh. This attracts flies that like to lay their eggs on rotting flesh. The flies pollinate the flowers.
  a What is the stimulus?
  b Explain why this is not good for the flies.

5 Millipedes feed on damp dead leaves, which are found in dark places. Describe the responses to stimuli that millipedes must have to find food.

Summary

Some animals _____ to changes inside their bodies to keep things at certain levels (e.g. _____). This is called _____. Small animals often respond to _____ by _____, to stay in good conditions. An animal may move positively (_____) food but _____ (away from) poison.

homeostasis	moving
negatively respond	stimuli
temperature towards	

Receiving a stimulus

What happens when a stimulus is received?

When we detect changes in our environments (stimuli) we say that we **sense** something. Most people think that humans have five senses – sight, hearing, taste, touch and smell. In fact we have six senses because we also have a sense of balance.

Sense organs contain cells that detect stimuli. Cells like this are called **receptor cells**.

?

1 What is a stimulus?

2 Draw a table like this to show which sense organs are used to detect which stimuli.

Sense	Sense organ	Stimulus detected

Your eye is a sense organ that contains receptor cells that sense light. Information from the **retina** is taken to the brain by a nerve.

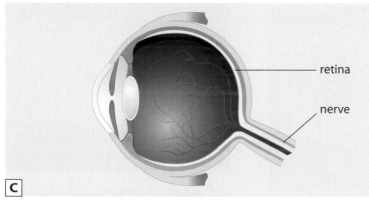

retina

nerve

C

Taste buds on your tongue contain receptor cells that sense chemicals in your food and drink. You can only taste chemicals that dissolve in the liquid in your mouth. If you have a cold you can't taste the difference between some things like tea and coffee, because your sense of smell is also involved in tasting things.

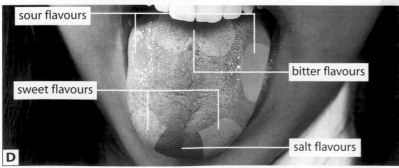

sour flavours

bitter flavours

sweet flavours

salt flavours

D

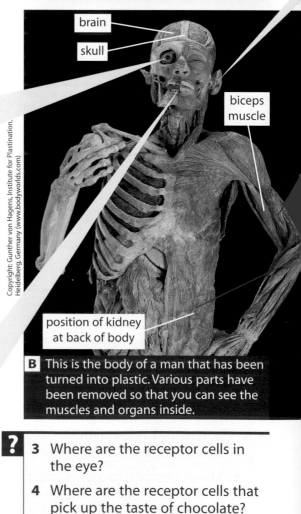

brain

skull

biceps muscle

position of kidney at back of body

Copyright: Gunther von Hagens, Institute for Plastination, Heidelberg, Germany (www.bodyworlds.com)

A

B This is the body of a man that has been turned into plastic. Various parts have been removed so that you can see the muscles and organs inside.

?

3 Where are the receptor cells in the eye?

4 Where are the receptor cells that pick up the taste of chocolate?

Your ear contains receptor cells for sound in the **cochlea** and for changes in your position (which help you keep your balance).

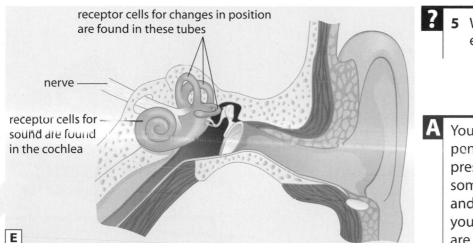

receptor cells for changes in position are found in these tubes

nerve

receptor cells for sound are found in the cochlea

E

? **5** What stimuli are detected in your ears?

A Your skin is a sense organ. If two pencils are held together and pressed gently onto the skin, in some areas you can feel two points and in others only one. How would you find out which parts of the skin are the most sensitive?

Effectors

Effector cells do something in response to a stimulus. Muscle cells in your muscles are effector cells because they can contract and cause you to move in response to a stimulus.

Sitting on top of each of your kidneys is an **adrenal gland**. Effector cells in this organ **secrete** (produce and release) a **hormone** called **adrenalin**. (A hormone is a chemical messenger that travels in your blood.)

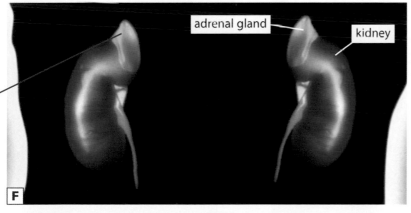

adrenal gland

kidney

F

Adrenalin increases your awareness and makes your heart beat faster, preparing you to defend yourself or run away from danger. Your adrenal glands are **effector organs** because they contain effector cells that secrete adrenalin in response to a stimulus, such as a fright.

? **6** What do effectors do?

7 Write one paragraph of a short story entitled *The Haunted Factory*. Mention all the senses and responses covered on these two pages.

Summary

Sense organs contain _____ cells that detect _____ . For example, receptor cells in the eye detect _____ and are found in the _____ . Effector cells can be found in _____ organs (e.g. the _____ glands). Effector cells or organs do something in response to a _____ (e.g. muscle cells _____ , adrenal glands release _____).

adrenal	adrenalin	contract
effector	light	receptor	retina
stimuli	stimulus

Receptors and effectors

How are receptors and effectors linked?

On 27 May 1995, actor Christopher Reeve fell off a horse and damaged his back. He became paralysed from the neck down.

The backs of all mammals (including humans) are made of many bones, which form a tube inside them. Running through this tube is a thick bundle of nerves called the **spinal cord**, which carries information between the brain, receptor cells and effector cells.

? **1** After the accident what was Christopher Reeve's spinal cord not able to do?

The brain and the spinal cord are the two organs that make up the **central nervous system** (**CNS**). The CNS controls how information travels around the body. The other nerves in the body form the **peripheral nervous system** (**PNS**) and these are linked to receptor cells and effector cells.

A Christopher Reeve as Superman in the 1980s.

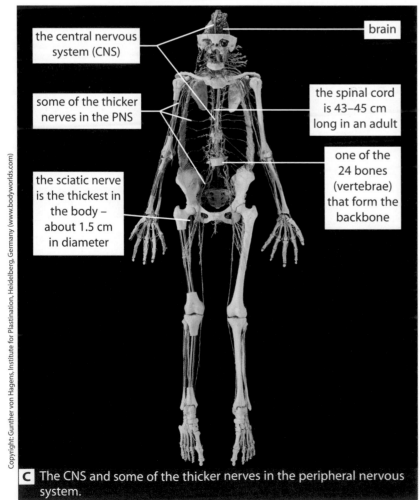

the central nervous system (CNS)

brain

some of the thicker nerves in the PNS

the spinal cord is 43–45 cm long in an adult

the sciatic nerve is the thickest in the body – about 1.5 cm in diameter

one of the 24 bones (vertebrae) that form the backbone

Copyright: Gunther von Hagens, Institute for Plastination, Heidelberg, Germany (www.bodyworlds.com)

C The CNS and some of the thicker nerves in the peripheral nervous system.

B After his accident he was unable to feel or move anything below his shoulders.

? **2** **a** Which organs are in the CNS?
b How does information get from a touch receptor cell in your foot to your brain?

Neurones

Nerves are made of bundles of cells called nerve cells or **neurones**, and it is these cells that carry information as signals called **impulses**.

Neurones that send impulses *from* receptor cells are called **sensory neurones** and those that take impulses *to* effector cells are called **motor neurones**. Nerves contain both types of neurones.

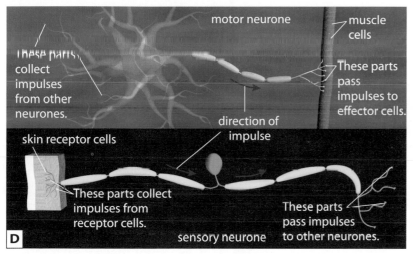

motor neurone

muscle cells

These parts collect impulses from other neurones.

These parts pass impulses to effector cells.

direction of impulse

skin receptor cells

These parts collect impulses from receptor cells.

These parts pass impulses to other neurones.

sensory neurone

D

Coordination

Impulses are sent from receptor cells, via nerves in the peripheral nervous system, to the CNS. Here, more neurones act on the information received, and send out impulses to effectors, telling part of the body to do something (this is the response). Diagram E shows what happens when someone picks something up.

Remarkably, with a great deal of determination, Christopher Reeve started to be able to move parts of his body again, especially his fingers. This was evidence that some of his motor neurones were reconnecting to neurones leading to his central nervous system. Sadly, he died on 10 October 2004.

?

5 Give one example of:
   a an effector   **b** a sense organ.

6 In drawing E, name:
   a the stimulus   **b** the response
   c the organ that coordinates the stimulus and response.

7 Diagram F shows the different bones in the backbone. Which vertebrae do you think were badly damaged in Christopher Reeve's accident? Explain your answer.

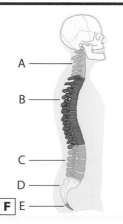

A

B

C

D

F E

?

3 What is the function of a neurone?

4 What is the difference between a nerve and a neurone?

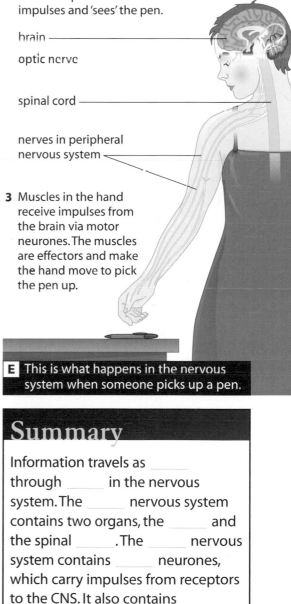

1 The eye contains receptor cells that pass information to the brain via sensory neurones in the optic nerve. The brain processes these impulses and 'sees' the pen.

2 The brain can send more impulses to tell parts of the body to do something.

brain

optic nerve

spinal cord

nerves in peripheral nervous system

3 Muscles in the hand receive impulses from the brain via motor neurones. The muscles are effectors and make the hand move to pick the pen up.

E This is what happens in the nervous system when someone picks up a pen.

Summary

Information travels as _____ through _____ in the nervous system. The _____ nervous system contains two organs, the _____ and the spinal _____. The _____ nervous system contains _____ neurones, which carry impulses from receptors to the CNS. It also contains _____ neurones, which carry impulses from the CNS to _____.

brain   central   cord   effectors
impulses   motor   neurones
peripheral   sensory

Impulses

How do neurones carry impulses?

After his accident, Christopher Reeve relied on a pump to push air into his lungs through a tube stuck into his windpipe. Then, in February 2003, he was fitted with a device that allowed him to breathe on his own.

When you breathe in, your diaphragm muscles receive an impulse from the brain and contract. This causes the diaphragm to move downwards, which makes the lungs bigger and air flows into them. When you breathe out the opposite happens.

To fit the breathing device, electrodes were attached to his diaphragm. Electrical pulses were sent from a battery pack to the electrodes and these pulses caused his diaphragm muscles to contract.

air pump

A

?

1 **a** Which of these is an impulse most like?
      electricity   a force   light
   b Explain your choice.

2 What happens in your body when you breathe out?

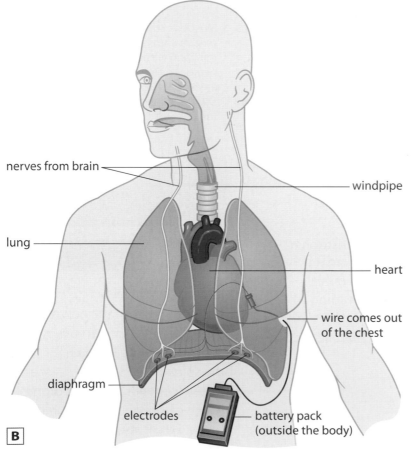

nerves from brain

windpipe

lung

heart

wire comes out of the chest

diaphragm

electrodes

battery pack (outside the body)

B

Neurones and electricity

The fact that electrical pulses can make muscles contract shows us that nerve impulses are electrical. Luigi Galvani (1737–1798) was the first to demonstrate this, but he couldn't show that the body made electricity.

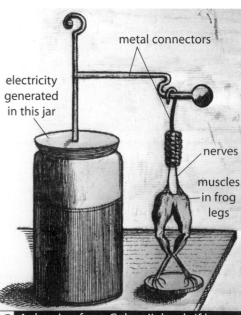

metal connectors

electricity generated in this jar

nerves

muscles in frog legs

C A drawing from Galvani's book. If he generated electricity in the jar, the frog legs twitched.

A device for measuring very small amounts of electricity (called a galvanometer) was invented in the 1820s. This allowed Emil du Bois-Reymond (1818–1896) to find tiny electrical currents in nerves. He showed that these tiny electrical currents (impulses) were made by receptors and flowed along nerves.

The main parts of a neurone

Nerves are bundles of long, thin cells called neurones. Diagram D shows the different parts of a motor neurone. Sensory neurones (see page 171) have the same main parts.

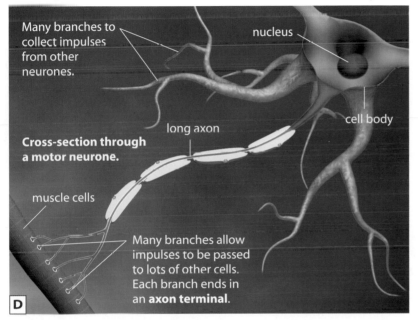

Many branches to collect impulses from other neurones.

nucleus

cell body

long axon

Cross-section through a motor neurone.

muscle cells

Many branches allow impulses to be passed to lots of other cells. Each branch ends in an **axon terminal**.

D

Some of the cytoplasm forms a long cylinder called the **axon** and the rest forms the **cell body**. Axons always carry impulses *away* from the cell body.

Neurones often have long axons so they can carry impulses for long distances. The neurones with the longest axons connect the bottom of your spinal cord to your big toes, and can be over a metre long.

The branches at the ends of neurones allow each one to connect with many other neurones or cells.

? 5 Look at diagram D.
   a In which direction will an impulse travel in this neurone?
   b How many muscle cells can this neurone pass its impulse to? Explain your answer.

6 How are neurones adapted to their function?

7 After people are struck by lightning, parts of their bodies may be paralysed. Explain why.

? 3 Why did the frog legs twitch in Galvani's experiment?

4 Why couldn't Galvani show that electrical currents were made by the body?

Summary

_____ impulses can be made by _____. Neurones can carry _____ a long way because they have long _____. They also have lots of _____ at their ends to connect with many other neurones or cells. The branches at the end of an axon end in axon _____. The _____ of a neurone is found in its _____ body.

axons   branches   cell
electrical   impulses   nucleus
receptors   terminals

Impulse speeds
How are impulses carried quickly?

One of Christopher Reeve's co-stars in the Superman films was Richard Pryor, who developed a nervous system disease called multiple sclerosis (MS).

MS affects about 85 000 people in the UK and stops neurones from carrying impulses properly. People with the disease often have difficulty in walking, talking and swallowing.

?

1 What does MS stand for?

2 **a** Name three symptoms of MS.
   b How are these symptoms caused?

A Richard Pryor (1940–2005) as Gus Gorman in the 1980s.

Myelin

Many neurones have axons that are covered in a yellowish, fatty substance called **myelin**. This **insulates** the axons and so stops impulses jumping from one axon into other axons next to it. The myelin **sheath** (covering) also increases the speed of impulses.

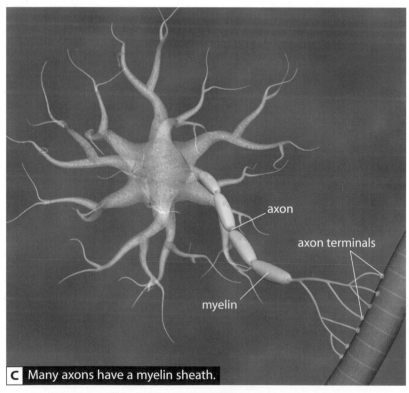

axon

axon terminals

myelin

C Many axons have a myelin sheath.

Neurones with myelin sheaths cannot carry impulses very well if the sheaths are damaged, and this is what happens in MS. Scientists are not sure how MS is caused, but it appears that the body starts destroying the myelin.

B In later life Richard Pryor suffered from multiple sclerosis.

?

3 In what ways is a nerve similar to an electrical cable?

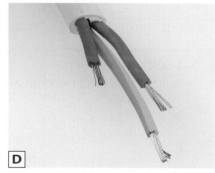

D

4 Why are large nerves yellow in colour?

Impulse speeds

In 1852, Hermann von Helmholtz (1821–1894) used frog nerves to measure impulse speeds and found that they were about 27 m/s. We now know that different neurones conduct impulses at different speeds; thicker ones and those with myelin sheaths conduct faster.

If you stub your toe, you quickly feel that your foot has hit something because sensory neurones from toe touch receptors carry impulses at 75 m/s. However, you don't feel pain for another second or two because the sensory neurones from toe pain receptors only carry impulses at 0.6 m/s. The fastest neurones in your body carry impulses at about 120 m/s.

Synapses

All impulses are slowed down slightly because neurones aren't joined to each other. There is a gap, called a **synapse**, between one neurone and the next. When an impulse arrives at a synapse it is detected in the next neurone, which then makes another impulse. This takes time.

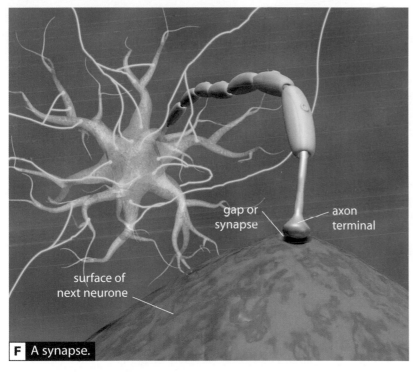

gap or synapse

axon terminal

surface of next neurone

F A synapse.

?

6 It is better to have one long sensory neurone running from a receptor cell to the CNS, rather than lots of shorter sensory neurones. Why?

7 In a disease called syringomyelia a fluid-filled hole forms at the top of the spinal cord. This slowly destroys the surrounding nerves. Suggest some symptoms of this disease, and explain your reasoning.

A How could you measure impulse speeds?

- What will you do?
- What calculations will you need to do?
- How will you get reliable results?

?
5 You feel pain quicker when you bang your thumb than when you stub your big toe. Why might this be? Give as many reasons as you can.

Summary

Neurones carry impulses _____ if they are thicker and if they have a fatty, _____ sheath. The _____ sheath also _____ axons from each other. _____ have gaps called _____ between them.

faster   insulates   myelin
neurones   synapses

Different responses

How are reflex actions different to normal responses?

In a driving test, you have to do an 'emergency stop'. When the examiner thumps the dashboard you have to stop the car quickly; you have to respond to a stimulus.

Diagram B shows how impulses travel in an emergency stop. It takes time for the impulses to travel through the driver's body and so there is a time delay between the stimulus and the response. This is the **reaction time**.

A An emergency stop.

B Impulse routes during an emergency stop.

? **1** In an emergency stop, name:
   a the response
   b two possible stimuli.

? **2** Draw a flow chart to show the route that impulses take during an emergency stop. Start with 'receptor cells' and include these words and phrases:
   effector cells   impulse   motor neurone
   neurones in the brain   sensory neurone

3 Alcohol slows down impulse speeds. Give one reason why it is against the law for people to drive if they've had more than a certain amount of alcohol.

Reflex actions

Reaction times vary between about 0.2 seconds and 0.5 seconds. However, sometimes your body responds quicker than this to stop damage occurring.

If you flick your fingers suddenly in front of somebody's face, they will blink. This blink is **involuntary**; it doesn't involve the brain deciding what the response should be. An automatic reaction like this is called a **reflex action**.

? **4** Why is the blink reflex useful?

Reflex arcs

To make sure that your neurones are working, doctors often test reflex actions – usually the knee reflex. If you let your lower leg hang freely, your leg will swing up automatically if the area just below your knee cap is tapped.

The knee jerk reflex takes about 0.05 seconds to occur and is faster than a normal response because the impulses from the sensory neurones connect directly to the motor neurones in the spinal cord and the brain is not involved. Neurone connections where a sensory neurone directly controls a motor neurone are called **reflex arcs**. Photos D, E and F show some more simple reflexes.

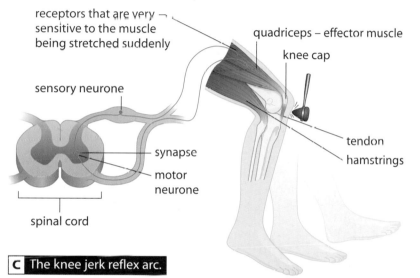

receptors that are very sensitive to the muscle being stretched suddenly
quadriceps – effector muscle
knee cap
sensory neurone
synapse
motor neurone
spinal cord
tendon
hamstrings

C The knee jerk reflex arc.

D The pain withdrawal reflex.

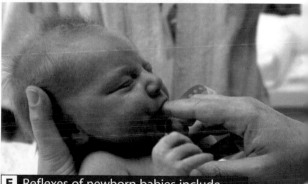

E Reflexes of newborn babies include gripping things and sucking things put in their mouths.

F Eye muscles cause your pupils to shrink in bright light. This stops too much light damaging your eyes.

?

5 a What is a reflex arc?
  b How many synapses are in the knee jerk reflex arc?
  c Why is it important to have fewer synapses in a reflex arc?

6 a What happens in the reflexes shown in photos D, E and F?
  b Explain why you think each reflex is useful.

7 Draw the reflex arc for the simple reflex that is occurring in photo D.

Summary

Simple _____ are quicker than normal responses because they don't require the brain to decide what to do. Examples include the _____ and pupil reflexes of the _____, and the knee _____ reflex. Impulses in simple _____ travel along a _____ arc, which is when a _____ neurone directly controls a motor _____.

blink   eyes   jerk   neurone   reflex   reflexes   sensory

Animal reflexes

How do animals use simple reflex actions?

A tiny water creature called a hydra feeds using tentacles, pulling food into its central mouth.

The tentacles usually move slowly but if water fleas or certain chemicals are placed nearby, the tentacles move faster. This is a reflex action.

The behaviour of small animals is mainly caused by reflexes which help them survive, including:
- finding food
- avoiding predators
- finding shelter
- finding a mate.

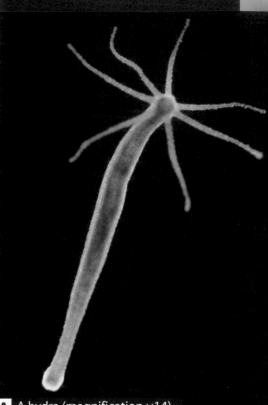

A A hydra (magnification ×14).

? 1 How does a hydra's reflex action help it to survive?

Avoiding predators

Some sea slugs have an escape reflex. Receptor cells on the sea slug detect chemicals produced by a starfish and instantly cause muscles to contract and relax. This causes a squirming movement that moves the sea slug upwards, where (hopefully) a water current will sweep it away from danger.

sea slug making squirming movements

starfish

B

? 2 Draw a diagram to show how neurones in a sea slug might make a reflex arc for its escape reflex.

Finding shelter

Cockroaches live in dark nooks and crannies, where they can hide from predators and find moist and warm conditions in which to breed. A reflex action causes them to move away from light.

C

A How would you use a **choice chamber** to find out what responses small animals (e.g. woodlice) have to various stimuli (e.g. light, warmth)?

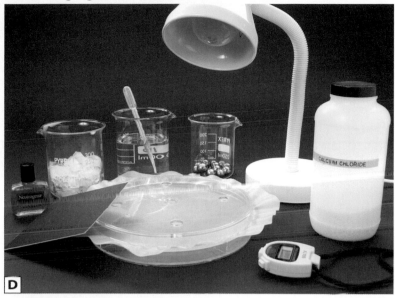

D

Finding a mate

Female moths produce a scent. Due to a simple reflex the males fly towards the scent.

Moths and lights

An experiment in Italy showed that over 5 million moths a year are attracted to lamps around a certain statue. Scientists aren't sure why moths fly towards lights. One theory is that moths keep the Moon on one side of their bodies when flying, so that they go in a straight line. A moth confuses a light for the Moon, and when it flies past the light, a simple reflex makes it turn, to keep the light in the same place. This results in the moth circling the light.

This is bad news for moths because they damage themselves and predators can easily find them. That's the problem with simple reflexes: they can't change and so animals can't learn how to respond to new situations.

?
4 Look back at page 167.
   a What reflex do *Euglena* have?
   b How does this help them survive?

5 How are lights a problem for moths? Write down as many ways as you can.

6 Nematode worms are often eaten by dogs. They then burrow out of the dog's intestines into the muscles and organs. Suggest what simple reflex would help them do this.

E Receptor cells in a male emperor moth's antennae can detect the scent of a female up to 6 miles away!

?
3 **a** List four things that simple reflexes allow small animals to do.
   b Give an example of each.

Summary

Small animals use simple _____ actions for most of their behaviour. These _____ allow them to survive by avoiding _____ and finding food, _____ and _____. However, _____ reflexes cannot _____ and so the animals cannot usually respond to new situations.

| change | mates | predators | reflex |
| reflexes | shelter | simple |

Learning

How do mammals learn?

What an animal does and how it reacts to things is known as its **behaviour**. More complex animals have large brains that allow them to learn things and to change their behaviour to adapt to new situations. Learned actions are **voluntary** because the animal can decide whether to do them or not.

?
  1 What has the squirrel in photo A learnt to do?

  2 Why can a squirrel adapt to new situations more easily than a flatworm?

The rat in photo C pushed the left hand lever by accident, which delivered food. The rat didn't instantly learn that the lever delivered food, but when it pushed the lever by accident again and got more food, it soon learnt.

A A squirrel learns from its experiences.

C

Many animals learn to do things by being given a reward. They also learn not to do things by being given something unpleasant. If the rat gets tasty food by pressing the left hand lever and bad-tasting food by pressing the right hand lever, it soon learns only to press the left hand lever.

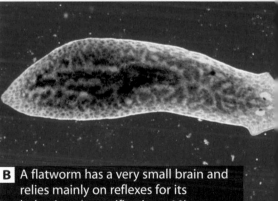

B A flatworm has a very small brain and relies mainly on reflexes for its behaviour (magnification ×10).

?
  3 Explain why cows don't try to leave a field that is surrounded by an electric fence.

When an animal experiences something, receptors send impulses to the brain. The brain contains billions of neurones and so there are billions of different routes, called

neurone pathways, which impulses can take. Each pathway results in the animal doing something different. If impulses follow a pathway that causes an animal to do something enjoyable or useful, impulses are more likely to follow this pathway again. This is one way that learning occurs.

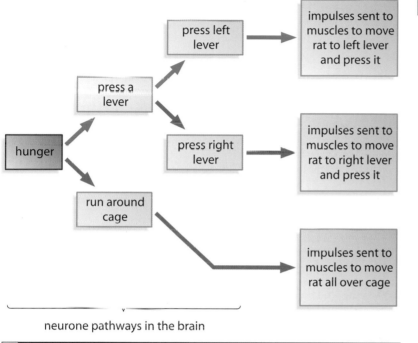

neurone pathways in the brain

D Some neurone pathways in a rat brain. As the rat learns, the pathway in blue is used more of the time.

Social behaviour

Some male animals fight to see who is the strongest and will mate with the females. The same males might fight a few times, but eventually the less strong one learns to avoid fighting the stronger one. Behaviour where animals in a group work, play or fight with one another is called **social behaviour**.

?

5 What is social behaviour?

6 Forensic scientists use a fake 'dead body smell' to train dogs to find dead bodies. Explain how you think these dogs are trained.

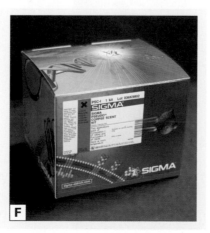

F

?

4 Look at diagram D.
   a Name three things the caged rat can do when it is hungry.
   b Explain why a hungry rat that has been in the cage for weeks only uses the blue pathway.
   c Explain why a hungry rat that is new to the cage may simply run around.

E Male ibexes fighting.

Summary

Brains contain billions of _____. Depending on which neurone _____ impulses travel along in the _____, an animal will do different things. When an animal _____ from its experiences, one _____ gets used all the time. What an animal does is called its _____. _____ behaviour is how an animal behaves around animals of the same type.

behaviour	brain	learns	neurones
pathway	pathways	social	

181

Learning as you grow

How do children learn new skills?

A A 10-month-old baby learning to walk.

B A young monkey watches another crack nuts with a stone.

C Cheetahs show their cubs how to hunt.

Baby mammals learn to do thousands of different things as they grow and develop. They learn from their own experiences and by copying other animals.

A human baby's brain contains about 100 billion neurones but many are not yet connected to one another. New synapses are being made in a baby all the time and new neurone pathways are developing. By the age of 3 each neurone may be connected by synapses to 15 000 other neurones, making a total of over 1000 trillion (1000 000 000 000 000) connections!

? **1** Name one thing that you learnt when you were young:
  a by yourself
  b by watching an adult.

D The brain contains billions of interconnected branching neurones.

? **2** What feature of brain neurones allows them to make so many connections?

A newborn baby has fuzzy eyesight and can only make out light, shapes and movement. As the neurones form synapses, sight gets better. While sight is developing, the baby sees its parents over and over, which causes the same neurone pathways to be used over and over. This repeated use makes those neurone pathways permanent and the baby recognises its parents after about 3 months. A baby's eyesight is fully developed after about 8 months.

E A baby's view at 1 week old. | A baby's view of the same scene at 8 months old.

A new baby's arm movements are fairly random but new neurone pathways form that gradually allow the baby to reach out and grab specific items. Once a baby has discovered how to do this, it will repeat the action many times and use that neurone pathway repeatedly. The pathway becomes permanent and the baby has learnt to reach out and grab things.

? 5 What happens in a baby's brain that allows it to reach out and grab specific things?

The more a neurone pathway is used, the more easily that pathway is able to carry impulses and the more permanent it becomes. This is why the more you practise something, the better you get at it. Neurone pathways that aren't used disappear because the synapses are destroyed.

? 6 When people want to remember something, they often repeat it to themselves. Why does this work?

7 A human needs different neurone pathways to make different sounds. Suggest why adults find it harder to learn languages than small children.

? 3 How long does it take a baby to recognise its parents?

4 List two ways in which a baby's eyesight changes between birth and 8 months.

F A baby learns to grab specific things by about 4 months.

Summary

As a young animal _____ it learns skills from experience and by _____ other animals. Newly learnt skills are _____ often and this helps the _____ pathway for that action to become stronger and _____. Neurone _____ that aren't used disappear because the _____ are destroyed.

copying grows neurone pathways
permanent repeated synapses

Parts of the brain

What do different parts of the brain do?

Phineas Gage was an American railway worker. In 1848, he was checking that a stick of dynamite was properly positioned in a hole, by prodding it with a long metal rod. The dynamite exploded, firing the rod upwards though his head. Remarkably, Gage could walk and talk immediately after the accident!

? 1 Apart from Gage's brain, what organ did the rod damage?

Before the accident, Gage had been hard-working and friendly. Afterwards he was lazy and ill-mannered. Gage's doctor, John Harlow (1819–1907), concluded that the front of the brain was used for personality.

Scientists then wanted to find out what the other parts of the brain did. In 1855 Bartolomeo Panizza (1785–1867) cut the nerves leading to the back of animal brains. This caused blindness.

Paul Broca (1824–1880) examined the brains of people who had been unable to speak. He found that they all had damage to a certain part of the brain.

People are often awake when they have brain surgery. In the 1950s this allowed Wilder Penfield (1891–1976) to apply small electrical currents directly to living brains and ask the patients what they felt. If the current made patients do a certain action or stopped them from doing an action, then he knew that brain area controlled that action.

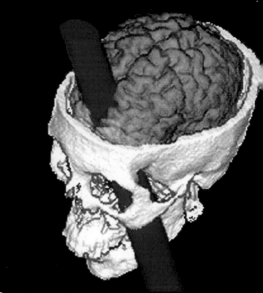

A The rod went through the front of Gage's brain.

? 2 **a** What did John Harlow conclude?
  b Why did he conclude this?

3 What do you think Panizza concluded from his experiments?

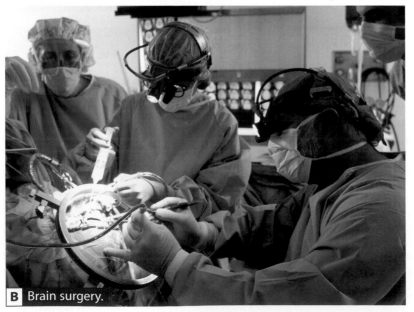

B Brain surgery.

Today scientists use machines that are able to 'see' inside the skull. There are many different types of these scanners and some produce images that show where electrical activity is occurring.

4 Gavin is looking carefully at a painting.
   a Where in his brain would you expect to find the most electrical activity?
   b Explain your answer.

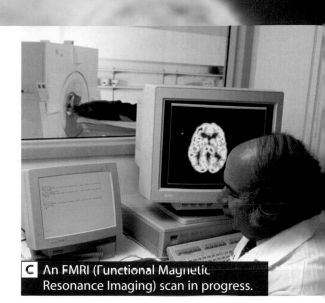
C An FMRI (Functional Magnetic Resonance Imaging) scan in progress.

A map of the brain

The main part of the brain is called the **cerebral cortex**. This part is used for most of our senses, behaviour and **consciousness** (our inner thoughts and feelings). Drawing D shows what the different parts do.

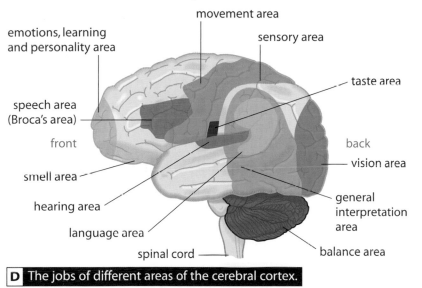

emotions, learning and personality area

movement area

sensory area

taste area

speech area (Broca's area)

front

back

vision area

smell area

hearing area

general interpretation area

language area

spinal cord

balance area

D The jobs of different areas of the cerebral cortex.

Brain mapping and phrenology

In some ways Franz Gall, who invented phrenology (see page 165), was right. However, his idea was not based on scientific evidence and he invented what each area of the brain was supposed to do.

5 In what way was Franz Gall right?

6 Photo E shows a scan of someone's brain. The brighter colours show more activity. Suggest one thing the person was doing during the scan. Explain your reasoning.

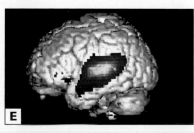
E

7 Find out how a PET scanner works.

Summary

The cerebral _____ controls our behaviour and our _____ (our inner thoughts and _____). Scientists know what different parts of the _____ do by studying people with brain _____, by putting electrical _____ through parts of the brain and by _____ (e.g. _____).

brain   consciousness   cortex
currents   damage   feelings
FMRI   scanning

Memory

What is memory?

Memory is storing and retrieving information. When we memorise something, a neurone pathway is created that leads to the place in the brain where the memory is stored. A single neurone pathway may get damaged or may disappear if it is not used enough. However, linking things to images or silly rhymes creates more pathways to the same memory and so you are more likely to remember it.

?
1 Why can linking things to images help you to remember things?

Verbal memory

Scientists have a theory that there are two types of **verbal memory** (remembering numbers and words). Your **short-term memory** holds a small amount of information for up to 30 seconds but your **long-term memory** can hold lots of information for a lifetime.

A
How could you find out how many pieces of information someone's short-term memory can hold?
• You could try different lengths of phone numbers.

A Using a 'linking method' Andi Bell can learn the order of cards in ten shuffled packs in 20 minutes.

Evidence to support the theory that you have different types of memory comes from scanning (picture B).

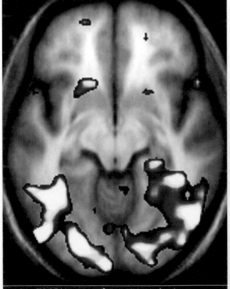

a An FMRI scan of a person being shown a face and being asked to remember it.

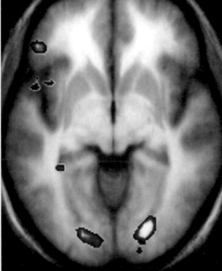

b As the person is asked to think about the face, the information is transferred to the long-term memory.

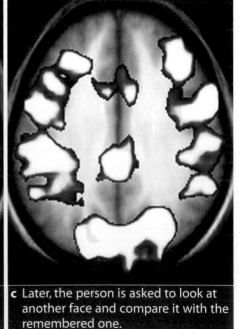

c Later, the person is asked to look at another face and compare it with the remembered one.

B

2 a Write down something that is often remembered using short-term memory.
b How long does this information take to be forgotten?

3 a How do the scans in picture B suggest that there are different types of memory?
b Why are areas at the back of the brain active when the person is looking at faces?

Drugs and memory

Memory uses the synapses between neurones. Drugs and poisons that alter how impulses travel across synapses can cause problems with memory

Picture C shows scan images of the brains of two different people, one who has never used ecstasy (MDMA) and one who does. These images are supposed to show that a brain exposed to ecstasy is less active (the lower set of images).

C The upper set of brain scan images are from someone who has never used ecstasy and the lower set is from someone who last used the drug 3 weeks ago.

Many scientists think that picture C is not good evidence because the images were taken using a method that caused some brains to 'glow' 40 times brighter in the scan pictures than others, even if ecstasy had not been taken. However, recent studies seem to confirm that ecstasy reduces brain activity and that ecstasy users have worse long-term memories than non-users, although scientists don't know how permanent the effect is.

4 a What is picture C supposed to demonstrate?
b Describe an alternative interpretation of these images.

5 Describe one way in which you would change the simple short-term/long-term theory of human memory. Explain why you would make this change.

Summary

Memory is being able to _____ and get back _____. Most people agree that we have a _____ verbal memory (that lasts for about 30 seconds) and a _____ verbal memory (that can last for a lifetime). Many _____ and poisons interfere with memory because they change the way _____ travel across _____.

drugs   impulses   information
long-term   short-term
store   synapses

Dr Frankenstein's lab

What do you know about the brain and mind?

A

Dr Frankenstein is at work in his lab trying to create a human from various parts of bodies that he has collected. He's got all the bits together and he now needs to 'wire up' the nervous system.

Dr Frankenstein starts by examining some nerves to try to find some neurones. He finds that the neurones are covered in a fatty substance.

1 Diagram B shows two neurones.

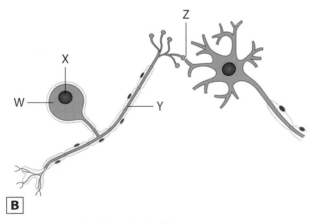

B

a What are the parts labelled W, X, Y and Z?
b What does a sensory neurone do?
c Describe two features of neurones that help them to carry out their functions (jobs).
d Name the two organs that make up in the central nervous system.

2 Which two of these sentences best describe the functions of a neurone's myelin sheath?
  - It is a yellow colour.
  - It is a non-fatty substance.
  - It insulates one neurone from another.
  - It speeds up impulses.
  - It is only found on neurones in the brain.
  - It makes neurones shorter.

Dr Frankenstein knows that some neurones take impulses to the brain and others take impulses away from the brain.

3 In order to 'wire up' some neurones, Dr Frankenstein has cut through his creature's brain.

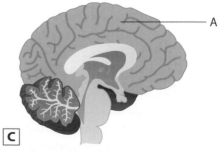

C

a What is the part marked A called?
b Describe two functions of this part.
c Describe one way in which the functions of this part have been studied.

4 a The information in this table has been muddled up. Redraw the table, organising the words into three columns, each with a heading. The words for the headings are already in the table.

bright light	receptor	muscle
cells in retina	effector	scary sound
adrenal gland	cells in inner ear	stimulus

D

b Describe what happens when the two effectors in the table are activated.

Dr Frankenstein now needs to give the creatures some reflex actions.

5 Draw a table to show which of the following actions Dr Frankenstein's creature should do as involuntary actions and which actions should be voluntary.

picking up some keys   blinking   sneezing
removing its hand from a flame   walking
taking a deep breath

6 Drawing E shows how Dr Frankenstein plans to install a pain reflex.

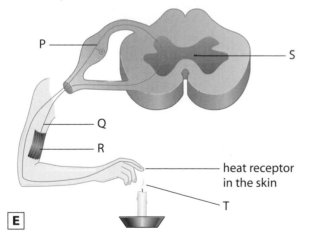

E

a What is this arrangement of neurones called?
b Which letter is each of the following?
  i sensory neurone   **ii** stimulus
  iii spinal cord   **iv** effector
c Explain what happens when a person accidentally touches the candle flame.
d List two ways in which this is different to a conscious movement of the hand.
e Give an example of a reflex action in a newborn baby.

7 Some of Dr Frankenstein's neurones come from animals, including a sea slug called *Aplysia* (picture F). If this sea slug is touched, a reflex pulls its delicate gill inside its body.

F   gill   head

a Explain why this simple reflex action is useful to the sea slug.
b State two other things that simple animals use reflexes for.

Dr Frankenstein is nearing the moment when he will pass electricity through his creation in an attempt to get it to live. As a keen cricketer, he wants his creation to be good at the game.

8 Cricket helmets protect batsmen's heads but slow their reaction times by about 16 milliseconds.
a What is a reaction time?
b Describe what happens in a batsman's nervous system as he or she goes to hit a ball. Start with the retina in the back of the eye.
c Explain why a shorter reaction time is better for batting.
d Suggest one way in which Dr Frankenstein could make his creature have a fast reaction time.

Success! Dr Frankenstein manages to get his creature to live but is disappointed to find that it behaves like a baby.

9 Complete the following sentences using words from the box.

As a baby is _____, _____ are connecting together and new neurone _____ are being formed. When the _____ has discovered how to do something it will repeat the _____ many times. In this way the _____ _____ becomes more able to carry impulses and so becomes _____.

| action   baby   learning |
| neurone   neurones   pathway |
| pathways   permanent |

Chemical synthesis

What does the chemical industry make?

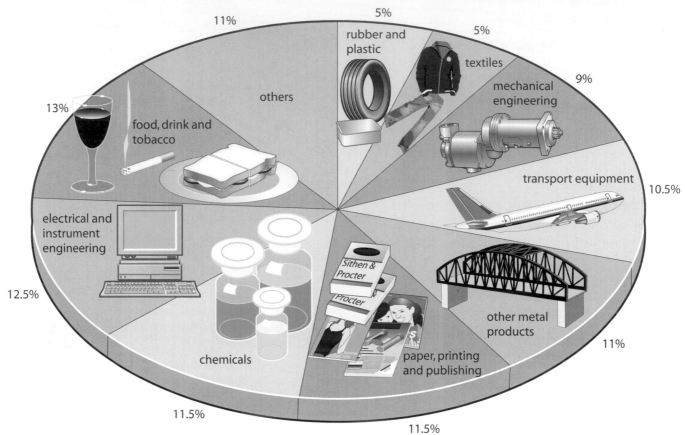

11%

5%
rubber and plastic

5%
textiles

9%

others

13%

food, drink and tobacco

mechanical engineering

transport equipment

10.5%

electrical and instrument engineering

Sithen & Procter

Procter

other metal products

11%

12.5%

chemicals

paper, printing and publishing

11.5%

11.5%

A All of these industries use chemicals made by the chemical industry.

The chemical industry is one of Britain's largest industries, making more than a tenth of the total substances produced in this country. It uses a wide range of **raw materials** and turns them into an enormous variety of useful substances. These substances can be divided into six types:

• fertilisers
• acids and chemicals used by other industries
• dyes, paints and pigments
• plastics
• medicines
• special chemicals such as food additives and liquid crystals for televisions.

? 1 Look at chart A. List four industries that use chemicals.

2 Look around the room and list four substances you see that have been made by the chemical industry.

B A chemist working for Terra Nitrogen, where they make fertilisers.

sea (water and salt)

oil

limestone

In this module you will look at how some of these substances are made. You will also find out how to make some of the reactions quicker. Some of the most important raw materials available in this country are:

• water
• air
• limestone (calcium carbonate)
• iron ore (iron oxide)
• coal
• oil and natural gas
• salt.

The chemical industry is now also trying to develop processes that use the principles of **green chemistry**. These include the use of sustainable raw materials and reducing the amount of dangerous waste.

Terra Nitrogen make the fertiliser ammonium nitrate. They use raw materials from the air and natural gas.

C These provide some of the raw materials from which many different chemicals are made.

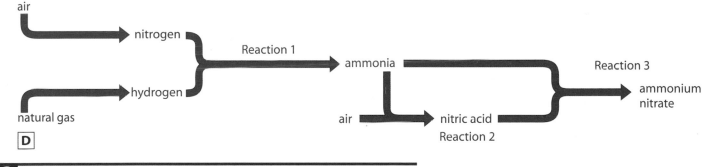

D

?

3 Which is the odd one out: oil, plastic, water? Explain your answers.

4 Look at diagram D.
   a What are the raw materials used in this process?
   b What are the reactants in the second reaction?
   c What is the product in the second reaction?
   d Write word equations for each of the three reactions.

5 Why is green chemistry important?

6 Ammonium chloride (NH_4Cl) is used to make batteries. This is made from ammonia (NH_3) and hydrochloric acid (HCl). Write a word equation and a symbol equation for the formation of ammonium chloride.

Summary

The chemical industry make things like _____, _____ and _____. It starts with raw materials like _____, _____, _____ and _____ and converts them into useful substances.

| air | coal | fertilisers | iron ore |
| limestone | medicines | plastics |

191

Acids

What are acids?

Acids are found in foods, and even in your stomach! You may be used to thinking of acids as liquids, but acidic compounds can be solids, liquids or even gases.

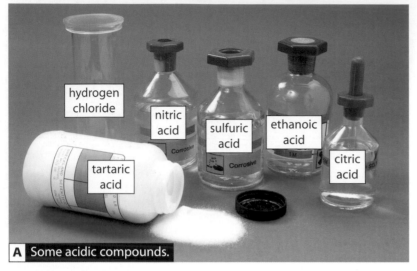

A Some acidic compounds.

?
1 Name two solid acidic compounds.

2 What type of fruit would contain citric acid?

3 Name three liquid acidic compounds.

4 Which acid can be found as a gas?

When these acidic compounds are dissolved in water, they have the following properties.
- They have a **pH number** below 7.
- They react with metals such as magnesium or zinc to form a salt and hydrogen.
- They react with bases (metal oxides and hydroxides) to form a salt and water. This is a **neutralisation** reaction.
- They react with carbonates to form a salt, carbon dioxide and water.
- They turn litmus red.

The acids that we usually use are hydrochloric acid (HCl), nitric acid (HNO_3) and sulfuric acid (H_2SO_4).

We can show these reactions as both word equations and as balanced symbol equations. For example:

sodium hydroxide + hydrochloric acid → sodium chloride + water
$$NaOH\ (aq)\ +\ HCl\ (aq)\ →\ NaCl\ (aq)\ +\ H_2O\ (l)$$

magnesium + hydrochloric acid → magnesium chloride + hydrogen
$$Mg\ (s)\ +\ 2HCl\ (aq)\ →\ MgCl_2\ (aq)\ +\ H_2\ (g)$$

B All of these foods contain acids.

Concentrated acids are corrosive and even the dilute acids used in most practicals can irritate the skin. Take care!

CORROSIVE

?

5 Copy and complete the word equations for the following reactions:
  a magnesium hydroxide + sulfuric acid →
  b calcium carbonate + hydrochloric acid →
  c potassium hydroxide + hydrochloric acid →
  d copper oxide + sulfuric acid →

6 Write symbol equations for these reactions. The formulae you need are given below.
  $CaCl_2$ $CaCO_3$ CuO $CuSO_4$
  KCl   KOH $Mg(OH)_2$ $MgSO_4$

7 What would you see if you mixed magnesium and orange juice?

C Terra Nitrogen makes this nitric acid to convert into fertilisers.

We can use hydrochloric acid to find out which rocks contain insoluble salts called carbonates. Calcium carbonate ($CaCO_3$) is found naturally in marble, limestone and chalk. The calcium carbonate reacts with hydrochloric acid like this:

  calcium carbonate + hydrochloric acid → calcium chloride + carbon dioxide + water

The carbon dioxide that is formed makes the acid fizz.

A Different rocks contain different amounts of calcium carbonate.
  • How can you compare the amounts of calcium carbonate in different rocks?
  • What apparatus would you need?
  • How will you make your experiment a fair test?

D

?

8 Think of a plus, a minus and an interesting point about this statement: Acids are really dangerous.

9 Find out what is in sherbet, and why it fizzes in your mouth.

Summary

Acidic compounds can be solids, _____ or gases. They have typical properties when dissolved in _____. Acids react with some metals to form a salt and _____. Acids react with _____ to form a salt and water. Acids react with carbonates to form a _____, _____ and water. Hydrochloric acid can be used to identify _____ in rocks.

bases	carbonates
carbon dioxide	hydrogen
liquids	salt water

Alkalis, bases and pH

What are bases and alkalis?

Bases are the opposite of acids. **Alkalis** are bases that dissolve in water. Alkalis have these properties:
• They have pH numbers greater than 7.
• They react with acids to form a salt and water.
• They turn litmus blue.

Alkalis used in the laboratory include sodium hydroxide ($NaOH$), potassium hydroxide (KOH), calcium hydroxide ($Ca(OH)_2$) and ammonium hydroxide (NH_4OH). Ammonium hydroxide is formed when ammonia reacts with water. Many chemicals used in the home contain alkalis or bases.

B All of these contain bases.

A The ammonia made at Terra Nitrogen is an alkali.

Strong alkalis are dangerous. They burn your skin on contact and can permanently blind you.

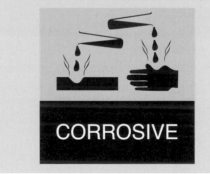

CORROSIVE

?

1 Name three common alkalis.

2 What colour will litmus paper go if you put sodium hydroxide on it? Explain your answer.

3 What safety precautions should you take when you use alkalis?

We all safely swallow some acids like citric acid in oranges and limes, and some alkalis like antacids and toothpaste. This means that these acids and alkalis are weaker and safer than strong ones like hydrochloric acid and sodium hydroxide.

Litmus will only tell us if a solution is an acid or an alkali. It does not tell us how strong or weak the acid or alkali is. **Universal indicator** is a mixture of many different indicators. The mixture changes to different colours depending on how acidic or alkaline the solution is. The different colours are put on a scale and given a number called the pH number. The stronger the acid, the lower the pH number. The stronger the alkali, the higher the pH number. Water is neutral and has a pH of 7.

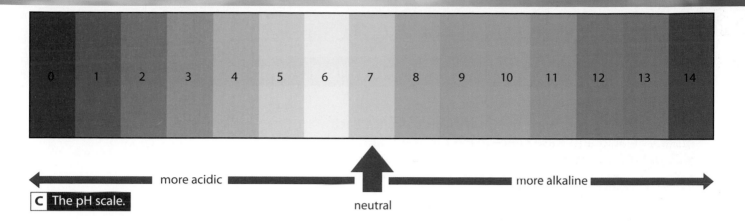

0 1 2 3 4 5 6 7 8 9 10 11 12 13 14

more acidic ◄━━━━━━━━━━━━ ━━━━━━━━━━━━► more alkaline

neutral

C The pH scale.

? **4** What does the pH scale tell us?

We can also use pH meters. These give a direct and accurate reading for the pH of a solution.

D Universal indicator comes as a solution or as paper.

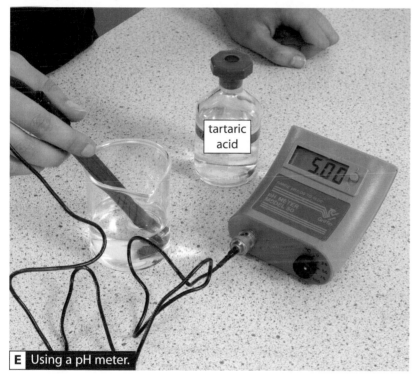

tartaric acid

E Using a pH meter.

? **5** What colour will universal indicator go with the two solutions shown in photo D?

6 Is the tartaric acid in photo E a strong or weak acid? Explain your answer.

7 What would be the pH of a solution of salt (sodium chloride) in water?

8 What would be an advantage of using a pH meter instead of universal indicator?

9 Ammonium hydroxide is a weak alkali. What pH value would it have?

Summary

Bases are the opposite to _____ . If they dissolve in water they form _____ . An alkali has a pH _____ than 7, and reacts with acids to form a _____ and water. Common alkalis are _____ hydroxide and sodium hydroxide.

acids   alkalis   greater
potassium   salt

Neutralisation reactions

What happens during neutralisation reactions?

When an acid reacts with an alkali, they neutralise each other. The acid and base cancel each other out and a salt and water are formed.

acid + alkali → salt + water

For example:

hydrochloric acid + sodium hydroxide → sodium chloride + water
$$HCl\ (aq)\quad +\quad NaOH\ (aq)\quad \rightarrow\quad NaCl\ (aq)\quad +\ H_2O\ (l)$$

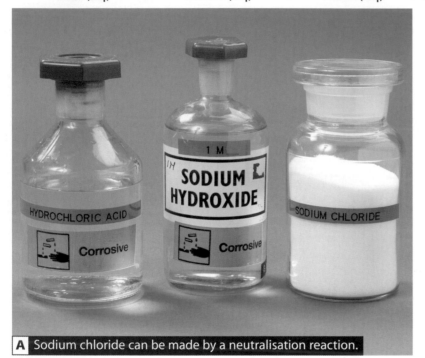

A Sodium chloride can be made by a neutralisation reaction.

When acids are dissolved in water, they form **hydrogen ions** (H^+). The hydrogen ions make the solution acidic. **Strong acids** like hydrochloric acid produce more hydrogen ions in water than **weak acids** like citric acid. This means that strong acids have a lower pH value than weak acids.

All alkalis contain **hydroxide ions** (OH^-). The hydroxide ions make the solution alkaline. **Strong alkalis** produce more hydroxide ions than **weak alkalis**.

During a neutralisation reaction, the hydrogen ions from the acid react with the hydroxide ions from the alkali. This can be shown as:

$$H^+\ (aq) + OH^-\ (aq) \rightarrow H_2O\ (l)$$

This is called an **ionic equation**, as it only shows the ions that have changed. This equation is the same, whatever the acid or alkali used.

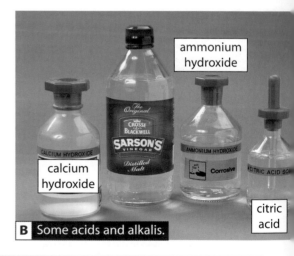

B Some acids and alkalis.

calcium hydroxide

ammonium hydroxide

citric acid

?

1 Which ions are formed when:
   a an acid dissolves in water
   b an alkali dissolves in water?

2 Which of the substances shown in photo B contain:
   a hydrogen ions
   b hydroxide ions?

3 Write the ionic equation for the reaction of nitric acid with potassium hydroxide.

These are the acids and alkalis that you are most likely to use.

Acids		Alkalis	
hydrochloric acid	HCl	sodium hydroxide	NaOH
nitric acid	HNO_3	potassium hydroxide	KOH
sulfuric acid	H_2SO_4	ammonium hydroxide	NH_4OH

C

As all acids contain hydrogen, a salt is prepared by replacing the hydrogen in the acid with a metal. The metal comes from the alkali.

The salt formed depends upon the acid and alkali used. If we know the formula of the acid and alkali used, we can write down the formula of the salt formed. We just swap the hydrogen for the metal ion (or ammonium NH_4^+ ion). Remember that hydrochloric acid forms chlorides, nitric acid forms nitrates and sulfuric acid forms sulfates.

Acid	Alkali	Salt
hydrochloric acid	potassium hydroxide	potassium chloride
nitric acid	ammonium hydroxide	ammonium nitrate
sulfuric acid	lithium hydroxide	lithium sulfate

D

Potassium chloride is KCl, ammonium nitrate is NH_4NO_3 and lithium sulfate is Li_2SO_4.

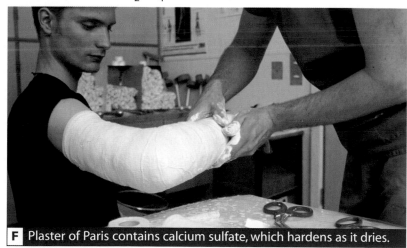

F Plaster of Paris contains calcium sulfate, which hardens as it dries.

? 4 Write down the name of the salts formed from:
   a nitric acid and barium hydroxide
   b hydrochloric acid and caesium hydroxide
   c sulfuric acid and sodium hydroxide.

E 'Lo Salt' contains potassium chloride as too much sodium is bad for our hearts.

? 5 What acid and alkali were used to make the 'Lo Salt' shown in photo E?

6 Which is the odd one out: carbon dioxide, sodium carbonate, sodium sulfate? Explain your answer.

7 Write down the formula of the calcium sulfate shown in photo F.

Summary

When an acid reacts with an _____ a salt is formed. The hydrogen _____ from the acid react with the _____ ions from the alkali. The _____ formed depends on the _____ and alkali used.

acid   alkali   hydroxide   ions   salt

Relative masses

What is relative atomic mass?

A This balloon is filled with helium as it is a very light element. Each atom of helium has a mass of 0.000 000 000 000 000 000 000 0067 g.

All chemicals are made of atoms. As atoms are so tiny we cannot work with their individual masses, but we can compare the masses of all of the different elements. Each element is given a number to show how the mass of an atom of that particular element relates (compares) to the masses of atoms of other elements. This is called the **relative atomic mass** (**RAM** for short). As hydrogen is the smallest element, hydrogen is said to have a relative atomic mass of 1. An atom of carbon is twelve times heavier than one of hydrogen, and therefore its relative atomic mass is 12. Relative atomic masses do not have units because we are comparing masses.

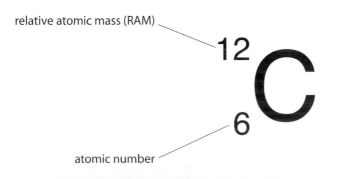

relative atomic mass (RAM)

atomic number

B The Periodic Table tells us the RAM of an element.

Molecules are made when atoms join together. Molecules may contain one type of atom only, for example the elements oxygen (O_2) and phosphorus (P_4). Most molecules are compounds with at least two types of element in them. For example sulfuric acid, H_2SO_4, contains two hydrogen atoms, one sulfur atom and four oxygen atoms.

?

1 a What is the relative atomic mass of hydrogen?
  b What is the relative atomic mass of carbon?

2 Why do we use relative atomic mass instead of the actual masses of elements?

3 Use the Periodic Table on page 242 to find out the names and relative atomic masses of these elements.
  a Na b U c Pb d Cs e Br

The **relative formula mass** tells us how heavy each molecule is compared to one hydrogen atom. This is called the **RFM** for short, and again has no units. The relative formula mass of a molecule can be found from the formula. We add up all the relative atomic masses of the elements in the molecular formula to find it.

The formula for water is H_2O.

atoms in formula	$2 \times H, 1 \times O$
RAMs for the elements	$H = 1, O = 16$
adding the masses	$(2 \times 1) + (1 \times 16) = 18$
therefore relative formula mass = 18	

RFMs are used to calculate how much product is made in a chemical reaction.

C This sulfur has been obtained from purifying natural gas. It contains S_8 molecules.

D Bromine has the formula Br_2.

Summary

As atoms are so _____ , we compare the masses of atoms by looking up their relative _____ masses. The smallest atom is _____ . For molecules we use _____ formula masses. These masses do not have _____ .

atomic	hydrogen	relative
	tiny	units

?

4 Work out the relative formula masses for the following molecules. Use the Periodic Table on page 242 to find the relative atomic masses.
 a bromine, Br_2
 b sulfur, S_8
 c sodium chloride, NaCl
 d propane, C_3H_8
 e calcium carbonate, $CaCO_3$
 f sodium carbonate, Na_2CO_3

5 Glucose is found in fizzy drinks and chocolate bars and has the formula $C_6H_{12}O_6$. What is its relative formula mass?

Yield calculations

How can we calculate the yield of a reaction?

One of the most useful rocks found in this country is limestone, which is mainly calcium carbonate.

When limestone is heated it forms calcium oxide (lime) and carbon dioxide. 1000 tonnes of *pure* calcium carbonate produces 560 tonnes of calcium oxide.

A Limestone is quarried from the ground.

B Lime can be used to neutralise acidic soils.

However, limestone is often impure. Manufacturers want to know how much calcium oxide they can get from 1000 tonnes of limestone. These impurities have to be taken into account when doing the calculations.

We know that 1000 tonnes of pure limestone gives 560 tonnes of calcium oxide. If the limestone is only 80% pure, then only 80% of 560 tonnes of calcium oxide will be produced.

$$\frac{80}{100} \times 560 = 448 \text{ tonnes}$$

The more impurities in the limestone, the less calcium oxide will be produced, so the manufacturer will make less money.

?

1   What is calcium oxide used for?

2   If the limestone was only 60% pure, how much calcium oxide would be obtained from 1000 tonnes of it?

We can work out the amount of product we should get using a balanced symbol equation and the RFMs of the different substances. This is called the **theoretical yield**. However many reactions do not produce this theoretical yield. This may be due to impurities or to the fact that not all of the reactants have turned into products.

The **percentage yield** of a reaction is the actual amount (**actual yield**) of product obtained, compared with the theoretical yield.

E
$$\text{percentage yield} = \frac{\text{actual yield}}{\text{theoretical yield}} \times 100\%$$

C The pharmaceutical industry makes thousands of compounds that are used in medicines.

Many medicines are complicated molecules, made in a series of reactions. Manufacturers need to know the yield of each reaction. For example, if each reaction only has a 50% yield (which is quite common), a lot of chemicals are not converted into the final product.

> For a two-step reaction, if the theoretical yield is 10 g:
>
> **Step 1:** actual yield = 50% of 10 g = 5 g
> **Step 2:** actual yield = 50% of 5 g = 2.5 g of product.

There are often different ways of making a compound, so manufacturers need to calculate the yield of each method so they can choose the best one.

?
4 There are three methods of making a medicine. The percentage yields are:
   method A: 51%, method B: 69% and method C: 43%.
   a Calculate the yield for each method if the theoretical yield is 200 g.
   b Which method should the company use? Explain your answer.

5 The iron ore in photo D contains iron oxide (Fe_2O_3). 800 tonnes of ore should contain 560 tonnes of iron. However, due to impurities in the ore, only 420 tonnes were obtained. What is the percentage purity?

?
3 a What is the difference between theoretical yield and actual yield?
   b What is percentage yield?

D Iron ore contains iron oxide, which is used to make iron.

Summary

Many reactions do not produce as much as the _____ yield. This is shown as the percentage _____. Manufacturers want as high a yield as possible for their _____. Often they only obtain a _____ of what they expect.

percentage	products
theoretical	yield

201

Making chemicals

How do we make chemicals on a large scale?

Many different chemicals are made in industry. In each case, the manufacturers have to choose how to make their product. This may involve just one reaction, or it may need a number of reactions. The first reaction must use raw materials that are always available. These are often obtained from the oil industry.

The manufacturers must also choose reactions that are safe. They will carry out a **risk assessment**, which looks at all of the safety risks involved, so that their workers are not in any danger.

?

1 What will happen if oil runs out?

2 What is a risk assessment?

New products are first developed by making small amounts in a laboratory. The process is then **scaled up** to make tonnes of product rather than a few grams.

A Plastics are just one group of substances made by the chemicals industry.

B Product development on a small scale.

C Large scale production of pigments for paint.

Once they have calculated the quantities of reactant needed, the chemical engineers must also consider the following.

• The type of apparatus to use. Industry needs large, strong containers rather than glassware, but these must be made from materials that are resistant to the chemicals being used.

• The conditions of temperature and pressure to use. A **catalyst** may be also used to speed up the reaction. (You will learn more about catalysts in Topic C6.12.)

• Methods of mixing and transferring chemicals automatically.

- Methods of heating and cooling. Something much more powerful than a Bunsen burner is needed to give the very high temperatures which may be needed.
- Methods for separating unused reactants or other impurities. Simple lab procedures such as fractional distillation have to be done on a much larger scale.
- A method of purifying the product.
- Measuring the yield and checking purity.

?

3 Why do you think that a manufacturing plant costs so much money?

4 What might happen if an impure medicine was sold?

5 What might happen if a fertiliser containing too much acid was sold to gardeners?

One example of a test on products is one to find out which antacid has the most active ingredient. Antacids contain bases that neutralise excess acid in our stomachs. We can react these with hydrochloric acid of the same concentration. The more 'active ingredient', the more acid is needed to neutralise it.

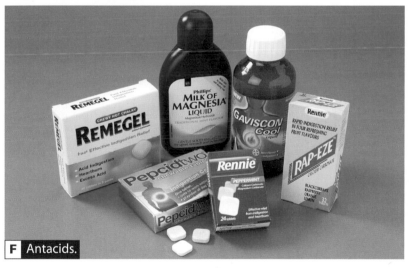

F Antacids.

Table G shows some sample results.

Brand	Active ingredient	Volume of acid needed to neutralise each tablet
X	aluminium hydroxide	30 cm³
Y	sodium carbonate	10 cm³
Z	magnesium hydroxide	20 cm³

G

?

6 a Which of these brands needs most acid to neutralise it?
b Which of these brands has the most base in it?

D Taking a sample of pigment for quality testing.

E Strict testing for purity is carried out on foods to make sure they do not contain any banned chemicals.

Summary

When new _____ are manufactured, the manufacturer has to consider what reactions to use, _____ and the reaction _____. The product must then be _____ from the reaction mixture, purified and then its _____ and _____ measured.

chemicals   conditions   purity
safety   separated   yield

Making a soluble salt

How can we make soluble salts?

A A solution of copper sulfate is used in a spray to protect these grapevines from insect pests.

B Sodium chloride in food tastes salty because it dissolves in the water on our tongue.

Soluble salts **dissolve** in water.

? 1 **a** Write down the names of two soluble salts
   b Explain what each salt is used for.

Soluble salts can be made by reacting an acid with a metal oxide or a metal carbonate.

metal oxide + acid → salt + water
metal carbonate + acid → salt + carbon dioxide + water

We can make the salt that we want by choosing the acid and the metal oxide or carbonate that we use. For example, we can make copper sulfate by adding copper carbonate (or copper oxide) to sulfuric acid.

Many metal oxides and carbonates do not dissolve in water. If we add the insoluble solid to the acid until solid is left over, we know that all the acid has reacted.

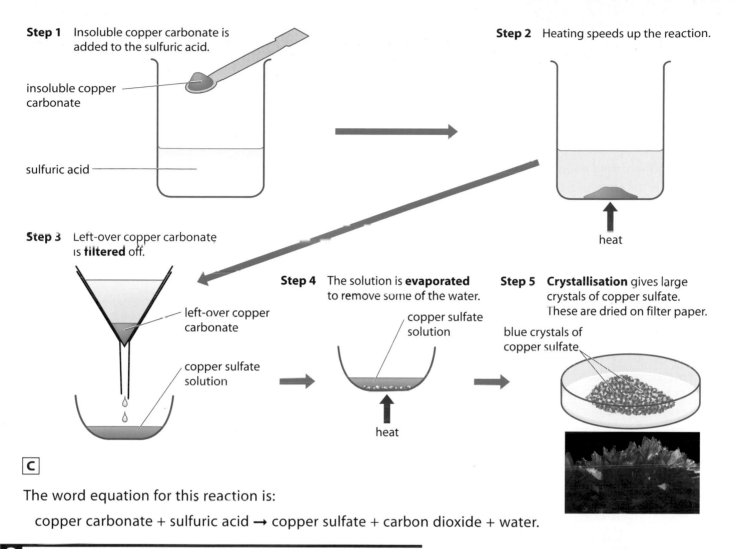

Step 1 Insoluble copper carbonate is added to the sulfuric acid.

insoluble copper carbonate

sulfuric acid

Step 2 Heating speeds up the reaction.

heat

Step 3 Left-over copper carbonate is **filtered** off.

left-over copper carbonate

copper sulfate solution

Step 4 The solution is **evaporated** to remove some of the water.

copper sulfate solution

heat

Step 5 **Crystallisation** gives large crystals of copper sulfate. These are dried on filter paper.

blue crystals of copper sulfate

C

The word equation for this reaction is:

copper carbonate + sulfuric acid → copper sulfate + carbon dioxide + water.

? Look at diagram C to help you answer these questions.

2 Bubbles form as the copper carbonate reacts with the acid in step 1. What causes the bubbles?

3 Which step separates the product from the reaction mixture?

4 Why is the solution above the crystals in step 4 still blue?

5 1.24 g of copper carbonate should give 2.50 g of copper sulfate crystals. Only 2.00 g of crystals were obtained. What is the percentage yield?

6 Write word equations to show how the following salts can be made:
   a cobalt chloride
   b zinc nitrate

7 A beaker contains a liquid and a solid. Think of as many reasons for this as you can.

8 Sodium carbonate is soluble in water. Explain why sodium chloride cannot be made by the method described above.

Summary

Soluble salts can be made by adding a metal _____ or _____ to an acid. Enough of the compound is added until all of the _____ has reacted. The _____ metal compound is filtered off and the solution heated to evaporate some of the _____. After cooling, _____ of the salt are formed. These are dried on _____ paper.

Salts made by this method include _____ sulfate.

acid   carbonate   copper   crystals
filter   oxide   unreacted   water

What is a titration?

Many reactions are carried out with the chemicals dissolved in water. This is because the dissolved chemicals can move about and react with each other.

Manufacturers need to know the concentrations of the solutions they use so they can work out the yields of reactions. The **concentration** of a solution is measured as the number of grams of **solute** dissolved in a **solvent** to make a *total volume* of 1 dm³ of solution. The units are g/dm³.

1 dm³ is the same as 1000 cm³ or 1 litre.

? **1 a** What does 'concentration' mean?
 b What are the units of concentration?

Titrations are used to find out the concentrations of solutions. In neutralisation reactions they are used to measure the precise volumes of acidic and alkaline solutions reacting together. We use an **indicator** which changes colour at the '**end-point**' (when the acid and alkali have exactly neutralised each other).

For example, you might need to find out the concentration of an acid, so you will need to use an alkali of known concentration.
A titration is carried out like this:
Step 1: Use a pipette to place a measured volume of alkali into a conical flask.
Step 2: Add an indicator and place the flask on a white tile. A common indicator is methyl orange, which is red in acid and yellow in alkali.

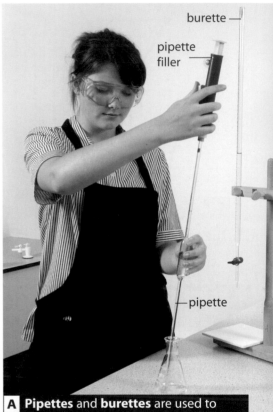

A **Pipettes** and **burettes** are used to measure accurate volumes of liquid.

Step 3: Pour the acid into the burette.

Step 4: Write down the reading on the burette, and then open the tap to let out 1 cm³ of the acid into the flask.

Step 5: Swirl the flask gently.

Step 6: Add another 1 cm³ of the acid and swirl the mixture again. Continue doing this until the indicator changes colour.

Step 7: Write down the volume of acid added. This is the end-point. This first titration gives the 'range-finder' reading.

Step 8: Wash out the conical flask and repeat steps 1–7, but this time add the acid from the burette drop by drop near the end-point. This will give a much more accurate result.

Step 9: Repeat the whole titration until you have two readings within 0.1 cm³ of each other. This will make the results more reliable.

If you know the volumes of the two solutions used, and the concentration of the alkali, you can calculate the concentration of the acid, using a special formula.

C

?

2 Why do you need to use a white tile in step 2?

3 Antacids are alkalis. What colour will methyl orange turn in a solution of an antacid?

4 Why do you need to swirl the flask in step 5?

5 Why do you need to do repeat readings within 0.1 cm³ in step 9?

6 Suggest some possible sources of error when you carry out a titration.

Summary

Titrations are used to find out the _____ of solutions. One solution is placed in a _____ using a _____. The other solution is placed in a _____. The _____ in the burette is added until an _____ changes colour. We can then work out the unknown concentration.

| burette concentration flask indicator pipette solution |

Rates of reaction

Can we measure the rate of a chemical reaction?

Manufacturers want to make as much of their product as possible in the shortest amount of time. They want reactions that are fast but safe, as well as having a high yield. This will help them to make the greatest amount of money.

?
1 Why do manufacturers want fast reactions?

2 Give an example of a very fast chemical reaction.

The speed of a reaction is called the **rate of reaction**.

We can follow the rate of a reaction by measuring how quickly the reactants are used up, or measuring how quickly the products are formed. This can be done in a number of ways:
• if the reaction produces a gas, it can be collected in a gas syringe
• we can weigh a reaction mixture
• we can watch the formation of a colour or an insoluble precipitate. For example, if iodine is formed the mixture will go brown.

Calcium carbonate reacts with hydrochloric acid to form carbon dioxide gas. Diagram B shows how you can measure the volume of gas given off.

A This reaction would be far too fast to use in industry.

calcium carbonate + hydrochloric acid → calcium chloride + carbon dioxide + water
$$CaCO_3 \text{ (s)} \quad + \quad 2HCl \text{ (aq)} \quad \rightarrow \quad CaCl_2 \text{ (aq)} \quad + \quad CO_2 \text{ (g)} \quad + H_2O \text{ (l)}$$

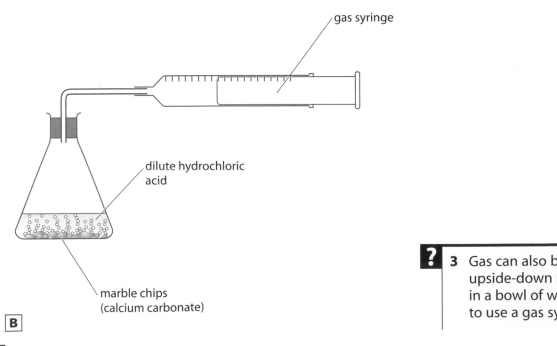

gas syringe

dilute hydrochloric acid

marble chips (calcium carbonate)

B

?
3 Gas can also be collected in an upside-down measuring cylinder in a bowl of water. Why is it better to use a gas syringe?

Graph C shows how much gas was given off in the reaction.

The graph is steepest at the start, which means that the rate of the reaction is the greatest here. This is because this is the point when there is most acid and marble chips. As the reactants are used up the reaction gets slower and the graph flattens off. When the graph is totally flat (after 250 seconds), the reaction has finished. One or both of the reactants has been used up.

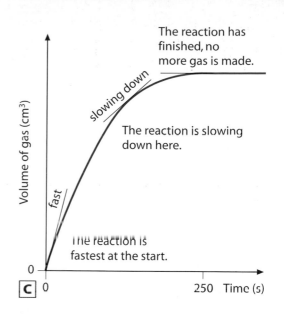

The reaction has finished, no more gas is made.

slowing down

The reaction is slowing down here.

fast

The reaction is fastest at the start.

C 0   250   Time (s)

Volume of gas (cm³)

? 4 Marble chips are usually left in the flask at the end of this reaction. Which reactant has been used up?

The reaction can also be followed by finding how the mass changes. Diagram D shows the same experiment carried out on a balance. The loss of mass can be measured every minute until the reaction has finished.

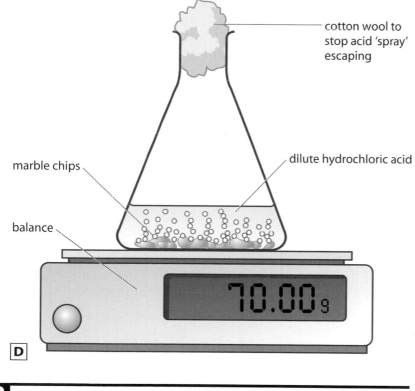

cotton wool to stop acid 'spray' escaping

dilute hydrochloric acid

marble chips

balance

70.00 g

D

? 5 a What gas is produced when marble chips react with acid?
   b Explain why the mass of the flask in diagram D will go down during the reaction.

6 Sketch a graph showing how the mass of the apparatus would change during this reaction.

Summary

The speed of a reaction is called the _____ of reaction. The reaction is _____ at the start and _____ down as the _____ are used up. The _____ finishes when one of the _____ has been completely used up. We can find out the volume of _____ given off or look at _____ changes.

fastest	gas	mass	rate
reactants	reaction	slows	

209

Speeding up reactions 1

How do concentration and surface area affect the rate of reaction?

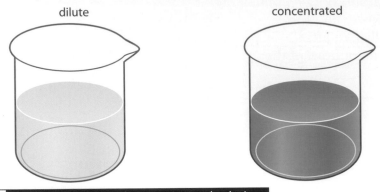

A A dilute solution and a concentrated solution.

Concentration

A concentrated solution has lots of solute dissolved in it. A concentrated solution has more particles of solute in each cm³ of solution than a dilute solution.

If we increase the concentration of one of the reactants, the reaction happens faster because there are more particles to react with each other. Table B shows the results of an experiment with marble chips and different concentrations of acid.

Solution	Volume of acid (cm³)	Volume of water (cm³)	Time to collect 20 cm³ of gas (s)
A	10	40	200
B	20	30	100
C	30	20	67
D	40	10	50
E	50	0	40

B

?

1 a Which solution is the most concentrated?

   b Which solution gives the fastest reaction?

2 Why didn't the experiment use a solution containing no acid?

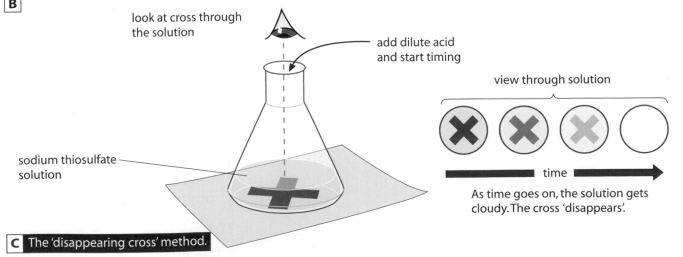

look at cross through the solution

add dilute acid and start timing

view through solution

sodium thiosulfate solution

time

As time goes on, the solution gets cloudy. The cross 'disappears'.

C The 'disappearing cross' method.

The effect of concentration on a reaction rate can also be studied using the 'disappearing cross' method shown in diagram C. As the two solutions are mixed, they react to form solid particles of sulfur. The sulfur makes the solution cloudy. As the solution gets cloudier it gets difficult to see through. If we time how long it takes for the cross to disappear, we can measure the rate of the reaction. The faster the cross disappears, the faster the reaction. We find that the more concentrated the solutions, the faster is the reaction.

Surface area

If you cut a potato into small pieces it will cook faster than a whole potato. This is because more surface is exposed to the boiling water. It is the same with chemical reactions. Graph D shows what happens if you react acid with marble chips of different sizes.

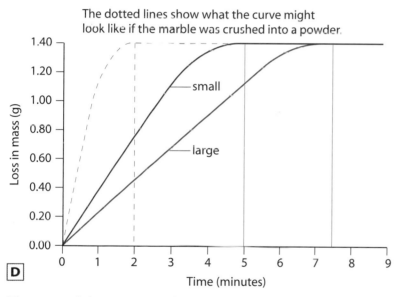

The dotted lines show what the curve might look like if the marble was crushed into a powder.

D

The rate of the reaction does not change the total amounts of the products – only the speed at which they are formed.

Summary

The _____ of a reaction depends on the _____ of a reactant solution. The higher the concentration, the _____ the reaction. If a solid reactant is broken into smaller pieces, its surface area _____. This means that the rate of _____ also increases.

concentration   faster   increases
rate   reaction

3 What should be kept constant in this reaction to make it a fair test?

4 Which reaction finished first?

5 How would you explain these results?

6 This is the symbol equation for the reaction between marble chips and hydrochloric acid.

$$CaCO_3 \text{ (s)} + 2HCl \text{ (aq)} \rightarrow CaCl_2 \text{ (aq)} + CO_2 \text{ (g)} + H_2O \text{ (l)}$$

a Why does the mass decrease as the reaction proceeds?

b 10 g of marble chips should give 4.4 g of carbon dioxide. How much carbon dioxide would be formed if the marble was only 90% pure?

7 This is the equation for the reaction between magnesium and hydrochloric acid.

$$Mg \text{ (s)} + 2HCl \text{ (aq)} \rightarrow MgCl_2 \text{ (aq)} + H_2 \text{ (g)}$$

24 g of magnesium gives 2 g of hydrogen. Why can't we study changes in mass if 0.24 g of magnesium is used?

Temperature

We keep food in the fridge to slow down the chemical reactions that occur when food 'goes off'. Just as lowering the temperature slows down reactions, heating speeds them up.

The experiment with the marble chips and acid can be repeated at different temperatures. Some results are shown in graph A. You can see that when the temperature of a reaction is increased, more gas is formed in the same time – the reaction is faster.

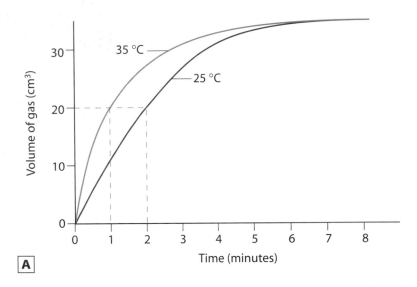

A

? 1 Name two things that should be kept constant during this reaction to make the comparison fair.

We can repeat the disappearing cross experiment at different temperatures. Table B has sample results showing how the time for the cross to disappear changes with temperature.

Temperature of reaction mixture (°C)	Time for cross to disappear (s)
20	360
30	180
40	91
50	46
60	23

B

? 2 Why has the mixture gone cloudy?

3 Plot a graph showing how the time taken for the cross to disappear changes as you increase the temperature. Plot temperature on the x-axis and time on the y-axis.

4 How long would the reaction take at 45 °C?

Catalysts

Many chemical reactions are very slow, but some can be speeded up using a catalyst. This is a chemical that is not used up in a reaction and remains unchanged at the end. It can therefore be removed and reused. Each catalyst only works on a particular reaction, so processes with several steps may need several different catalysts.

We can show the effect of a catalyst by looking at this reaction:

hydrogen peroxide → water + oxygen

$$2H_2O_2 \text{ (aq)} \rightarrow 2H_2O \text{ (l)} + O_2 \text{ (g)}$$

Hydrogen peroxide solution only decomposes very slowly. However, as soon as a catalyst called manganese dioxide is added, bubbles of oxygen can be seen.

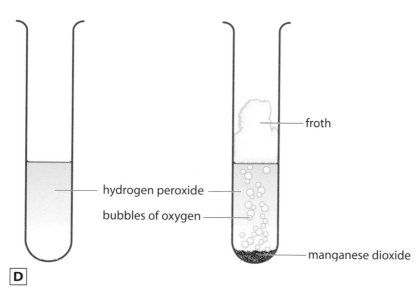

— froth

— hydrogen peroxide

— bubbles of oxygen

— manganese dioxide

D

Catalysts are important in industry because they help to speed up reactions without having to heat the reactants to high temperatures. Heating costs a lot of money. Manufacturers change the conditions of temperature and concentration, or vary the catalysts they use, to control the rates of their chemical reactions.

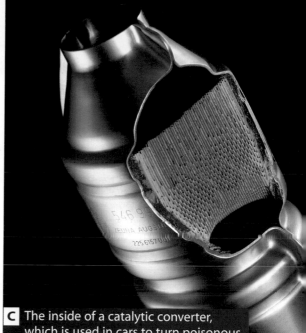

C The inside of a catalytic converter, which is used in cars to turn poisonous exhaust gases into harmless ones.

E Nickel is a catalyst used to obtain the hydrogen needed for the Haber process.

?

5 a What is a catalyst?
  b What is the advantage of using a catalyst in industry?

6 a How could you show that there was no change in the mass of the manganese dioxide during the experiment in diagram D?
  b How could you measure the volume of oxygen formed?

7 Liver contains a biological catalyst which also decomposes hydrogen peroxide. How could you show this practically?

Summary

Chemical reactions are faster at _____ temperatures. _____ speed up reactions without being used up, and are very important in _____ .

catalysts   higher   industry

Using calculations

What do you know about making chemicals?

Emma and Ravi decided that they wanted to set up a small company to make special chemicals.

A

Ravi and Emma have been asked to make titanium dioxide, TiO_2. This will be used to make pavements for some streets in London. The titanium dioxide absorbs acidic exhaust fumes from cars, and so reduces air pollution.

B The first anti-pollution paving slabs being laid in London.

1 Cars produce a lot of acidic gases when they burn petrol.
   a Why do some cars have a catalytic converted fitted to their exhaust?
   b What is a catalyst?
   c Why are catalysts important in industry?

C Black ilmenite and white titanium dioxide.

Ravi found that titanium dioxide was extracted from an ore called ilmenite, $FeTiO_3$. The first step is to react the ilmenite with sulfuric acid, H_2SO_4.

Ravi and Emma decide to try out the reactions on a small scale first. Ravi starts by calculating the amounts of the different reactants that he needs.

2 **a** What does 'relative atomic mass' mean?
   b Why do we use RAMs instead of the real masses of atoms?

3 Use the Periodic Table on page 242 to help you to answer these questions.
   a Write down the relative atomic masses of iron, titanium and oxygen.
   b What is the relative formula mass of ilmenite?
   c What is the relative formula mass of titanium dioxide.

4 The theoretical yield from 304 g of ilmenite is 160 g of titanium dioxide.
  a What does 'theoretical yield' mean?
  b Why is the actual yield usually less than the theoretical yield?
  c What is the actual yield if the ilmenite is only 60% pure?

5 Why does Ravi want as high a yield as possible of titanium dioxide?

6 Titanium dioxide reacts with acid.
  a Is titanium dioxide a base or a salt?
  b Write a word equation for the reaction of titanium dioxide with hydrochloric acid.

Emma and Ravi want the reaction to happen quickly. They crush the solid ilmenite before reacting it with sulfuric acid.

7 a How does crushing the ilmenite help to speed up the reaction?
  b Will crushing the ilmenite increase the yield from the reaction? Explain your answer.

8 Emma uses a high concentration of acid when she reacts it with the ilmenite.
  a What does 'concentration' mean?
  b Why does Emma use a high concentration of acid?
  c Why must this process have a risk assessment?

9 Only the ilmenite reacts with the acid. The rest of the ore is left as a solid waste.
  a Describe how the reacted solution can be separated from the waste.
  b Draw a diagram to show how you could do this in a school laboratory.

Emma wants to check the concentration of the sulfuric acid she is using. She has some sodium hydroxide, and she knows its concentration.

10 a How can Emma use litmus paper to find out which bottle contains sulfuric acid and which contains sodium hydroxide?
  b What will happen if she adds sodium hydroxide solution to the sulfuric acid?
  c Write an ionic equation to show this reaction.

d Diagram D shows some of the apparatus Emma will need to check the concentration of the acid. What are the names of A and B?

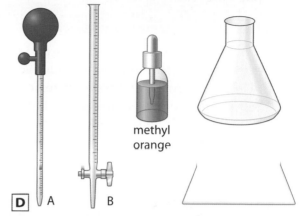

methyl orange

D A   B

e Describe how Emma can use the sodium hydroxide and the apparatus shown in D to find the concentration of the sulfuric acid.

Once Emma and Ravi know how to carry out the reactions, they need to work out how they will produce larger quantities of the product.

11 Write down three things they will have to think about when they scale up the reactions.

Ravi found another supplier of sulfuric acid. The supplier provided some details of how their sulfuric acid was made.

12 Sulfuric acid is made in a three-step process, which can be summarised as:

sulfur + oxygen + water → sulfuric acid
$$2S + 3O_2 + 2H_2O \rightarrow 2H_2SO_4$$

  a What raw material would supply the oxygen for this reaction?
  b 64 tonnes of sulfur should produce 196 tonnes of sulfuric acid. However only 147 tonnes were produced. What is the percentage yield for this reaction?

13 a Describe how sulfuric acid would react with magnesium.
  b Write a word equation for this reaction.
  c Write a symbol equation for this reaction.
  d What would you see when sulfuric acid reacts with calcium carbonate?
  e Write a word equation for this reaction.
  f Write a symbol equation for this reaction.

The wave model of radiation

How do we use different kinds of radiation?

We see things around us when our eyes detect light waves. These are a form of **electromagnetic** radiation. There are other kinds of electromagnetic radiation such as radio waves, infrared radiation and X-rays. These electromagnetic waves have different properties, which means that they can be used for different purposes.

Astronomers use radio telescopes to look for radio waves from outer space. These can tell us about the stars and galaxies. They could also give us signs of intelligent life elsewhere in the Universe, but we have not picked up any messages yet. The radio waves that we detect from outer space are similar to the ones that carry radio and television signals to your home.

I work in a factory that makes microwave ovens. Microwaves are absorbed by water molecules in food and produce heat. Microwaves allow food to be cooked very quickly. Microwaves are also used for satellite communication.

A Gareth.

B Keiko.

I am a telephone engineer. Information can be sent down fibre optic cables as visible light or infrared radiation. This information can be sound, pictures, video or text. My hobby is photography, which also involves using visible light. I took this photo of my two boys.

C Mike.

James and Tom.

All objects give out infrared radiation. The hotter the object is, the more infrared radiation it emits. We use infrared cameras to try and find people who are trapped in buildings or under rubble or snow.

D Sam.

?

1 How are radio waves useful?

2 What can microwaves be used for?

3 a Which emits more infrared radiation, a cup of tea or the Sun?
   b Explain your answer.

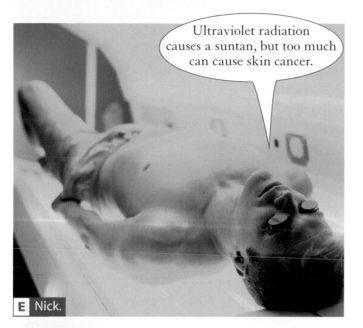

Ultraviolet radiation causes a suntan, but too much can cause skin cancer.

E Nick.

I use X-rays to produce pictures of broken bones.

F Judith.

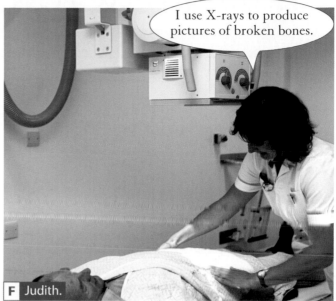

I use ultrasound to look at unborn babies. Ultrasound is better than X-rays for looking at babies because X-rays have more energy and can harm the fetus.

G Coral.

I use gamma radiation to treat people who have cancer. The gamma rays have enough energy to kill the cancer cells. Gamma rays are also used to sterilise surgical equipment.

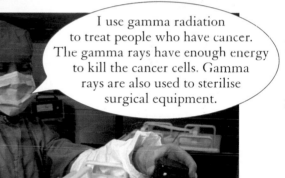

H Giacomo.

?

4 a Which types of radiation are used in hospitals?
   b How are these types of radiation used?

5 Which of the people mentioned on these two pages are most likely to be:
   a safe when using radiation
   b at risk when using radiation?

6 Explain how people who might be at risk of being harmed by radiation in their job make sure that they are not harmed.

Summary

_____ waves are used to transmit radio and TV signals. All hot objects give out _____ radiation. _____ is used to look at unborn babies. _____ radiation can be used to cook food quickly. _____ light gives you a suntan and _____ radiation is used to kill cancer cells.

gamma   infrared   microwave
radio   ultrasound   ultraviolet

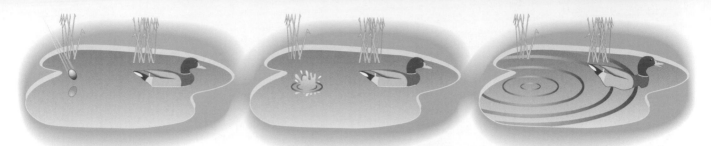

A When waves spread out across the surface of the pond, the duck will move up and down because the waves are transferring energy. The duck will not move outwards with the waves because the water itself is not moving outwards.

Waves are disturbances that carry **energy** from one place to another without any material, or **matter**, being transferred.

Transverse waves

If you shake a rope up and down the energy in the rope is transferred horizontally, at right angles to the direction of shaking. The same is true if you drop a stone into a pond. The stone causes the water to move up and down, but the wave energy spreads out horizontally across the surface of the pond. In both examples, the vertical movement is at right angles to the direction that the energy is being transferred. Water waves, waves on ropes and light waves are all examples of **transverse** waves.

?
1 What are waves?

2 Why don't the water waves move the duck across the pond?

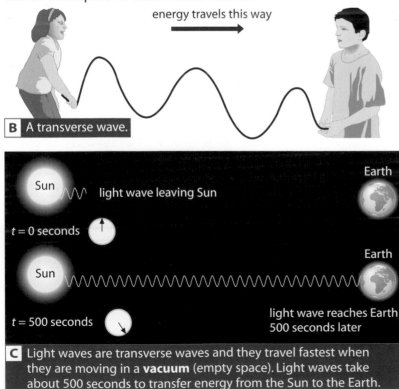

energy travels this way

B A transverse wave.

Sun ⋀⋁⋀ light wave leaving Sun

Earth

$t = 0$ seconds

Sun

Earth

$t = 500$ seconds

light wave reaches Earth 500 seconds later

C Light waves are transverse waves and they travel fastest when they are moving in a **vacuum** (empty space). Light waves take about 500 seconds to transfer energy from the Sun to the Earth.

?
3 **a** What is a transverse wave?
   b Give three examples of transverse waves.

Longitudinal waves

Sound waves, ultrasound and some waves in springs are **longitudinal** waves. Longitudinal waves in springs are a series of places where the spring is stretched or squashed. Sound waves are a series of pressure changes. All longitudinal waves need a **medium** or material to travel through. Longitudinal waves cannot travel through a vacuum.

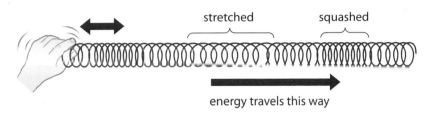

stretched   squashed

energy travels this way

D A longitudinal wave in a spring.

In longitudinal waves the direction of travel of the wave is in the same direction as the disturbance that caused the wave.

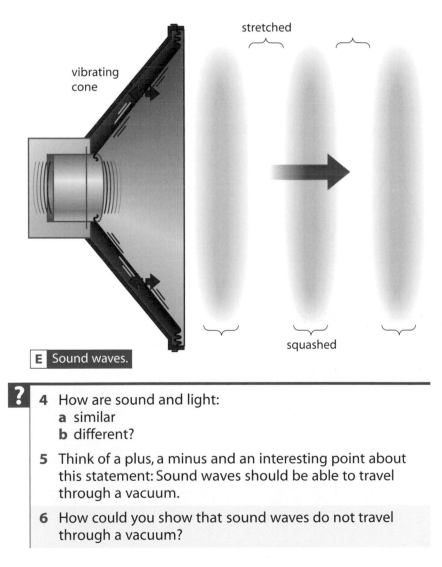

stretched

vibrating cone

squashed

E Sound waves.

?

4 How are sound and light:
  a similar
  b different?

5 Think of a plus, a minus and an interesting point about this statement: Sound waves should be able to travel through a vacuum.

6 How could you show that sound waves do not travel through a vacuum?

Summary

Waves transfer _____ from one place to another without any overall movement of _____. Light waves are _____ waves and sound waves are _____. Light waves can travel through a _____ but sound waves need a _____ to travel through.

energy	longitudinal	matter
medium	transverse	vacuum

Describing waves

How can we describe waves?

We can describe any wave by its **wavelength**, **frequency** and **amplitude**.

Wavelength

The wavelength is the distance between the same points on two waves.

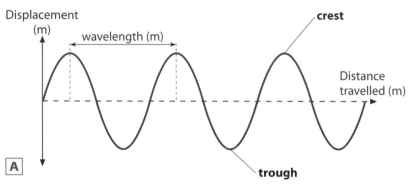

Displacement (m)

wavelength (m)

crest

Distance travelled (m)

A

trough

Amplitude

The amplitude of a wave is its height. The amplitude is always measured from the undisturbed position. The units for amplitude are metres.

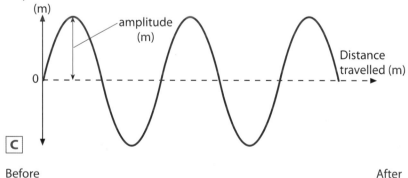

Displacement (m)

amplitude (m)

Distance travelled (m)

0

C

1 What is the wavelength of a wave?

2 What unit is wavelength measured in?

3 What is the wavelength of each of the waves in diagram B?

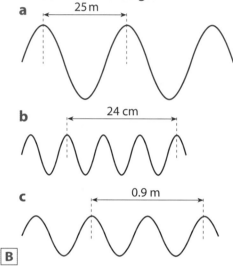

a   25 m

b   24 cm

c   0.9 m

B

Before

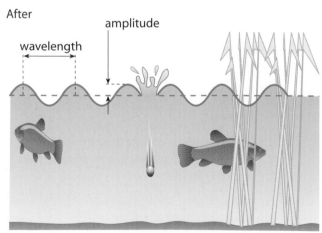

stone

surface of pond

After

amplitude

wavelength

D

4 What is the amplitude of a wave?

5 What is the amplitude of each of the waves shown in diagram E?

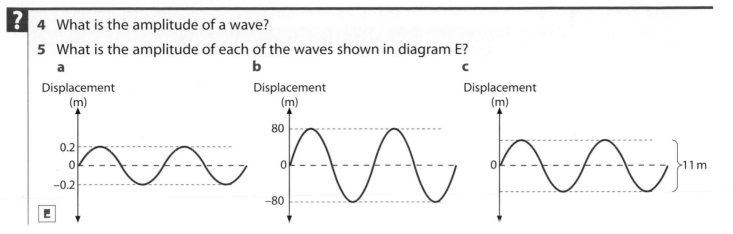

a   **b**   **c**

E

Frequency

The frequency of a wave is the number of complete waves that are produced by the source in one second. This is the same as the number of waves that pass a point each second. Frequency is measured in **hertz (Hz)**.

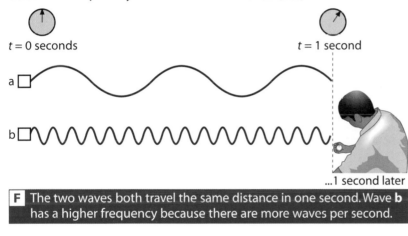

$t = 0$ seconds $t = 1$ second

a ☐

b ☐

...1 second later

F   The two waves both travel the same distance in one second. Wave **b** has a higher frequency because there are more waves per second.

6 What does the word 'frequency' mean?

7 Find the frequency of each of the following waves:
  a 10 water waves pass a point each second
  b 160 sound waves pass a point in 20 seconds
  c a person makes four waves on a rope in 0.5 seconds.

Changing the amplitude of a sound wave affects its loudness. A sound wave with a large amplitude is loud. A sound wave with a small amplitude is quiet. Changing the frequency of a sound wave affects its pitch. A sound wave with a low frequency has a low pitch and a sound wave with a high frequency has a high pitch.

8 Radio waves, microwaves and X-rays all travel the same distance in one second. Explain how this is possible if they all have different wavelengths.

Summary

The _____ is the distance between two crests on a wave. The _____ is the distance from the middle of a wave to its highest point. The number of complete waves passing a fixed point each second is called the _____ of the wave and it is measured in _____. Amplitude and wavelength both have units of _____ .

amplitude   frequency   hertz
metres   wavelength

The speed of waves

How fast do waves travel?

The distance that a wave travels in one second is called its **wave speed**. You can work out the speed of a wave if you know its frequency and its wavelength.

E | wave speed = frequency × wavelength
  (m/s)   (Hz)   (m)

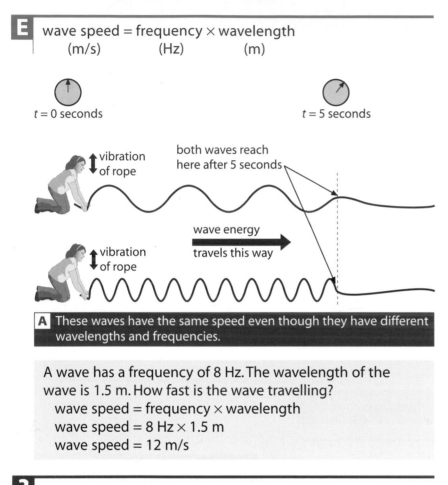

A These waves have the same speed even though they have different wavelengths and frequencies.

A wave has a frequency of 8 Hz. The wavelength of the wave is 1.5 m. How fast is the wave travelling?
wave speed = frequency × wavelength
wave speed = 8 Hz × 1.5 m
wave speed = 12 m/s

? 1 A water wave has a frequency of 4 Hz and a wavelength of 2.5 metres. Calculate its wave speed.

2 What are the speeds of the following waves:
   a a wave of wavelength 15 m and frequency 12 Hz
   b a wave of wavelength 25 m and frequency 8 Hz?

The speed of sound

All sound waves travel at approximately 330 m/s in air. This means that a sound wave will travel a distance of 330 metres through air in one second. The speed of a sound wave is not affected by its frequency. If the frequency of the sound wave increases, then the wavelength of the sound wave decreases by the same factor so that the wave speed is not changed.

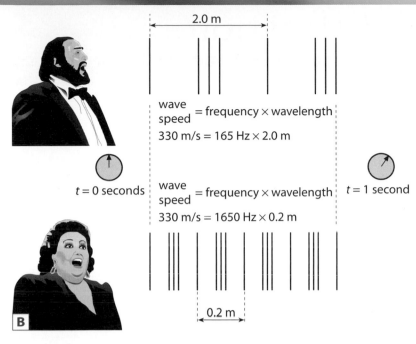

$$\text{wave speed} = \text{frequency} \times \text{wavelength}$$
$$330 \text{ m/s} = 165 \text{ Hz} \times 2.0 \text{ m}$$

$$\text{wave speed} = \text{frequency} \times \text{wavelength}$$
$$330 \text{ m/s} = 1650 \text{ Hz} \times 0.2 \text{ m}$$

$t = 0$ seconds $t = 1$ second

2.0 m

0.2 m

B

?

3 The frequency of a sound wave is doubled. What will happen to its wavelength?

4 A wave has a wavelength of 11 metres and a frequency of 30 Hz.
 a What is its speed?
 b Could it be a sound wave? Explain your answer.

5 Pablo says that doubling the frequency of a water wave makes it travel twice as fast. Is he right or wrong? Explain your answer.

The speed of light

Light waves travel at approximately 300 million metres per second in air. Just as with sound waves, changing the frequency of the wave does not change the speed of the light wave. Changing the frequency or wavelength of light causes the colour to change, but light of all colours travels at the same speed.

The other types of electromagnetic radiation also travel at this speed. This speed is called the **speed of light**.

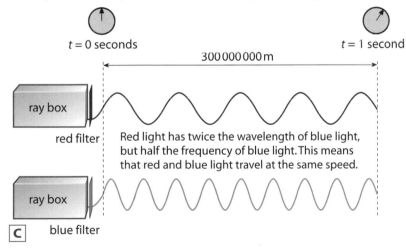

$t = 0$ seconds $t = 1$ second

300 000 000 m

ray box
red filter

Red light has twice the wavelength of blue light, but half the frequency of blue light. This means that red and blue light travel at the same speed.

ray box
C blue filter

?

6 How do red light and blue light compare in terms of their:
 a wavelength
 b frequency
 c speed?

7 **a** Which travels the fastest in air – light or sound?
 b Describe a simple experiment you could carry out to show that your answer is correct.

Summary

The wave speed is the _____ that a wave travels in one _____. It can be calculated by multiplying frequency and _____. Changing the amplitude or _____ of a wave does not affect its speed. As the frequency of a wave increases, the wavelength _____ so the speed remains the _____.

decreases	distance	frequency
same	second	wavelength

Reflection and diffraction

What are reflection and diffraction?

Waves carry energy from one place to another. When these waves come into contact with a **plane** (flat) surface, they will be **reflected**. This happens for water waves, light waves and sound waves.

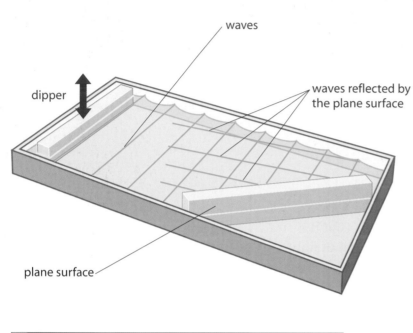

waves

waves reflected by the plane surface

dipper

plane surface

A A ripple tank is used to show how water waves behave.

The same thing happens for light waves and sound waves. When a beam of light hits a plane surface, the light waves are reflected. We can sometimes hear reflected sound waves as echoes.

> The angle of reflection is equal to the angle of incidence for all waves that are reflected.

? 1 What is a 'plane' surface?

2 What happens when water waves hit a plane surface?

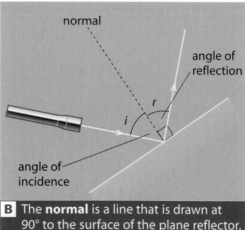

normal

angle of reflection

angle of incidence

r

i

B The **normal** is a line that is drawn at 90° to the surface of the plane reflector. It is used as a reference line for measuring the sizes of the angles of incidence and reflection.

? 3 a What is a normal?
   b How is it used?

4 A ray of light hits a plane mirror. Its angle of incidence is 48°. What is the angle of reflection?

5 What is angle x in diagram C?

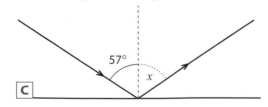

57°

x

C

Diffraction

Waves can spread out when they pass through a gap. This is called **diffraction**. The most diffraction occurs when the size of the gap is similar to the wavelength of the wave that is passing through it. Light can be diffracted, but it needs a very small gap to pass through as the wavelength of light is very small.

D The gap between the cliffs is similar in size to the wavelength of the waves. They are being diffracted as they go through the gap.

E Sound waves can be diffracted through doorways or other gaps.

?

6 Draw diagrams to show what happens when:
  a a light wave hits a mirror at 34° and is then reflected
  b a water wave bounces off a wall at an angle of 55° to the normal.

7 Look at drawing E. Why can the boy hear what the people are saying but not see them?

8 'Reflection can take place at a plane surface.' Write down all the possible ways this could happen.

9 Explain how you could use plane mirrors to see a friend who is hiding from you around a corner.

Summary

_____ waves, light waves and sound waves can all be _____ at a plane surface. The angle of _____ is always the same as the angle of reflection. These angles are measured from the _____, which is a line drawn at _____ to the mirror. Waves can be _____ when they pass through a gap that is a similar size to their _____.

diffracted   incidence   90°   normal
reflected   water   wavelength

Refraction

What is refraction?

The speed of a wave depends on what it is travelling through. For example, when water waves travel from deeper to shallower water they change speed. Water waves travel fastest in deep water and slowest in shallow water. The frequency of the water waves does not change, but the wavelength does.

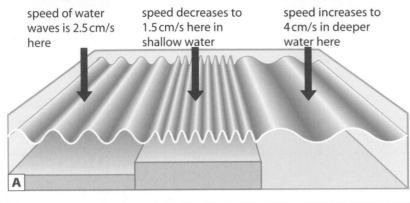

speed of water waves is 2.5 cm/s here

speed decreases to 1.5 cm/s here in shallow water

speed increases to 4 cm/s in deeper water here

A

B You can't see the boy clearly because light bends as it leaves the water.

 1 What happens to the speed of a water wave when it moves from shallow water into deep water?

The change in speed *can* also lead to a change in direction. This change in direction is called **refraction**.

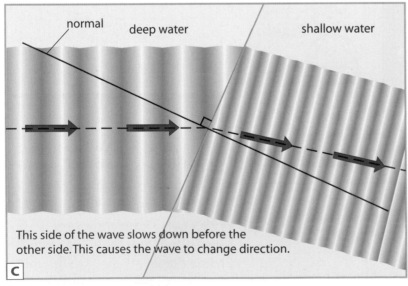

normal   deep water   shallow water

This side of the wave slows down before the other side. This causes the wave to change direction.

C

Sound waves travel faster in water than they do in air and they will travel even faster in a solid metal such as copper. The material that the wave is travelling through is called the medium. If you change the medium that the wave is travelling through, or along, then you will change the speed of the wave.

? **2** What is a 'medium'?

3 Through which medium do sound waves travel fastest?

Light waves slow down when they go from air into glass or water. As the light waves slow down, they also change direction and bend towards the normal. The light waves will speed up and bend away from the normal when they re-enter the air.

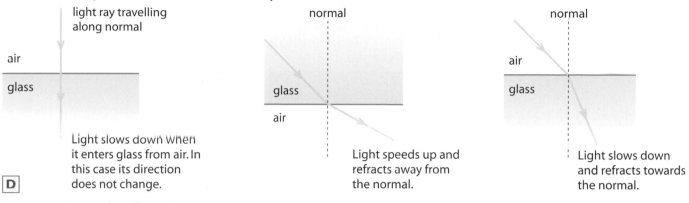

light ray travelling along normal

air

glass

Light slows down when it enters glass from air. In this case its direction does not change.

normal

glass

air

Light speeds up and refracts away from the normal.

normal

air

glass

Light slows down and refracts towards the normal.

D

At a certain angle of incidence, called the **critical angle**, the angle of refraction is 90° and the refracted ray of light travels along the boundary between the two materials. If the angle of incidence is bigger than this, the ray of light is reflected at the boundary and stays inside the medium. This is known as **total internal reflection**.

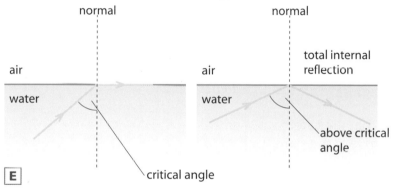

normal

air

water

critical angle

normal

total internal reflection

air

water

above critical angle

E

A How could you find out if light refracts more in different materials?

F

Summary

When light waves travel from air to glass they _____ down and change _____. This is called _____. Water waves change speed and direction if the _____ of the water changes. If the angle of _____ is big enough the wave will be _____ and stay inside the medium. This is called total _____ reflection.

depth   direction   incidence
internal   reflected   refraction   slow

?

4 Why do light waves change direction when they go from air into glass?

5 What is total internal reflection?

6 What two changes can happen to waves when they move from one medium into another?

7 Draw diagrams to show:
   a water waves changing direction and speed
   b a light ray refracting when it travels from air into glass.

8 Which is the odd one out in each of these lists? Explain your answers.
   a sound wave, light wave, water wave
   b reflection, refraction, diffraction.

9 How are refraction and reflection:
   a similar
   b different?

What is interference?

Waves carry energy from one place to another, without any overall movement of matter. When two waves overlap they can affect each other. This is called **interference**.

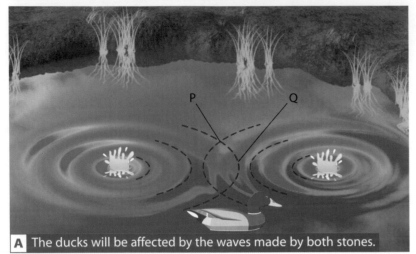

B The colours on a butterfly's wings are due to interference effects.

A The ducks will be affected by the waves made by both stones.

If the two waves are 'in step' with each other so that the crests of both waves arrive at the same point, they will combine to form a bigger wave. This is called **constructive interference**. The resulting wave produced has twice the amplitude of either of the initial waves.

If the two waves overlap with one another so that they are 'out of step', then a crest from one wave will arrive at the same time as a trough from the other. The two waves will cancel each other out. This is called **destructive interference**.

Constructive interference.

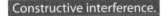

C Destructive interference.

?

1 What is:
   a constructive interference
   b destructive interference?

2 Look at diagram A. What would the motion of a beach ball be like if it were placed at:
   a position P
   b position Q?

Interference of light waves

When light waves overlap, the interference that occurs will produce changes in the brightness of the light. The brightest light will be where constructive interference occurs, and there will be dark areas where destructive interference occurs. The light and dark stripes produced when this occurs are called interference 'fringes'.

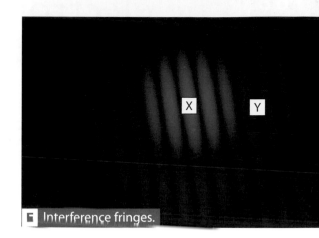
E Interference fringes.

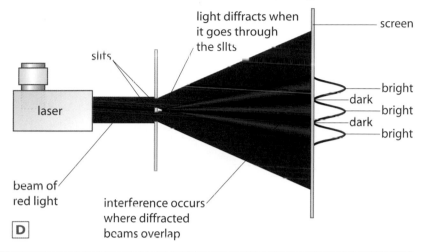
D

Labels in diagram: light diffracts when it goes through the slits; slits; screen; bright; dark; bright; dark; bright; laser; beam of red light; interference occurs where diffracted beams overlap

?
3 Look at photo E.
  a Two waves have arrived at point X. Are these waves in step or out of step?
  b Explain how you worked out your answer to part **a**.
  c Is the interference at point X constructive or destructive?

4 Explain what is happening at point Y in photo E. Give as much detail as you can.

Interference of sound waves

Sound waves from two sound sources can produce interference. The sound will be loudest when constructive interference occurs and quietest when destructive interference occurs.

We can see diffraction and interference happening directly in water waves. We can also see or hear the effects of diffraction and interference in light waves and sound waves. This is evidence that light and sound travel as waves.

?
5 Look at diagram F. What would you hear if you were sitting at:
  a position X
  b position Y?

6 What would you expect to happen if a sound wave and a light wave were to overlap? Explain your answer.

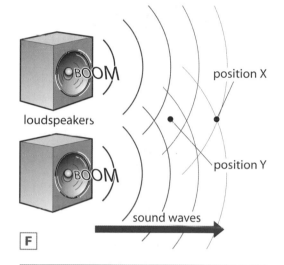
F

Labels in diagram: loudspeakers; position X; position Y; sound waves

Summary

When waves _____, they produce an effect called _____. When waves overlap in step, _____ interference occurs. When waves overlap out of step they _____ out and _____ interference occurs. Constructive interference results in _____ loudness for sound waves. Destructive interference for light waves produces _____ fringes.

cancel   constructive   dark
destructive   interference
increased   overlap

The electromagnetic spectrum

What is electromagnetic radiation?

Light is part of a family of waves called the electromagnetic spectrum. Electromagnetic waves (or EM radiation) do not need a medium to travel through. All electromagnetic waves travel 300 000 000 metres every second in a vacuum.

A beam of electromagnetic radiation delivers energy in packets called **photons**. Photons of high frequency electromagnetic radiation deliver more energy than photons of low frequency radiation. The **intensity** of a beam of electromagnetic radiation is the energy that arrives at a surface each second and depends on the number of photons arriving each second.

A

? **1** How fast do light waves move in a vacuum?

radio waves	microwaves	infrared	visible	ultraviolet	X-rays	gamma rays
lowest photon energy			increasing photon energy			highest photon energy
longest wavelength lowest frequency			wavelength decreases frequency increases			shortest wavelength highest frequency
• emitted by radio and TV transmitters • used to send radio and TV programmes • detected by aerials and radios/TVs	• emitted by radio transmitters, mobile phones and microwave cookers • used to carry information and to cook food • can damage living tissue by heating the water in it • detected by aerials and radios/mobile phones	• emitted by warm and hot objects, and by TV remote controls or car locks • detected by skin and thermometers • too much infrared can burn the skin	• emitted by hot objects • detected by eyes and photographic film	• emitted from very hot objects including the Sun • causes human skin to tan but can also cause skin cancer • detected by photographic film	• go through flesh but not bone • used to look at bones inside the body • can cause cancer • detected by photographic film	• emitted from radioactive substances • used to sterilise medical instruments • can penetrate deep inside the body • can cause cancer

B The electromagnetic spectrum.

? **2** Name three different types of electromagnetic wave.

3 How are radio waves and microwaves different?

The different colours of visible light all have different frequencies. As they all travel at the same speed, they must also have different wavelengths.

? **4** What changes when you change the colour of light?

5 Look at diagram C.
   a Which colour of light will have the highest energy photons?
   b Which will have the lowest energy photons?

wavelength

red
wavelength = 0.000 000 70 m
frequency = 4.2×10^{14} Hz

yellow
wavelength = 0.000 000 55 m
frequency = 6.0×10^{14} Hz

purple
wavelength = 0.000 000 40 m
frequency = 7.5×10^{14} Hz

C Red light has the longest wavelength and the lowest frequency.

The different types of EM radiation are **emitted** (given out) by different **sources**. We can **detect** the radiation in different ways. For example, radio waves that are emitted by radio transmitters can be detected by radio aerials. Our skin can detect infrared radiation as heat, and ultraviolet radiation is absorbed by our skin to give us a suntan.

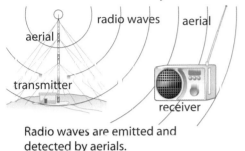

Radio waves are emitted and detected by aerials.

D | Sources and detectors.

Fires give out infrared radiation which our skin can detect.

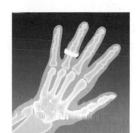

X-rays are emitted by special machines, and can be detected using film or cameras.

The different types of radiation can pass through different materials. This process is called **transmission**. For example, radio waves can be transmitted through brick walls, but visible light cannot.

When EM radiation hits an object, the radiation can be reflected or **absorbed**. Light hitting the food in a microwave oven is reflected, which is why we can see the food. Microwaves hitting the food are absorbed by water in the food. This heats up the food and cooks it.

A | How do different detectors respond to a light source?

E

?

6 What do the following words mean:
  a transmission **b** absorption **c** photon **d** intensity?

7 What could happen when the human body absorbs ultraviolet radiation?

8 Baldev thinks that radio waves are the most dangerous type of EM radiation. Gill thinks gamma rays are the most dangerous. Who do you think is right and why?

Summary

Light is an _____ wave. Other parts of the electromagnetic _____ include _____ waves (with the longest wavelength), then microwaves, _____, visible light, _____, X-rays and then _____ rays. The _____ of the radiation increases as more _____ strike a surface each second.

electromagnetic gamma infrared
intensity photons radio
spectrum ultraviolet

Long wavelength electromagnetic waves
How do we use long wavelength electromagnetic waves?

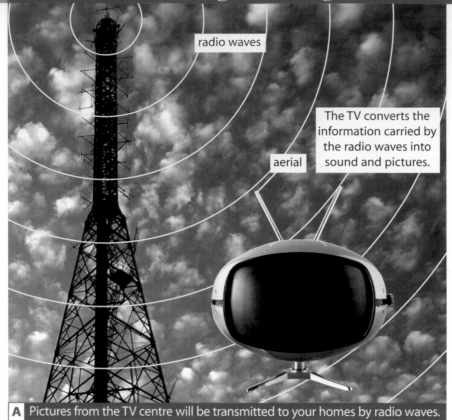

radio waves

The TV converts the information carried by the radio waves into sound and pictures.

aerial

A Pictures from the TV centre will be transmitted to your homes by radio waves.

There are many uses for the different types of electromagnetic radiation, which depend on how they are transmitted, absorbed or reflected.

Radio waves

Radio waves have low frequencies and wavelengths longer than 50 cm. They are used to carry information which can be converted into sound and pictures by a TV. Radio waves are easily transmitted through the atmosphere.

?
1 How long are radio wavelengths?
2 Describe one use for radio waves.

Microwaves

Short wavelength radio waves, from about 0.1 cm up to about 50 cm, are called microwaves. Some wavelengths of microwaves are transmitted very well through the atmosphere, whatever the weather. These wavelengths are used for long distance communication, such as sending messages via satellites. Microwaves are also used in mobile phones and by the radars used in air traffic control centres.

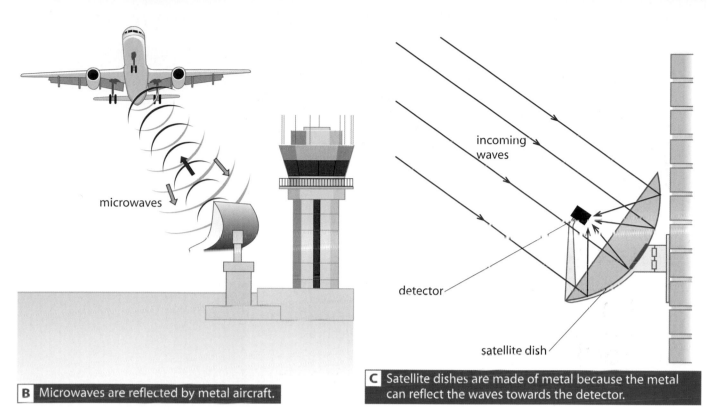

B Microwaves are reflected by metal aircraft.

C Satellite dishes are made of metal because the metal can reflect the waves towards the detector.

Other wavelengths of microwaves are used to cook food because they are strongly absorbed by the water molecules in food. The water heats up and cooks the food. Cells in our bodies contain water and they could be cooked in the same way, so microwave ovens have metal cases to reflect the microwaves and keep them inside the oven.

?
3 Give two uses for microwaves.

4 How could a microwave oven boil water for a cup of tea?

5 Why are microwave ovens and satellite dishes made from metal?

Infrared radiation

Infrared (IR) waves have wavelengths between microwaves and red visible light. All objects emit infrared radiation – the hotter the object, the more infrared radiation it emits. Infrared radiation is transmitted easily through air. Remote controls for TVs and DVD players transmit instructions using infrared radiation. Infrared radiation can also be used to send information along optical fibres.

?
6 List two uses of infrared radiation.

7 How are radio waves and microwaves:
   a similar
   b different?

Summary

Radio waves are EM waves with the longest wavelengths. They can be used to carry information for _____ and TV sets. Radio waves have a low _____. Microwaves can be used to cook food as they are strongly _____ by molecules of _____. Satellites and microwave ovens are made of _____ because it _____ microwave radiation well.

| absorbed | frequency | metal |
| radios | reflects | water |

An **optical fibre** is a fibre made from glass. Light can be shone in one end, and will be reflected from the edge of the fibre by total internal reflection. This allows the light to travel along the fibre even if the fibre is bent. Infrared radiation can be sent down optical fibres in a similar way. The light or infrared radiation does not become significantly weaker as it travels along the optical fibre, so these types of electromagnetic waves are very useful for carrying information for long distances.

? 1 a Which types of EM radiation can travel along optical fibres?
   b Why do these types of radiation stay inside the fibres?

A This ornament has a light bulb in the middle. Visible light is travelling along the optical fibres and shining out of the ends.

Ultraviolet

Ultraviolet radiation can give us a suntan, but it can also cause skin cancer. It is more dangerous than visible light because its photons have more energy. It is used in sun beds, and can also be used to check for forged bank notes.

B The stars show up in ultraviolet light and show this is a genuine bank note.

X-rays

X-rays have a higher frequency than visible light and ultraviolet radiation, so their photons carry more energy. X-rays can pass through some materials, such as the soft parts of our bodies, but cannot pass through more dense materials like bone. Doctors can use X-rays to 'see' the bones inside our bodies.

X-rays do not pass through metal, so they can be used to look for things like knives or guns in luggage at airports.

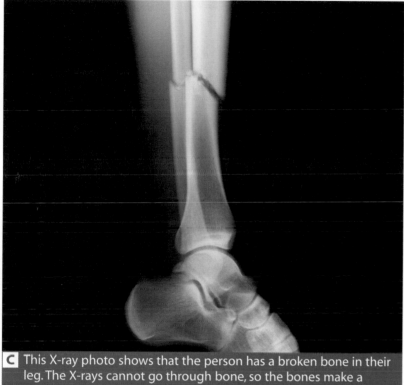

C This X-ray photo shows that the person has a broken bone in their leg. The X-rays cannot go through bone, so the bones make a 'shadow' on the picture.

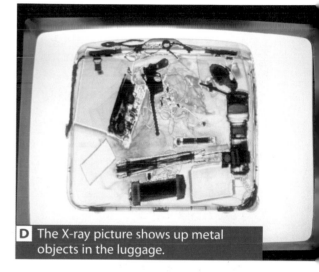

D The X-ray picture shows up metal objects in the luggage.

2 Why can X-rays be used to make shadow pictures of bones?

3 a Why don't swimming trunks show up on an airport luggage scanner?
  b Imagine that someone had invented a gun that could be made completely from plastic. Why would this be a problem for airport security?

Gamma radiation

Gamma radiation has the highest frequency of the whole electromagnetic spectrum, and the highest energy photons. The high energy of gamma radiation means it can kill living cells, so it is useful for things like sterilising surgical equipment.

4 Write out the parts of the electromagnetic spectrum in order, starting with the radiation with the highest photon energies. You may need to look back at page 230 to help you.

5 At one time, X-ray machines were used in shoe shops to look at the bones in the feet. Why is this no longer allowed?

6 Explain how the world might look different if we could see all of the waves in the EM spectrum.

Summary

Visible light and _____ radiation can travel along _____ fibres without becoming weaker, so they are useful for carrying _____. X-rays have a _____ frequency. They do not pass easily through _____ materials, so they can be used to make _____ pictures to look inside the _____, or inside luggage.

| body | dense | high | information |
| infrared | optical | shadow | |

Analogue signals

What are analogue signals?

When you talk or sing, the amplitude and frequency of the sounds you make are changing all the time. Anything that changes continuously like this is an **analogue** signal. Other things that vary continuously include the speed of the wind and the temperature of the air. All of these things could be described as being analogue.

Radio waves can be used to transmit the sounds made by your voice. The signal carried by the radio wave varies continuously in exactly the same way as the information it is carrying. Radio waves are also analogue signals. The receiver converts the radio signals back into sound waves.

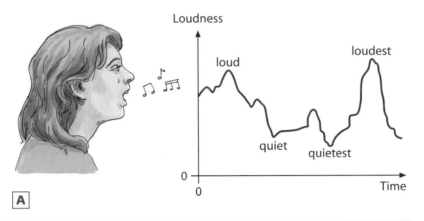

A

B

? **1** What is an analogue signal?

Radio waves have a much higher frequency than sound waves, so the amplitude and frequency of the radio wave cannot match the sound wave exactly. The microphone and transmitter take the sound wave and change the amplitude of the radio wave to make a pattern that matches the frequency of the sound wave.

? **2** Why can't the radio waves have the same frequency as the sound waves?

3 Look at photo B. Why are radio waves needed to transmit the reporter's voice?

① Sound waves are detected by the microphone and converted into analogue radio waves.

② Radio waves are transmitted and detected by aerials.

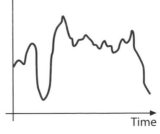

③ The radio waves vary in the same way as the sound waves did.

④ The receiver converts the radio waves back to sound waves again.

C

The process of changing the amplitude of a radio wave like this is called **amplitude modulation**. The shape of the sound wave that is to be sent as a radio wave is 'added' to another wave called the **carrier wave**. The carrier wave has a higher frequency than the signal being transmitted.

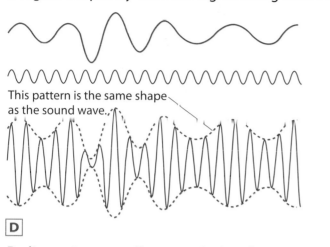

sound wave

carrier

This pattern is the same shape as the sound wave.

modulated carrier

D

? 4 What does amplitude modulation mean?

Radio stations usually transmit signals representing music or speech. Radio sets receive the signal and turn it back into a copy of the original sound. However, bits of other radio signals may also be picked up by a receiver, and these reduce the quality of the sound produced. The extra sounds in a radio signal are called **noise**.

Radio waves decrease in intensity the further they travel, so the receiver needs to **amplify** them (make their amplitude bigger). Unfortunately, this also amplifies any noise the signal has picked up.

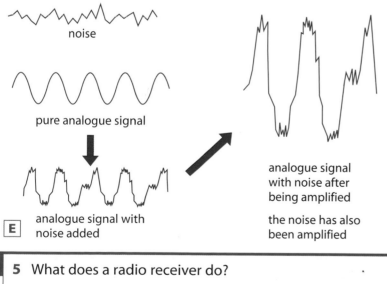

noise

pure analogue signal

analogue signal with noise added

analogue signal with noise after being amplified

the noise has also been amplified

E

? 5 What does a radio receiver do?

6 Which is the odd one out: radio wave, microwave, sound wave?

7 Write down as many examples of analogue signals as you can.

Summary

Analogue signals are constantly _____ . The _____ of someone's voice is an analogue signal. A radio _____ gives a radio wave the same pattern as a _____ wave. A radio _____ turns a radio wave back into a copy of the _____ sound.

changing   loudness   original
receiver   sound   transmitter

Digital signals

What are digital signals?

Many devices can be either 'on' or 'off'. There are no 'in-between' states. A torch is either on or off; so is a switch. Devices that are either on or off are **digital** devices.

Sound, and other information, can be transmitted as an analogue radio signal with a continuously changing amplitude or frequency. However, this information can also be transmitted as a digital signal. Sound waves can be converted into a digital code made up from just two values: 0 and 1.

A The light is providing a digital signal because it is either on or off.

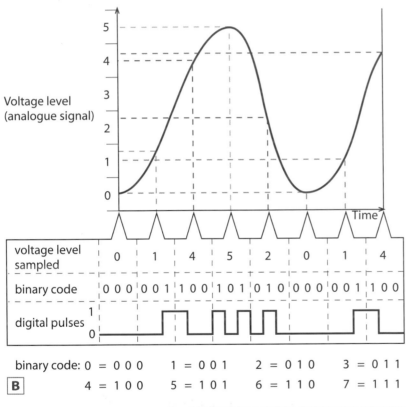

Voltage level (analogue signal)

voltage level sampled	0	1	4	5	2	0	1	4
binary code	0 0 0	0 0 1	1 0 0	1 0 1	0 1 0	0 0 0	0 0 1	1 0 0

binary code: 0 = 0 0 0   1 = 0 0 1   2 = 0 1 0   3 = 0 1 1

B   4 = 1 0 0   5 = 1 0 1   6 = 1 1 0   7 = 1 1 1

?

1 What is a digital signal?

2 Name five devices that can be only on or off.

Digital information can be transmitted by using it to control short bursts of waves, or **pulses**. There is a pulse when the digital signal is 1, and no pulse when the digital signal is 0. Once this digital signal has been received, it is decoded by the receiver and changed back into a copy of the original information.

?

3 What do 0 and 1 mean in a digital signal?

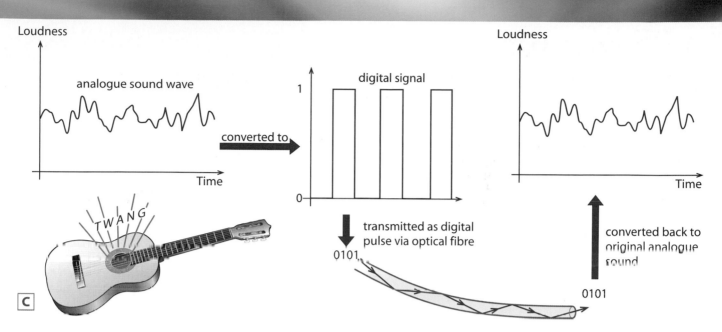

C

Why are digital signals better than analogue signals?

When a digital signal is received and converted to sound, the quality of the signal is better than when it is transmitted as an analogue signal. Both analogue and digital signals suffer from noise which can **distort** (change) the signal. This can spoil the sound of music transmitted using an analogue signal.

However, a digital signal can only be a pulse (1) or no pulse (0). When the noise is added to the digital pulse, the 0s and 1s can still be recognised and decoded as clearly as the original signal. This means that noise on a digital signal does not spoil the sound being transmitted.

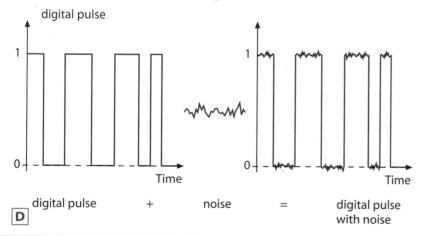

digital pulse + noise = digital pulse with noise

D

? **4** Why are digital signals better than analogue ones?

5 Think of a plus, a minus and an interesting point about this statement: All signals should be digital signals.

6 How are analogue signals:
a similar to digital signals
b different from digital signals?

Summary

A digital signal is either on or _____. Digital signals are a higher _____ than _____ ones, because they are not as affected by _____ as analogue ones. Digital signals are converted back into the _____ signal by a _____.

| analogue | noise | off | original |
| quality | receiver | | |

Using waves

What do you know about waves?

Greg and Ursula Wilson live in the new town of Ashbrooke with their three children, Adam, Robert and Abigail. Greg is a telephone engineer and Ursula works in a local hospital. Adam and Robert are both studying for their GCSE exams and Abigail has just returned home from university, where she is studying Sports Science.

I am so pleased with our new digital TV and radio.

A Greg

It's great living here! The X-ray department is just around the corner, so I can walk to work.

B Ursula

1 Which type of electromagnetic radiation do these devices in the house use:
   a satellite TV
   b microwave oven
   c radio
   d lights
   e toaster?

2 a What would Ursula use X-rays for in her job?
   b What other uses are there for X-rays?

Robert is having problems with his Physics homework.

I've forgotten what frequency, wavelength and amplitude are!

C

3 Explain what is meant by the terms *frequency*, *wavelength* and *amplitude*. Draw diagrams to help you to explain.

4 a Write down the equation that you use to work out wave speed.
   b Use the equation to work out the speed of a wave that has a wavelength of 3.5 m and a frequency of 2.5 Hz.
   c What type of wave is it most likely to be – sound, light or water wave? Explain your answer.

Adam is doing an electronics project at school. He has designed a device that can send and receive music in the form of light.

This will transmit music as a series of digital pulses down an optical fibre.

D

Abigail is training to be a PE teacher. Her favourite sport is diving.

E

5 a What is a digital signal?
  b What is an analogue signal?
  c Which is best for transmitting music programmes – digital or analogue?
  d Explain your answer to part **c**.

6 What is the purpose of:
  a a transmitter
  b a receiver?

7 a What kinds of radiation can be sent down an optical fibre?
  b Why does the radiation stay inside the optical fibre?
  c What can optical fibres be used for?

8 Why does the beach ball not move horizontally once the waves reach it?

9 Would the waves in the pool be faster if Abigail made a bigger splash when she entered it? Explain your answer.

10 a What happens to the speed of water waves as they move from the deeper water into shallow water?
   b What is the name given to the change of direction of a wave?

11 If you drop something into a pond, transverse waves spread out across the surface. If you make a noise under water, longitudinal waves spread out through the water. Draw diagrams to show what these two different waves will look like when produced in water.

Periodic Table

Key

| mass number |
| **symbol** |
| name |
| atomic number |

Example: H (hydrogen), mass number 1, atomic number 1

Group numbers: 1 2 3 4 5 6 7 0

Group 1	Group 2											Group 3	Group 4	Group 5	Group 6	Group 7	Group 0
																	4 **He** helium 2
7 **Li** lithium 3	9 **Be** beryllium 4											11 **B** boron 5	12 **C** carbon 6	14 **N** nitrogen 7	16 **O** oxygen 8	19 **F** fluorine 9	20 **Ne** neon 10
23 **Na** sodium 11	24 **Mg** magnesium 12											27 **Al** aluminium 13	28 **Si** silicon 14	31 **P** phosphorus 15	32 **S** sulphur 16	35.5 **Cl** chlorine 17	40 **Ar** argon 18
39 **K** potassium 19	40 **Ca** calcium 20	45 **Sc** scandium 21	48 **Ti** titanium 22	51 **V** vanadium 23	52 **Cr** chromium 24	55 **Mn** manganese 25	56 **Fe** iron 26	59 **Co** cobalt 27	59 **Ni** nickel 28	63.5 **Cu** copper 29	65 **Zn** zinc 30	70 **Ga** gallium 31	73 **Ge** germanium 32	75 **As** arsenic 33	79 **Se** selenium 34	80 **Br** bromine 35	84 **Kr** krypton 36
85 **Rb** rubidium 37	88 **Sr** strontium 38	89 **Y** yttrium 39	91 **Zr** zirconium 40	93 **Nb** niobium 41	96 **Mo** molybdenum 42	[98] **Tc** technetium 43	101 **Ru** ruthenium 44	103 **Rh** rhodium 45	106 **Pd** palladium 46	108 **Ag** silver 47	112 **Cd** cadmium 48	115 **In** indium 49	119 **Sn** tin 50	122 **Sb** antimony 51	128 **Te** tellurium 52	127 **I** iodine 53	131 **Xe** xenon 54
133 **Cs** caesium 55	137 **Ba** barium 56	139 **La*** lanthanum 57	178 **Hf** hafnium 72	181 **Ta** tantalum 73	184 **W** tungsten 74	186 **Re** rhenium 75	190 **Os** osmium 76	192 **Ir** iridium 77	195 **Pt** platinum 78	197 **Au** gold 79	201 **Hg** mercury 80	204 **Tl** thallium 81	207 **Pb** lead 82	209 **Bi** bismuth 83	[209] **Po** polonium 84	[210] **At** astatine 85	[222] **Rn** radon 86
[223] **Fr** francium 87	[226] **Ra** radium 88	[227] **Ac*** actinium 89	[261] **Rf** rutherfordium 104	[262] **Db** dubnium 105	[266] **Sg** seaborgium 106	[264] **Bh** bohrium 107	[277] **Hs** hassium 108	[268] **Mt** meitnerium 109	[271] **Ds** darmstadtium 110	[272] **Rg** roentgenium 111							

Elements with atomic numbers 112–116 have been reported but not fully authenticated.

* The Lanthanides (atomic numbers 58–71) and the Actinides (atomic numbers 90–103) have been omitted.

The mass numbers for Cu and Cl have not been rounded to the nearest whole number.

Glossary

absorbed Taken in. Infrared radiation is absorbed by most materials, leading to a rise in temperature.

accelerate To change velocity.

acid A chemical that will neutralise a base. Acids produce hydrogen ions in water.

action A force produced by an object.

actual yield The amount of products that are actually made during a chemical reaction.

adrenal gland An effector organ that releases adrenalin. Found on top of the kidney.

adrenalin A hormone that causes increased awareness and increased heartbeat rate.

air The mixture of gases in the lower part of the atmosphere mainly made up of nitrogen (78%) and oxygen (21%).

alkali A soluble base that neutralises an acid.

alkali metal Metal elements in Group 1 of the Periodic Table, starting with lithium.

alkaline A solution with a pH greater than 7.

alternating current (a.c.) A current whose direction changes many times a second.

amino acids Small molecules which are joined together to make proteins.

ammeter An instrument used to measure the size of electric current in a circuit.

amp (A) Short for ampere, the unit of electric current.

amplify To increase the amplitude of a signal.

amplitude The height of a wave from its undisturbed position.

amplitude modulation The process of changing the amplitude of a wave.

amylase An enzyme that digests starch into a sugar called maltose. It is produced by the salivary glands.

analogue A signal which is continuously varying.

atmosphere The mixture of gases that surround the Earth.

atom The smallest particle of a substance. All substances are made from atoms.

atomic number The number of protons in an atom (same as the proton number).

attract When two things try to pull towards each other.

average speed Speed calculated using the total distance travelled and the total time taken when the speed may have been changing during the journey.

axon Long tube of cytoplasm in a neurone that carries impulses away from a cell body.

axon terminal The end of an axon splits into branches, each of which ends in a thickening called the axon terminal.

balanced symbol equation A symbol equation is balanced when there are the same number of atoms of each element on both sides.

base (biology) One type of chemical found in DNA.

base (chemistry) A chemical that will neutralise an acid in water.

battery A number of cells connected together.

behaviour What an animal does and how it reacts to things.

biomolecules Large complex molecules found in living things.

biosphere All living things, including plants and animals.

bleach To remove the colour from a material.

bond The force of attraction which holds atoms together.

brain Organ that controls the body.

burette Apparatus used to measure out accurately the amount of a liquid in a titration, consisting of a glass tube with a measuring scale and a tap at the end.

carrier wave A wave to which another wave is added so that it can be transferred as a radio wave. The carrier wave has a higher frequency than the wave that is being sent.

catalyse Speed up a chemical reaction.

catalyst A chemical that speeds up a reaction but is not used up during the reaction.

cell (biology) The basic unit which living things are made of.

cell (electricity) A source of electrical energy needed to make electrons move around a circuit; two or more cells connected together form a battery.

cell body Part of a neurone where the nucleus is found and where most of the cytoplasm is.

cell cycle A series of stages that occur as a cell divides.

cell growth A stage in the cell cycle in which a cell copies its chromosomes and doubles its organelles.

cell specialisation When a stem cell turns into another sort of cell to do a certain job (such as a muscle cell).

cell surface membrane A thin layer on the outside of a cell which controls what goes into and out of the cell.

central nervous system Contains the brain and spinal cord and is responsible for coordinating the body's responses to stimuli.

cerebral cortex The major part of the brain with a crinkled outer surface.

change in momentum Produced when a force is applied to an object.

characteristics Features that an organism has, such as curly hair.

chemical equation A way of showing the reactants and products in a chemical reaction using symbols and formulae.

choice chamber A chamber in which the environmental conditions can be changed to observe the responses of small animals.

chromatid When a chromosome copies itself, the copies remain stuck together for a while. In this form the two copies are called chromatids.

chromosome Thread-like strands found in the nucleus of a cell. Chromosomes are made of DNA and contain the 'instructions' for a living thing.

clone An organism with exactly the same genes as the organism it was produced from.

CNS Short for central nervous system.

cochlea The part of the ear that contains receptor cells for sound.

components The parts that make up an electric circuit other than connecting wires, e.g. lamps, resistors, motors, switches, etc.

compound A substance made from atoms of different elements chemically joined together.

concentration The amount of a substance dissolved in a certain volume of water. It is measured in grams of solute in each 1 dm^3 of solvent.

conductor Material that allows an electric current to pass easily. Conductors have electrons that are free to move.

consciousness Your inner thoughts and feelings, including the feeling that you are you.

conservation of energy Energy cannot be created or destroyed, it can only be transferred from one form to another.

constructive interference When waves overlap in step and reinforce.

control system An automatic system that keeps conditions constant.

core (biology) The central part of the body which contains the major organs.

core (Earth) The centre or innermost part of the Earth's structure.

corrosive Substances that can attack metals and living material.

covalent bond Bond formed between non-metal atoms when atoms share electrons so each gains a full outer shell of electrons.

critical angle The angle, for a given material, above which total internal reflection occurs.

crumple zone Section of a vehicle designed to collapse when it experiences a large impact.

crust The outer solid layer of the Earth and main part of the lithosphere.

crystal A solid with a regular shape and flat surfaces that reflect light.

crystalline A substance made of crystals.

crystallisation The formation of crystals from a solution.

current A flow of electric charge (usually electrons).

cutting Part of a plant (usually a leaf) that can be used to make an identical copy of the plant.

cytoplasm The jelly-like part of a cell where most of the chemical reactions happen.

data Information (often the results of experiments).

daughter cells The two cells formed from a parent cell that divides.

decomposed When a substance is broken down into simpler substances.

dehydration When something has lost a lot of water.

denature When an enzyme stops working properly because the temperature is too high.

density The mass of a certain volume of a substance (usually the mass of 1 cm^3, measured in g/cm^3) (density = mass ÷ volume).

destructive interference When waves overlap out of step and cancel each other out.

detect When radiation is registered by a device it has been detected. Visible light is detected by the eye; infrared is detected by the skin.

diamond Form of carbon with a lattice structure which is a gemstone.

diatomic molecule A molecule made up of two atoms joined together.

diffraction The spreading out of waves as they pass through a gap.

diffusion The way molecules spread from an area of high concentration to an area of low concentration, without anything moving or mixing them.

digital Information coded as a series of digits. These digits are 0s and 1s, which represent off and on states, respectively.

direct current (d.c.) A current that flows in one direction only, such as the current provided by a cell.

directly proportional Two factors are directly proportional when doubling one of them doubles the other.

dissolve Mix into a liquid and seem to disappear.

distort To change a signal by the adding of noise.

divide When a cell splits into two it divides.

DNA The chemical that chromosomes are made from.

double helix Two spirals wrapped around each other.

effector The part of a control system which changes the conditions.

effector cell A cell that does something in response to a stimulus. Examples include muscle cells and secretory cells in glands.

effector organ An organ that does something in response to a stimulus.

efficiency The measure of how much energy is usefully converted by a component, rather than converted to unwanted forms.

egg cell The female gamete.

electric charge The property of electrons that causes electrical effects.

electric circuit An unbroken conducting path from one terminal of a battery to the other.

electrolysis The breaking down of a substance by passing electricity through it.

electrolyte Substance that conducts electricity when molten or in solution as it contains freely moving ions.

electromagnetic The electromagnetic spectrum is the family of transverse waves ranging from radio waves at the long wavelength end to gamma rays at the short wavelength end.

electromagnetic induction The process that creates a voltage or current in a coil when the magnetic field around it is changing.

electron A negatively charged particle moving around the nucleus of an atom.

electron arrangement The way in which electrons are arranged in shells around the nucleus of an atom.

electron shells Regions in which electrons move around the nucleus in an atom. Sometimes called energy levels.

electrostatic force The force between electric charges.

element A simple substance made up of only one type of atom.

embryo A ball of cells which will grow and develop into a new organism.

embryo splitting When an early embryo is split up into separate cells, each of which is allowed to grow into a new embryo.

embryonic stem cell A stem cell from an embryo. It can develop into all the different sorts of cells found in a baby.

emitted Something that is given out is emitted. Light is emitted by a lamp; radio waves are emitted by a radio transmitter.

end-point Where the acid and alkali have exactly reacted together during a titration.

energy Something that is needed to make things happen. The potential to do work.

energy levels Regions in which electrons move around the nucleus in an atom. Sometimes called electron shells.

environment The surroundings of an organism including all living and non-living factors.

enzyme A protein made by living things that speeds up chemical reactions in them.

evaporate Turn from liquid into gas.

excrete Get rid of waste materials from the body.

fertilisation The time when a male and a female gamete join.

filter Remove a solid from a liquid.

flame tests Technique of identifying the presence of certain elements by the colours they produce in a flame.

flower A plant organ that is used for reproduction in many plants.

formula The number of atoms in a molecule or the ratio of elements in a compound.

frequency The number of complete waves produced by a source in one second, measured in hertz.

friction Force due to the interaction between surfaces moving or trying to move over each other.

gamete A cell that only contains one set of chromosomes, such as a sperm cell or an egg cell.

gas State in which substances have no fixed volume or shape, but spread out in all directions.

gemstone Hard, shiny crystal of a rare and expensive mineral.

gene Part of a chromosome. A gene contains the 'instructions' for making a protein.

generator A device for converting movement energy into electrical energy.

genetic code The sequence of bases that makes up the DNA of a gene. This code contains the instructions for a protein.

genetic screening When one cell is taken from an early embryo and its DNA is examined for problems with its genes.

giant covalent structure A large regular arrangement of atoms, sometimes called a lattice structure.

GPE Short for gravitational potential energy.

gravitational potential energy The energy of an object due to its height above the ground.

green chemistry Attempts by the chemical industry to become more environmentally friendly.

group A vertical column in the Periodic Table.

halide A compound of a metal and a halogen.

halogen Non-metal elements in Group 7 of the Periodic Table, starting with fluorine.

harmful Substances that can make you ill if swallowed or breathed in.

hazard symbol Standard symbols that are used throughout the world to show the hazards of different chemicals.

heart Organ that pumps blood.

heat exhaustion A condition where someone has become too hot and dehydrated.

heat stroke A condition where the body temperature rises out of control.

hertz (Hz) The unit of frequency.

highly flammable Substances that catch fire easily.

homeostasis The way our bodies keep certain factors constant (such as temperature and water levels).

hormone A chemical messenger produced by glands in the body and carried in the bloodstream.

hydrogen ions Ions (H^+) formed when acids dissolve in water.

hydrosphere The surface water, such as oceans, seas, rivers and lakes.

hydroxide ions Ions (OH⁻) formed when alkalis dissolve in water.

hypothermia A condition where the core body temperature has dropped below 35°C.

implantation When an embryo buries itself in the lining of the uterus.

impulse An electrical signal carrying information which travels along neurones (nerve cells).

in parallel Components connected in a circuit so that there is more than one path for current between two points in a circuit.

in series Components connected in a circuit one after another so the same current passes through each.

indicator A substance that is a different colour in acidic and alkaline solutions.

induce To cause a voltage or a current in a wire.

instantaneous speed The speed at a given time during the journey.

insulate To prevent energy (for example electrical energy) from passing into or out of something.

insulators Materials that do not allow electricity to flow through them.

intensity The amount of energy from radiation reaching a certain area. For example, more intense infrared radiation feels hotter.

interact Things that interact have an effect on each other.

interference The overlapping of waves that are in the same place at the same time.

involuntary An action that your body just does automatically is said to be involuntary.

ion A charged atom or molecule formed by the loss or gain of electrons.

ionic bond Strong bond formed by the attraction between positive and negative ions.

ionic compound A substance which contains ions that are attracted to each other.

ionic equation An equation that only shows ions that have changed.

ionic lattice A giant regular structure made up of many oppositely charged ions held together by electrostatic forces.

irritant Substance that can make the skin red or cause blisters.

joule (J) The unit of energy.

keratin A type of protein that forms hair.

kg m/s The unit of momentum.

kidney tubules The parts of the kidneys that filter and reabsorb substances.

kidneys Organs in the body that produce urine.

kilowatt (kW) A unit of power, equal to 1000 joules per second. 1 kW = 1000 W.

kilowatt-hour (kWh) A unit of energy used by the electricity supply companies.

kinetic energy Energy of a moving mass.

lattice structure A regular arrangement containing billions of atoms or ions.

leaf A plant organ that makes food for the plant using photosynthesis.

light-dependent resistor A circuit component whose resistance decreases as the intensity of the light shining on it increases.

liquid State in which substances have a fixed volume but no fixed shape – they take the shape of the container.

lithosphere The crust of the Earth and the top part of the mantle.

liver Organ that converts amino acids into urea.

'lock and key' model The idea that only molecules with the right shape can fit into an enzyme.

longitudinal Waves, such as sound and ultrasound, where the direction of energy transfer is parallel to the direction of vibration which causes them.

long-term memory A memory store in the brain that can hold a huge number of memories for the whole of a life time.

lubricant Liquid used between moving surfaces to reduce friction.

mantle Layer of the Earth's structure between the crust and the core.

mass number The number of protons plus the number of neutrons in an atom.

matter Material – solid, liquid or gas.

medium Something through which waves travel.

meiosis A type of cell division that produces cells with only one set of chromosomes.

memory The storing and retrieving of information.

meristem A part of a plant where unspecialised meristem cells are dividing rapidly.

meristem cell An unspecialised cell found in plants.

metallic bond Strong bond formed in metals where outer electrons are freely moving through a lattice of positive metal ions.

metallic lattice Large regular arrangement of metal atoms held together by metallic bonds.

metals Elements which are generally hard, shiny and conduct electricity and heat easily. They are found on the left-hand side of the Periodic Table.

milliamp (mA) 1/1000th of an amp.

mineral An element or compound found in the lithosphere.

mitochondria Organelles which release energy for the cell to use.

mitosis When a cell divides to form two cells that are both identical to the original cell.

model A model is a way of comparing a scientific idea to something we are familiar with to help us to understand or visualise the scientific idea.

molecular formula A formula showing the number of atoms of each element in a molecule of a substance.

molecular structure Structure made up of particles containing two or more atoms joined together.

molecule A particle containing two or more atoms joined together.

momentum Mass × velocity. Its units are kg m/s.

motor neurone Neurone that carries impulses to effector cells from the CNS.

myelin A fatty substance that insulates neurones and makes them carry impulses more quickly.

negative distance A distance in the opposite direction to a positive distance.

negative ion Charged atom formed by the gain of electrons.

negative velocity A velocity in the opposite direction to a positive velocity.

negligible Unimportant; so small it can be ignored.

nerves Fibres that carry information around the body. Nerves are formed from bundles of neurones (nerve cells).

neurone A cell that can carry an electric current (impulse).

neurone pathway A route taken by impulses through neurones in the brain.

neutral Having no charge, neither positive nor negative.

neutralisation The reaction of an acid with an alkali to form a neutral solution (pH 7).

neutron A neutral particle inside the nucleus of an atom.

newton (N) The unit of force.

nitrogen cycle Natural cycle of nitrogen atoms in the soil, in plants and animals and in the air.

noise Unwanted signal or waves that accompany the information to be transmitted.

non-metals Elements which are generally not shiny and do not conduct electricity or heat easily. They are found on the right-hand side of the Periodic Table.

normal A line drawn at 90° to a mirror or glass block.

nuclear membrane Membrane around the nucleus.

nucleus (biology) The 'control centre' of a cell. It contains the chromosomes.

nucleus (chemistry) The central part of an atom (made up of protons and neutrons).

ohm (Ω) The unit of resistance.

optical fibre Glass fibre used when transmitting information in the form of visible or infrared radiation.

optimum temperature The temperature at which enzymes work best.

ore Rock or mineral from which a metal can be extracted.

organ A part of an organism that is made out of different tissues and has an important job.

organelle A small important part of a cell, for example mitochondria.

organic chemistry The study of the large number of compounds based on carbon including all biological molecules.

osmosis When water diffuses through a partially permeable membrane so that the concentrations on each side become more equal.

oxidation reaction Reaction in which a substance gains or combines with oxygen.

oxidised When a substance gains oxygen during a reaction.

oxidising Substance that releases oxygen (and so can encourage other materials to burn).

paper (scientific) The report a scientist writes to explain what experiments were done, what the results are and what the results show.

parallel circuit A circuit in which at least two components (other than voltmeters) are connected so that there is more than one path between the two points.

parent cell A cell that divides.

partially permeable membrane A thin barrier with tiny holes in it that lets small molecules through but not large ones.

percentage yield The actual yield of a substance as a percentage of the theoretical yield.

period A horizontal row in the Periodic Table.

Periodic Table A table showing all the elements in order of their proton number.

peripheral nervous system The nerves that connect the central nervous system to effectors and receptors.

pH number A number that shows how strong an acid or alkali is.

phloem A specialised plant cell that forms a channel to carry sugars and other materials dissolved in water.

photon A 'packet' of energy carried by electromagnetic radiation.

phototropism The growth of a plant towards light.

pipette Apparatus used to measure out accurately a known volume of liquid during a titration.

plane A plane surface is a flat surface.

plant hormone A chemical produced by a plant which affects other cells and 'tells' them what to do.

plasma The liquid part of blood.

PNS Short for peripheral nervous system.

positive distance A distance in a direction that has been defined as a positive direction.

positive ion Charged atom formed by the loss of electrons.

positive velocity A velocity in a direction that has been defined as a positive direction.

potential difference (p.d.) The difference in energy of the electrons in two points in a circuit.

power The rate at which energy is transferred to a component.

processing centre The part of a control system which receives information and decides what to do.

products The new substances formed in a chemical reaction.

property A description of what a substance does or looks like.

protein Proteins are important substances found in all organisms and are made of amino acids linked together. Many important structures are made using proteins; enzymes are proteins.

proton A positively charged particle found inside the nucleus of an atom.

proton number The number of protons in an atom (same as the atomic number).

pulses Short bursts of waves.

quartz Pure crystalline form of silicon dioxide.

RAM Short for relative atomic mass.

rate of reaction The speed of a reaction.

raw materials Naturally occurring substances from which other chemicals are made.

reactants The substances that take part in a chemical reaction.

reaction (physics) A force on the object in the opposite direction to the action the object is producing.

reaction time The time between a stimulus being received and a response occurring.

receptor The part of a control system which detects changes in conditions.

receptor cell A cell that detects a stimulus.

reduced When oxygen is removed from a substance during a reaction.

reduction reaction Reaction in which a substance loses oxygen.

reflected The ray that leaves a mirror or surface after the incident ray has hit it.

reflex action An automatic response to a stimulus.

reflex arc A simple connection between neurones so that a sensory neurone controls a motor neurone without the brain being involved.

refraction The changing of direction of a wave as it travels from one medium into another. Refraction is also accompanied by a change in speed of the wave.

relative atomic mass (RAM) The mass of an atom of an element compared to the mass of a hydrogen atom.

relative formula mass (RFM) The sum of the RAMs of all the elements in a molecule of a substance.

repel When two things push each other away.

resistance How difficult it is for current to pass through a component.

resistor A component that provides resistance to control the amount of current in a circuit.

respiration The reaction which combines glucose and oxygen to release energy, and produces carbon dioxide and water as waste products.

response The action taken by a processing centre in a control system as a reaction to a stimulus.

resultant force The sum of all forces acting on an object taking account of those acting in opposite directions.

retina Area at the back of the eye that contains receptor cells for light.

RFM Short for relative formula mass.

risk assessment Assess the risks involved in a process.

rock Solid mineral or mixture of minerals found in crust.

root A plant organ that takes water and mineral salts from the ground, and anchors the plant.

salt A compound formed from a metal and a non-metal.

scaled up A reaction carried out in a chemical factory, where tonnes of product may be made.

scientific journal A magazine that scientific papers are published in. The most famous is called *Nature*.

secrete To produce and release a substance.

sense Detecting a stimulus.

sense organ An organ that is involved with detecting a stimulus.

sensory neurone Neurone that carries impulses from receptor cells to the CNS.

series circuit A circuit in which all the components (other than voltmeters) are connected one after another in line.

sex cell Another name for a gamete.

sheath Something that wraps around something else, covering it. For example, the myelin sheath is a covering of fatty material that surrounds the axons of many neurones.

shiver Shaking of the muscles to produce more heat energy.

short-term memory A memory store in the brain that can hold a small number of memories for up to 30 seconds.

skull Set of bones that protect the brain.

social behaviour How an animal reacts to other animals of the same type.

solid State in which substances have a fixed volume and a fixed shape.

soluble Able to dissolve in water.

solute The solid that dissolves in a solvent to form a solution.

solvent The liquid in which a solute dissolves to form a solution.

sources Devices or objects which give out waves.

spectroscopy The study of substances using the colours/wavelengths of light they emit or absorb.

spectrum An image showing the colours/wavelengths of light given out by a substance.

speed A measure of the distance travelled in a given time.

speed of light The speed of light (and other kinds of electromagnetic radiation) in a vacuum. Equal to 300 million metres per second.

sperm cell The male gamete.

spinal cord Thick column of nerves leading out of the brain and running through the centre of the spine.

staining Dyeing things to make them show up better. You can stain genes to make them show up.

state symbols Symbols used in equations to indicate state: solid (s), liquid (l), gas (g) and dissolved in water (aq).

stem A plant organ that transports substances around the plant and provides support.

stem cell A cell that can develop into many different types of cells.

stimulus A change in the environment of something.

strong acid An acid that produces many hydrogen ions in water.

strong alkali An alkali that produces many hydroxide ions in water.

structural formula A way of drawing a molecule, in two dimensions, using lines to stand for bonds.

sweat Liquid that cools the skin by evaporation.

sweat glands Where sweat is produced.

symbol equation A way of showing a chemical reaction using symbols for each reactant and product.

synapse A gap between one neurone and the next.

tachograph A speed–time graph used to monitor vehicle journeys.

tarnish When the surface of a metal reacts and becomes dull.

taste buds Parts of the tongue that contain receptor cells for different types of dissolved chemicals.

temperature control system An automatic control system to keep the temperature of something constant.

theoretical yield The mass of products that should be produced during a chemical reaction, calculated using the chemical equation.

theory Scientific idea which has evidence (for example data from experiments) that suggests it is correct.

thermistor A circuit component whose resistance decreases when its temperature increases.

tissue A group of the same type of cells working together.

tissue culture A way of cloning plants by using meristem cells.

titration A process used to find out the concentration of a solution.

total internal reflection The process by which light and infrared radiation is continually reflected down an optical fibre.

toxic Substances that can kill you if swallowed or breathed in.

trace elements Elements (other than carbon, hydrogen, oxygen and nitrogen) which are required in small amounts to produce the chemicals essential for life. Trace elements include calcium, sulfur, phosphorus and potassium.

transformer A device consisting of two coils on an iron core, which can change the voltage of an alternating electricity supply.

transition metals Metals found in the central block of the Periodic Table.

transmission The sending of information.

transverse Waves, such as electromagnetic waves and waves on the surface of water, where the direction of energy transfer is at right angles to the vibration which causes them.

universal indicator A coloured solution used to measure the pH of other solutions.

urea A chemical made in the liver from waste amino acids, and excreted by the kidneys.

urine Liquid produced by the kidneys that contains waste substances and water.

vacuum Empty space.

variable resistor A circuit component whose resistance can be changed by turning a knob or moving a slider.

velocity Tells you the speed of an object and also the direction in which it is travelling.

verbal memory A memory containing words.

volt (V) The unit of voltage.

voltage The amount of energy transferred to or from charges when they pass between two points.

voltmeter An instrument to measure the voltage between two points in a circuit.

voluntary An action that you can do if you want to is said to be voluntary.

water cycle The movement of water between the land, sea and sky.

watt (W) The unit of power, equal to one joule per second.

wave speed The distance that a wave travels in one second.

wavelength The distance between successive identical points on a wave.

weak acid An acid that only produces a few hydrogen ions in water.

weak alkali An alkali that only produces a few hydroxide ions in water.

weathering The breaking up of rocks by natural processes.

wind chill The cooling effect of the wind.

word equation A way of showing the changes which occur during a chemical reaction, giving the reactants and products in words.

work The process by which energy is converted from one form to another. The units are joules (J).

xylem A specialised plant cell that forms a tube to carry water.

zygote The cell formed by fertilisation (a fertilised egg cell).

Index

Pearson Education
Edinburgh Gate
Harlow
Essex
CM20 2JE
UK
www.longman.co.uk

First published 2007

ISBN: 978-0-582-85340-9

Project manager and
development editor: Sue Kearsey
Editors: Liz Jones, Anne Trevillion
Design and production: Roarr Design
Illustration: Oxford Designers & Illustrators Ltd
Picture research: Charlotte Lippmann
Indexer: Indexing Specialists (UK) Ltd
Printed In China   SWTC/01

The publisher's policy is to use paper manufactured from sustainable forests.

Acknowledgments

The publisher would like to thank the following for their help in reviewing this book:

Basil Donnelly; Christina Garry, Second in Science, Alder Community High School, Hyde, Cheshire; Mr Ben Green, Head of Science, Wheatley Park School, Holton, Oxford; Mary Jones, Educational Consultant/Author, Banbury, Oxon; Colin Lever, Freelance writer and educational consultant, Jersey, Channel Islands; Leonie Lisle, Assistant Team Leader for Science, Lyndon School, Solihull, West Midlands; David McKean, Teaching and Learning Adviser, Darlington L.A.; Dr Michael O'Neill, Director of Educational Strategies, UCST; Dr Kim Quigley, AHT, Lyndon School, Solihull; Dorothy Warren; Steve Woolley.

We are grateful to the following for permission to reproduce photographs:

Action Plus: pg22(t) (Neil Tingle), pg67(m) (Neil Tingle), pg73 (Glyn Kirk), pg76 (Neil Tingle), pg82(b) (Chris Brown), pg236 (Chris Barry); **Alamy** pg14 (Bubbles Photolibrary), pg16 (Stock Connection Distribution), pg18(bl) (FAN travelstock), pg22(b) (Arclight), pg24(br) (Dynamic Graphics Group / IT Stock Free), pg31 (Arclight), pg32(b) (Marion Bull), pg33(b) (Simon Belcher), pg33(t) (Peter Davey), pg34 (Stephen Frink Collection), pg35(tl) (Chris Fotoman Smith), pg35(r) (Lesley White), pg46 (Sciencephotos), pg55 (Simon Cross), pg55 (Sue Cunningham), pg56(t) (Imagestopshop), pg60 (Jim Lane), pg65 (Terry Oakley), pg70(b) (Tom Payne), pg70(t) (Justin Kase), pg71 (Superstock), pg77 (Stock Image/Pixland/Jim Boorman), pg79 (Picture Contact/Jochem Wijnands), pg81(t) (Transtock Inc./Glenn Paulina), pg83 (ImageState/david Mackie), pg99(b) (AGStockUSA, Inc./Rick Miller), pg107(m) (G.P Bowater), pg110(mr) (BananaStock), pg113 (Justin Kase), pg126(r) (Phil Degginger), pg131 (Andy Arthur), pg134(tr) (Doug Houghton), pg138(l) (Mediacolor), pg138(r) (Des Kilfeather), pg140 (picturesbyrob), pg143(r) (Mark Bourdillon), pg147(tml) (Ian M Butterfield), pg148 (Leslie Garland), pg154(t) (Sciencephotos), pg156(b) (The Photolibrary Wales), pg159(b) (Leslie Garland), pg159(t) (Clynt Garnham), pg160(m) (Brian Hamiliton), pg191(b) (Vincent Lowe/LGPL), pg198 (Rodolfo Arpia), pg199(l) (Gunter Marx), pg200(l) (geogphotos), pg201(l) (Imagestate), pg202(br) (Phototake/Maximilian Stock Ltd.), pg204(l) (Scotstock), pg208 (David Hoffman), pg214(tl), pg216(bl) (Chris Howes/Wild Places Photography), pg216(br) (Paul Glendell), pg216(t), pg216(tr) (Stockbyte Gold), pg230 (plainpicture GmbH & Co.KG), pg231(l), pg234(tl) (Doug Steley); **Albert Bonniers:** pg98(tr); **Andy Rouse:** pg92; **Ardea:** pg62 (John Daniels), pg78(b) (Tom & Pat Leeson), pg81(m) (Jean Paul Ferrero), pg84 (Francois Gohier), pg228 (Duncan Usher); **Bill Frost:** pg178(l); **Bridgeman Art Library:** pg57(l) (Bibliotheque Nationale, Paris, France), pg165(t) (Prado, Madrid, Spain); **British Museum/Image of Nesperennub produced by SGI Inc Permission to reproduce granted by SGI/British Museum 2006:** pg164(b); **Bryan & Cherry Alexander Photography:** pg9, pg32(t), pg82(t); **Bubbles Photo Library:** pg203(br); **Collections:** pg118(b) (Keith Pritchard); **Corbis:** pg48(r) (Mika/Zefa), pg78(t) (The Military Picture Library/Robin Adahead), pg101 (Michaela Rehle/Reuters), pg104(br) (Louie Psihoyos), pg104(t) (Bettmann), pg105(r) (Royalty Free), pg108(t) (Wu Dongjun/epa), pg155 (Lester Lefkwitz), pg165(b) (Bettmann), pg166(l) (Nicolas Cotto), pg167(br) (Gray Hardel), pg170(r) (Sygma Ohlinger Jerry), pg172(b) (Bettmann), pg172(t) (Marko Shark), pg176 (Royalty Free), pg182(tl) (Rick Gomez), pg184(b) (Roy Ressmeyer), pg201(r) (James L.Amos), pg202(l) (Patrick Bennett), pg231(r); **Crown Copyright 2006:** pg238;

Dornsife Neuroscience Imaging Center: pg184(t); **Dr. E.S. Pierson:** pg104(bl); **Dynamic Graphics Group:** pg216(tr) (IT Stock Free); **EPSON:** pg95(b); **Eurofighter GmbH:** pg134(tr); **FLPA:** pg94(b) (Norbert Wu/Minden Pictures), pg182(tm) (Pete Oxford/Minden Pictures), pg191(br) (Martin H Smith), pg191(tl) (David Hosking); **Food Features:** pg30, pg122, pg192(b), pg197(r), pg204(r); **Garden World Images:** pg106(t); **Getty Images:** pg18(tl) (Patrik Stollarz/AFP), pg186(t), pg187, pg197(l) (Stone/Ben Edwards); **Gunther von Hagens, Institute for Plastination, Heidelberg, Germany (www.bodyworlds.com):** pg168(br), pg170(bl); **Johnson Matthey:** pg213(t); **Macmillian Publishers Ltd: Nature 1953:** pg87(m), Mark Levesley: pg102(m), pg107(t), pg110(bl), pg174(b), pg183(l), pg183(r), pg216(bm); **Mountain Camera:** pg18(tr) (John Cleare), pg25(r) (John Cleare), pg27 (John Cleare), pg68(b) (John Cleare), pg225 (John Cleare); **NASA:** pg8(l), pg98(insert), pg98(tl) (Galaxy Picture Library), pg114 (Galaxy Picture Library); **Natural Visions:** pg178(t) (Heather Angel); **Nature PL:** pg94(t) (Michael Richards/John Downer), pg182(tr) (Anup Shah); **New Media Ltd.:** pg45(tr); **NHPA:** pg20 (Ann and Steve Toon), pg26(r) (Nigel J. Dennis), pg93 (Daniel Heuclin), pg96(br) (M.I. Walker), pg180(tl) (Daniel Zupanic); **Oxford Scientific Films:** pg109; **PDB: Ramasubbu, N., Paloth, V., Luo, Y.G., Brayer, G.D., Levine, M.J. Structure of human salivary alpha-amylase at 1.6 angstrom resolution: Implications for its role in the oral cavity. Acta Crystallogr D Biol Crystallogr v52 pp.435-446 , 1996.:** pg95(t); **Pearson Education:** pg108(tr); **Photo Library Wales:** pg18(bl); **Photo Researchers Inc.:** pg106(b) (Sinclair Stammers); **Photofusion:** pg24(tr) (Ulrike Preuss); **Photographer's Direct:** pg167(tl) (Adam Eastland), pg178(b) (Louise Batalla Duran); **PhotoTake:** pg102(t) (P.Dumas/Eurelios); **Ranganath C, Cohen MX, Dam C, D'Esposito M. Inferior temporal, prefrontal, and hippocampal contributions to visual working memory maintenance and associeteive memory retrieval. Journal of Neuroscience, 2004 Apr 21;24(16):3e917-25.:** pg186(b); **Reuters:** pg118(t), pg164(t) (Teddy Blackburn), pg170(mr), pg174(m) (Fred Prouser); **Rex Features:** pg24(bl) (David Bebber), pg24(tl) (Jon Santa Cruz), pg48(l) (Sipa Press), pg68(t), pg74, pg168(l) (Christian Schou), pg214(bl); **Sigma-Aldrich Co.:** pg181(l); **Simon Watts:** pg166(m); **SkyScan:** pg145, pg200(r); **Science Photo Library:** pg8(r) (NASA), pg17 (Publiphoto Diffusion), pg19(r) (Tony McConnell), pg35(ml) (Andrew Entwistle), pg35(mr) (TEK Image), pg37(l) (Dirk Wiersma), pg37(r) (Martyn F. Chillmaid), pg45(ml) (Charles D. Winters), pg45(tl) (Andrew Lambert), pg45(tm) (Andrew Lambert), pg47(l) (Andrew Lambert), pg52 (Charles D. Winters), pg55 (Ton Kinsbergen), pg56(b) (Andrew Lambert), pg57(r) (James Braidwood), pg58 (Scott Camazine), pg59 (Andrew Lambert), pg67(t) (Simon Lewis), pg72 (Starsem), pg75(t) (TRL Ltd.), pg75, pg80 (Dr.Gary S. Settles & Stephen S. McIntyre), pg87(t), pg88 (James Stevenson), pg90 (Simon Fraser/MRC Unit Newcastle General Hospital), pg91(t) (Michael Abbey), pg98(b) (Dr Yorgos Nikas), pg99(t) (Pascal Goetgheluck), pg100(bl) (Steve Gschemissner), pg100(br) (David Scharf), pg100(l) (Steve Gschemissner), pg100(m) (CNRI), pg100(ml) (Eric Grave), pg100(mr) (Eye of Science), pg103(b) (Herve Conge,ISM), pg103(t) (J.C. Revy), pg105(l) (Dr. Jeremy Burgess), pg108(b) (Martyn F. Chillmaid), pg110(bl) (BSIP Jolyot), pg111 (M.I.Walker), pg112(b) (Canada- France- Hawaii Telescope/Jean-Charles Cuillandre), pg120(b) (Dr. Jeremy Burgess), pg120(tl) (Alex Bartel), pg120(tr) (Dirk Wiersma), pg123 (Prof.K.Seddon & Dr.T.Evans, Queen's University Belfast), pg126(l) (Andrew Lambert), pg127(b) (Charles D. Winters), pg127(tl) (Charles D. Winters), pg127(tr) (George Bernard), pg128(tl) (John Heseltine -), pg128(tr) (Martin Land), pg129(l) (Alfred Pasieka), pg129(r) (Andres McClenaghan), pg130(bl) (Robert Brook), pg130(mr) (John Mead), pg130(tl) (Ben Johnson), pg130(tlm) (Arnold Fisher), pg130(tm) (Martin Land), pg130(tr), pg130(trm) (Biophoto Associates), pg134(ml) (Martin Bond), pg139 (Will & Deni Mcintyre), pg143(b) (Tek Image), pg147(tl) (Andrew Lambert), pg147(tm) (Andrew Lambert), pg147(tr) (Andrew Lambert), pg152(t) (Steve Allen), pg156(tr) (HeineSchneebeli), pg167(tr) (Sinclair Stammers), pg169 (Roger Harris), pg177(m) (BSIP Astier), pg179(r) (Claude Nuridsany & Marie Perennou), pg180(bl) (Walter Dawn), pg182(b) (David McCarthy), pg185(b) (Wellcome Dept. of Cognitive Neurology), pg185(m) (Hank Morgan), pg199(r) (Andrew Lambert), pg202(t) (Philippe Psaila), pg203(t) (Maximian Stock Ltd.), pg205 (Martin Dohern), pg214(tr) (Jerry Mason), pg216(tl) (P.Gontier), pg217(br) (David Parker), pg217(bl) (Samuel Ashfield), pg217(tr) (Antonia Reeve), pg226 (Mark Clarke), pg234(bl) (Mauro Fermariello), pg235(l), pg235(r) (Alexander Tsiaras); **Still Pictures:** pg181(r) (John Cancalosi); **UK Terra Industries:** pg190, pg193(t), pg194(t); **Warner Bros DC comics:** pg174(t) (Courtesy Ronald Grant); **Wellcome Library:** pg96 (M I Walker), pg152(br).

The following photographs were taken on commission © **Pearson Education Ltd. by Trevor Clifford:**

pg13(l), pg13(m), pg15, pg19(m), pg21, pg25(l), pg26(l), pg36(bl), pg36(br), pg36(t), pg37(r), pg41(l), pg41(r), pg44(l), pg47(r), pg48(tr), pg49, pg93, pg107(b), pg112(t), pg119, pg121, pg134(mr), pg141(b), pg141(t), pg142, pg146, pg152(bl), pg154(b), pg156(tl), pg156, pg160(t), pg161, pg167(bl), pg175, pg177(b), pg177(t), pg179(t), pg192(t), pg193(b), pg194(l), pg195(l), pg195(r), pg196(b), pg196(t), pg203(bl), pg206(l), pg206(r), pg207, pg227, pg231.

Front cover photos:
Main image: (c)David Trood/The Image Bank/Getty Images.
Inset: (top) Getty Images/ Steven Hunt (middle) Getty Images/Images Makers (bottom) Getty Images/ David Chasey.

Licence Agreement: *21st Century Science GCSE Additional Science Foundation CD-ROM*

Warning:
This is a legally binding agreement between You (the user) and Pearson Education Limited of Edinburgh Gate, Harlow, Essex, CM20 2JE, United Kingdom ('PEL').

By retaining this Licence, any software media or accompanying written materials or carrying out any of the permitted activities You are agreeing to be bound by the terms and conditions of this Licence. If You do not agree to the terms and conditions of this Licence, do not continue to use the Disk and promptly return the entire publication (this Licence and all software, written materials, packaging and any other component received with it) with Your sales receipt to Your supplier for a full refund.

21st Century Science GCSE Additional Science Foundation CD-ROM consists of copyright software and data. The copyright is owned by PEL. You only own the disk on which the software is supplied. If You do not continue to do only what You are allowed to do as contained in this Licence you will be in breach of the Licence and PEL shall have the right to terminate this Licence by written notice and take action to recover from you any damages suffered by PEL as a result of your breach.

Yes, You can:
1. use *21st Century Science GCSE Additional Science Foundation CD-ROM* on your own personal computer as a single individual user;

No, You cannot:
1. copy *21st Century Science GCSE Additional Science Foundation CD-ROM* (other than making one copy for back-up purposes);

2. alter *21st Century Science GCSE Additional Science Foundation CD-ROM*, or in any way reverse engineer, decompile or create a derivative product from the contents of the database or any software included in it;

3. include any software data from *21st Century Science GCSE Additional Science Foundation CD-ROM* in any other product or software materials;

4. rent, hire, lend or sell *21st Century Science GCSE Additional Science Foundation CD-ROM*;

5. copy any part of the documentation except where specifically indicated otherwise;

6. use the software in any way not specified above without the prior written consent of PEL.

Grant of Licence:
PEL grants You, provided You only do what is allowed under the Yes, You can table above, and do nothing under the No, You cannot table above, a non-exclusive, non-transferable Licence to use *21st Century Science GCSE Additional Science Foundation CD-ROM*.

The above terms and conditions of this Licence become operative when using *21st Century Science GCSE Additional Science Foundation CD-ROM*.

Limited Warranty:
PEL warrants that the disk or CD-ROM on which the software is supplied is free from defects in material and workmanship in normal use for ninety (90) days from the date You receive it. This warranty is limited to You and is not transferable.

This limited warranty is void if any damage has resulted from accident, abuse, misapplication, service or modification by someone other than PEL. In no event shall PEL be liable for any damages whatsoever arising out of installation of the software, even if advised of the possibility of such damages. PEL will not be liable for any loss or damage of any nature suffered by any party as a result of reliance upon or reproduction of any errors in the content of the publication.

PEL does not warrant that the functions of the software meet Your requirements or that the media is compatible with any computer system on which it is used or that the operation of the software will be unlimited or error free. You assume responsibility for selecting the software to achieve Your intended results and for the installation of, the use of and the results obtained from the software.

PEL shall not be liable for any loss or damage of any kind (except for personal injury or death) arising from the use of *21st Century Science GCSE Additional Science Foundation CD-ROM* or from errors, deficiencies or faults therein, whether such loss or damage is caused by negligence or otherwise.

The entire liability of PEL and your only remedy shall be replacement free of charge of the components that do not meet this warranty.

No information or advice (oral, written or otherwise) given by PEL or PEL's agents shall create a warranty or in any way increase the scope of this warranty.

To the extent the law permits, PEL disclaims all other warranties, either express or implied, including by way of example and not limitation, warranties of merchantability and fitness for a particular purpose in respect of *21st Century Science GCSE Additional Science Foundation CD-ROM*.

Governing Law:
This Licence will be governed and construed in accordance with English law.

© Pearson Education Limited 2007